THE ENGLISH NOVEL AT MID-CENTURY

The English Novel at Mid-Century

From the Leaning Tower

Michael Gorra

Assistant Professor of English Language and Literature
Smith College, Northampton, Massachusetts

St. Martin's Press   New York

© Michael Gorra 1990

First published in the United States of America in 1990

Printed in Hong Kong

ISBN 0-312-04023-7

Library of Congress Cataloging-in-Publication Data

Gorra, Michael Edward.
    The English novel at mid-century: from the leaning tower/
Michael Gorra.
    p. cm.
Includes bibliographical references.
ISBN 0-312-04023-7
1. English fiction—20th century—History and criticism.
2. Green, Henry, 1905–1974—Criticism and interpretation.
3. Powell, Anthony, 1905- —Criticism and interpretation.
4. Greene, Graham, 1904- —Criticism and interpretation.
5. Waugh, Evelyn, 1903–1966—Criticism and interpretation.
I. Title.
PR881.G58   1990   89–70055
823'.91209—dc20   CIP

In memory of my father

Contents

Acknowledgements

This study began as a dissertation at Stanford University, where my first year of research was supported by a teaching fellowship. My thanks to my director at Stanford, William M. Chace, and to my readers there, Robert M. Polhemus and Peter Stansky.

William H. Pritchard and Hilary Schor read an early draft of the chapter on Waugh. Martin Green shared the galleys of his *The English Novel in the Twentieth Century* with me before publication. Jefferson Hunter gave me several essential suggestions during a late stage of revision.

A portion of the chapter on Evelyn Waugh appeared in *Contemporary Literature* for Summer 1988, and is copyright by the Board of Regents of the University of Wisconsin Press. It is reprinted here with their permission. An additional section of that chapter appeared in *The Threepenny Review* for Autumn 1986, and some of my ideas on Waugh were first developed in a review essay in that journal for Autumn 1981; my thanks to its editor, Wendy Lesser. My argument about Anthony Powell began to take shape in an essay review on his memoirs for *The Hudson Review* (Winter 1981–82) and I am grateful to its editors, Frederick Morgan and Paula Deitz.

I would like to thank Laurence Pollinger Ltd and The Bodley Head for allowing me to quote from Graham Greene's *The Heart of the Matter*, and to thank Simon & Schuster for permission to quote from *Monsignor Quixote*. Passages from Evelyn Waugh's *Decline and Fall*, *Vile Bodies*, *A Handful of Dust*, *Brideshead Revisited*, and *The Ordeal of Gilbert Pinfold* are reprinted here with the gracious permission of Little, Brown and Co., as are passages from Anthony Powell's *A Question of Upbringing* and *The Acceptance World*. I am grateful to Chatto and Windus for permission to quote from Henry Green's *Loving*, *Living*, and *Party Going*. Viking Penguin, a division of Penguin Books USA, Inc have given permission to quote from *Doting* by Henry Green (copyright 1952 by The Viking Press Inc, copyright renewed © 1980 by Adelaide Yorke) and from the following works by Graham Greene: *Brighton Rock* (copyright 1938, renewed © 1966 by Graham Greene); *The Power and the Glory* (copyright 1940, renewed © 1968 by Graham Greene); *The Heart of the Matter* (copyright 1948, renewed © 1976 by Graham Greene); *The End of the Affair* (copyright 1951, renewed © 1979 by Graham Greene); *The Quiet American* (copyright 1955, renewed © 1983 by Graham Greene); *The Comedians* (copyright © 1965, 1966 by Graham Greene).

Preparation of the manuscript was aided by a grant from the Dean of the Faculty's office at Smith College. Laura Brewer, Jerri Higgins, Bobbie Kozash, and Dottie Pietraskiewicz gave me help with the word-processing.

I am grateful for the many kinds of support my parents, John and Dorothy Gorra, have given me.

My greatest debt is to my wife Reina Calderon.

MICHAEL GORRA
Northampton, Massachusetts

Introduction

This study does two things. First, it characterizes the English novel as written by the 'second generation' of this century's novelists, those born just after the turn of the century, who were too young to fight in the Great War, and who began publishing in the late 1920s.[1] Second, it describes the careers of four members of that generation: Henry Green, Anthony Powell, Graham Greene, and Evelyn Waugh. I was first drawn to these writers by a fondness for their novels and a sense that in biographical terms they 'fit' together. All four of them were born into the professional classes between 1903 and 1905, were educated at public schools and Oxford, and had ties of personal friendship to the other men in the group. Henry Green and Powell went to prep school and Eton together and shared digs at Oxford, where both became friends of Waugh's; Henry Green later served as the best man at Waugh's second wedding. Powell and Graham Greene overlapped at Balliol, and both moved after the Second World War through the pub-crawling literary world of Fitzrovia. Waugh and Graham Greene became friends in the late 1930s, when both worked on *Night and Day*, that short-lived British answer to *The New Yorker*; they became particularly close after the war, when they both criticized and admired each others' attempts to write about Catholicism. None of them, moreover, could be associated in any consistent way with the group of their contemporaries whom Samuel Hynes has dubbed 'the Auden generation', those writers who in the 1930s sought an accommodation between their art and leftist politics.[2]

As I read, however, I became convinced that these writers went together in more interesting ways. For the formal similarities between their work made them fit together as well, and above all in the way that they avoid, in their early novels in particular, any close exploration of their characters' interior lives. William H. Pritchard has described those novels as 'short, cool or opaque in [their] tone, suspicious of eloquence, committed to terse conversations among characters, neither genial nor "sincere" in [their] overall manner.'[3] I take that coolness, that suspicion, as a mark of the difficulty these writers had in representing the relation between subjective experience and the objective world – 'the antagonistic duality of soul and world' in Georg Lukacs' classic formulation[4] – in a period when both the operations of history and modernist experimentation had so combined as to make the conventional fictional relation between them no longer seem valid or interesting.

Halfway through *Howards End* (1910) E. M. Forster imagines placing a spectator on top of the Purbeck Hills, from which that viewer could see 'system after system of our island . . . roll together under his feet' from the 'valley of the Avon' to the Isle of Wight, spread out like a map before him.[5] Such a stance, Virginia Woolf argues in her 1940 essay, 'The Leaning Tower', is characteristic of her own generation's writers. They regard society from a tower of 'middle-class birth and expensive education',[6] held so steady by the confidence born of a youth in the Edwardian afternoon, that they could persuade themselves they saw 'the whole of life'[7] rolling under their feet, even in the aftermath of the Great War. But their successors, the generation with whom I am concerned, came to maturity during that aftermath itself. They too enjoyed that middle-class birth, that expensive education, but for them the tower had begun to lean under the weight of historical change, producing a 'slanting, sidelong' view of the world. And that view, Woolf argues, made them 'acutely conscious'[8] of both their position and its precariousness, and of their consequent inability fully to survey the world around them; an inability they sought to compensate for through a variety of artistic strategies or political and religious beliefs.

Woolf's immediate concern in that essay is with 'the Auden generation'. Hynes' group includes such writers as Auden himself, Christopher Isherwood, Stephen Spender, Edward Upward, C. Day Lewis, Rex Warner, and Louis MacNeice, with George Orwell standing some distance away from the main body. That group has set the terms in which the literary history of the 'thirties has been written. As Orwell wrote in his 1940 essay 'Inside the Whale', while there are 'many contemporary writers who are outside the current . . . there is not much doubt about what *is* the current. For the middle and late 'thirties, Auden, Spender & Co, *are* "the movement", just as Joyce, Eliot & Co. were for the 'twenties.'[9] The terms in which that movement is discussed have grown increasingly complex since Orwell wrote about it. Hynes in particular shows that writers like Auden and Isherwood were far more ambivalent about their political engagement than at the time they appeared to be. But it still dominates any discussion of the decade, as the photographs of Auden, Isherwood and Spender on the cover of Valentine Cunningham's encyclopaedic *British Writers of the Thirties* suggest, even though writers like MacNeice, Day Lewis, and Spender himself now go increasingly unread.[10] It's salutary, therefore, to recall that Orwell noted some writers swam outside the current, and praised the American Henry Miller for not trying to make his work an agent of social change. Or to remember the controlled scorn of Waugh's attack on the standard conception of 'the thirties' in his review of Spender's 1951 autobiography, *World Within World*, in which he describes how 'Certain young men ganged up and captured the decade' even though they 'by no means comprised the best of the period.' And he compares that conception to that of the 1890s, which 'means, and always will mean, Ernest Dowson and the decadence' and not Hardy, James, and Conrad.[11]

The four writers with whom I deal all swam outside the current of the decade in which they began their careers. But they are of the same age and background as the Auden group, and I contend that Woolf's terms provide a lens through which to view the writers of that generation as a whole, regardless of political involvement or allegiance. It is, in fact, the attempt to compensate for the limitations that the leaning tower imposes, rather than the specific choice of solution, that characterizes the writers of this generation. Auden does, after all, remain a characteristic figure even after – or precisely because – he begs forgiveness for the treason of all clerks and becomes an Anglican. But Waugh is equally as characteristic, in both his superb despairing scepticism and the Catholicism through which he sought to conquer it.

Critical attention has turned lately to what has been called 'minor literature' – minor not in terms of its quality, but in terms of its producer's marginal and subversive position within his or her society. The classic example is Kafka's position as a member of both German-speaking and Jewish minorities in Czech culture.[12] In those terms, the novels of Joyce, Lawrence, and Woolf, the three great British modernists – an Irishman, a miner's son, and a woman – are all minor literature. And in those terms both Hynes' grouping and the writers I deal with are representatives of what one might call 'major literature'. Isherwood and Auden – and Isherwood more than Auden – may be somewhat marginalized by their homosexuality. Nevertheless they, like Powell and Waugh, were born on that tower of middle-class birth and educated at public schools and ancient universities. Indeed, these writers belong to the first generation in which one can assume that the author of that once marginal and pushy middle-class form, the novel, will have had a gentleman's education, will have been to Oxford or Cambridge. Orwell's decision not to go to university makes him as much the exception in this generation as Forster's enrolment at King's made him in the age of Bennett and Wells.

In consequence these writers remain insiders in English society, even when in revolt against it, members of what would later be called the Establishment, in ways that a writer like Lawrence could never be. And they face, as Woolf's metaphor suggests, certain problems as writers because of those advantages. I've chosen to deal with such an homogenous group of novelists out of the belief that in doing so I might suggest certain constants about the 'major' fiction of this period, might establish a point of reference from which other critics might consider those writers who don't fit into this group. To the degree that I emphasize their homogeneity, I treat these writers as an example of what Lucien Goldmann would call a 'collective subject'.[13] Goldmann argues that 'the *structures* of the world of the work are homologous with the mental structures of certain social groups'.[14] An understanding of the 'world vision'[15] – or of what Raymond Williams has more elegantly called the 'structure of feeling'[16] – expressed by that homology cannot explain why an individual member of a social group becomes a great writer. But it can, Goldmann argues, explain why he becomes a particular kind of great writer.

In its account of their childhoods and education, Hynes' *The Auden Generation* remains the best account of the social group with which both he and I are concerned. He has little room, however, for those writers whose work does not embrace the political issues of the 1930s, and in consequence does not deal with the formal problems the novel as a genre confronted in that period, even when it shares some of the iconography – bombs, borders – of the poetry he so ably describes. Yet those formal problems are as much an expression of the period as Auden's call to action in 'Spain', and unlike the political issues of the 'thirties, those problems did not vanish with the coming of the Second World War. For the novelists I deal with, that is, their generation's crisis of belief became one with the aesthetic difficulties faced by the novel in the aftermath of the modernist revolution, and it is with those difficulties that I shall be most explicitly concerned. I have therefore extended my consideration of them to embrace their careers as a whole, to follow them as they move toward the mid-century and beyond. While I inevitably begin with the work these writers produced in the first decade of their careers, this is not a study of 'the 'thirties' alone.

The question of the novel's 'death' after Joyce bothers critics far more than it does novelists themselves. In this generation, for example, it was the book reviewer Cyril Connolly, and not Waugh or Greene, who wrote that 'Flaubert, Henry James, Proust, Joyce and Virginia Woolf have finished off the novel. Now all will have to be re-invented as from the beginning.'[17] Yet Connolly's words do suggest that however liberating modernism might be, that liberation depended on forestalling the young novelist's access to the genre's past, so that modernism itself became one more force that made the tower lean, one more thing that had to be compensated for. And the way the modernists 'finished off' the novel, Iris Murdoch has argued, was by making it turn inward, toward a fascination with an interior life that it depicts in isolation from, rather than in relation to, the world.[18] In the process, she writes in her 1961 essay, 'Against Dryness', the culture lost what, outside of the great nineteenth-century novel, it had never really had, 'a satisfactory Liberal theory of personality, a theory of man as free and separate and related to a rich and complicated world from which, as a moral being, he has much to learn'. In consequence, Murdoch suggests, the English novel at mid-century tended toward one of two extremes. It could be 'journalistic . . . a large shapeless quasi-documentary object, the degenerate descendant of the 19th-century novel, telling, with pale conventional characters, some straightforward story enlivened with empirical facts'. C. P. Snow and J. B. Priestley come to mind. Or it could be 'crystalline . . . a small quasi-allegorical object portraying the human condition and not containing "characters" in the 19th-century sense'.[19] One thinks of William Golding or, even more appropriately, of Samuel Beckett, in whose abstract consideration of an absurd human condition the social world hardly exists. But Murdoch ignores the possibility of a middle-ground, of that ground occupied by Beckett's contemporaries, the less extreme and more accessible writers I've chosen to deal with here. They gave the novel a way to go on by creating an idiom, suitable for the social conditions of post-Great War England, that simultaneously attempted to restore, and yet acknowledged the difficulties of maintaining, the novel's traditional function as a mediator between subjective experience and the objective world.

In making that claim I am, I know, resisting the apocalyptic internal logic of modernism. I am resisting above all its belief in the continuing necessity of a rigorous and radical experimentation, whose quasi-scientific purpose is to make the past obsolescent, that has produced the line of descent from Joyce to Beckett to the *nouveau roman*. But modernism is not the absolute standard of artistic achievement that until recently most criticism has made it seem, so much as the product of a particular era whose cultural imperatives may have little to do with those of a later period. My opening chapter will discuss the differences between the second generation's situation and that of their modernist predecessors, differences that made the modernist aesthetic unavailable to the writers with whom I am concerned. Each subsequent chapter provides something like the biography of a literary sensibility, whose relation to my historical model is a flexible one. Yeats writes that 'We make out of the quarrel with others, rhetoric, but of the quarrel with ourselves, poetry';[20] a statement that one can gloss by citing Clive James' observation that writers 'find their guiding principles by assessing the implication of what they have done already'.[21] My account of each novelist describes that process of assessment, treating each major work as a revision of the books that preceded it, in which the writer attempts to work out his quarrels with himself and so address the implications – or the limitations – of his own style, and through that of his historical period as well.

1

The English Novel:
Modernism and After

By the time Woolf published *Mrs Dalloway* in 1925, the English novel appeared to have come to a simultaneous fruition and dissolution that paralleled that of the liberal society on which it was based. Throughout the nineteenth century the novel had been one of the chief ways through which European society both explored the meaning, and affirmed the value, of what Lionel Trilling describes as liberalism's chief tenet, 'the value of individual existence in all its variousness, complexity, and difficulty'.[1] With the new century the novel itself became an embodiment of that ideal. The late style of Henry James, so demanding to read that one is flattered by his sense of one's adequacy to it, provided an expression of a more far-ranging liberalism, of a greater generosity of spirit, than any society could hope to reach in practice. And with that style what Lawrence called 'the one bright book of life'[2] achieved a peculiar democratization of spirit. I say peculiar because it had nothing to do with the novel's accessibility to the common reader, but depended instead upon the novelist's declaration of his or her own independence, the right to choose whatever subject matter or prose style he or she wanted, even the right to make the novel readable only by the fit and the few. Yet most modern novelists did not use this new sense of freedom to transform the novel into an object of its own self-regard, but employed it to extend the breadth of the novel's understanding, its sense of the range of human life and of the variety of ways in which that life could be seen and experienced and expressed and interpreted.

Such freedom fulfilled the promise of the nineteenth-century novel as, perhaps, the welfare state fulfilled the promise of nineteenth-century liberalism. Yet there were costs as well as gains in the fulfilment, in the transition from the individualism of Emma Woodhouse to Bloomsbury's cult of personal relations. The modernists used their new freedom to make an increasingly detailed exploration of their characters' interior lives, an exploration

1

the terms of which differ markedly from those of their predecessors. The nineteenth-century novel, Lukacs writes in *The Theory of the Novel*, had described 'the adventure of interiority'[3] in terms of 'the antagonistic duality of soul and world', which creates the self-consciousness out of which that interiority grows. In describing that adventure, Lukacs argues, the novelist must attempt to construct a harmonious relationship between the world of objects and the subjective imagination. Yet while the genre longs for an identity between the soul and world, the word and the world, it remains suspicious of it as well. For the novel's concern is with the life of a 'problematic'[4] individual, often a woman, flayed into a self-consciousness that both damns and distinguishes her by the gap between her desires and the world's failure to fulfil them, an unhappy soul 'that seeks adventures in order . . . to find its own essence'.[5] Such a quest for what Lukacs calls the 'concealed totality of life'[6] must inevitably fail, for the hero learns 'through experience that a mere glimpse of meaning is the highest that life has to offer'.[7] Yet in that failure, the novel 'shows polemically the impossibility of achieving [its] necessary object',[8] and so provides a potent criticism of the life from which it grows. Nor is that search the character's alone. In *Madame Bovary*, Emma's quest for a way to make the world fit the requirements of her imagination is also Flaubert's. The needs of her soul coalesce with his search for a form, and the novel's ethic becomes its aesthetic as well.[9]

For Lukacs, then, the novel is built upon the irrevocable split between subjective consciousness and the objective world. With Henry James, however, the novel began to deal with the 'adventure of interiority' in a way that subordinated the world to the soul. James' innovations in the management of point of view combined with the late-Victorian loss of belief in the existence of objective truth to produce the impressionism of his disciples Conrad and Ford, in which the characters' 'adventures' matter less than the interpretation placed on them by the character through whose eyes the author reveals those adventures. And Woolf, of course, chose to describe what she calls 'character in itself',[10] divorced from the objects – houses, clothing, 'hot-water bottle[s]'[11] – that she felt determined it for those writers who had not absorbed James' lessons, people such as Arnold Bennett or H. G. Wells. She concentrates on describing the mind in the act of receiving the 'myriad impressions' of an ordinary day, 'an incessant shower of innumerable atoms'. For 'Life', she argues in this famous passage:

. . . is not a series of gig lamps symmetrically arranged; but a luminous halo, a semi-transparent envelope surrounding us from the beginning of consciousness to the end. Is it not the task of the novelist to convey this varying, this unknown and uncircumscribed spirit, whatever aberration or complexity it may display, with as little mixture of the alien and external as possible?[12]

The house of fiction may have many windows, but for Woolf, as for the late James, it seems to have only one. She provides, Graham Greene says, not 'Regent Street . . . but Regent Street seen by Mrs Dalloway',[13] cuts the soul free from the material world that had so completely absorbed her predecessors. The soul and the world may in her work remain antagonistic. But there is no duality between them, for the claims of the soul take precedence over those of a world which is judged, and condemned, like Mr Ramsay's insensitivity to emotion in *To the Lighthouse*, according to the degree that it fails to fulfil them. If, as such different critics as Lukacs and Trilling argue, the novel traditionally describes a search for authentic values among what Trilling calls the 'inferior objects offered by the social world',[14] then with *Mrs Dalloway* its work appears complete. That search is no longer necessary, for the soul has in itself become the novel's supreme value, and the world exists only in relation to it.

One must pause to examine just how this happened. Roman Jakobson has argued that realistic prose fiction is largely metonymic. 'The realistic author', he writes, 'metonymically digresses from the plot to the atmosphere and from the characters to the setting in space and time',[15] from the part to the whole it suggests, so that the narrative is 'forwarded essentially by contiguity'.[16] A writer moves from one object or scene to the next because they are either spatially or chronologically contiguous, and in that movement suggests an entire world, as George Eliot does in making *Adam Bede*'s Arthur Donnithorne travel from his grandfather's manor house to the Poyser's farmhouse kitchen. Yet Eliot describes only the various stops Arthur makes on that trip, and not the trip itself. She moves from one of Woolf's 'gig lamps' to another, without pausing to examine the 'innumerable atoms' in the space between; atoms whose existence one must assume the metonymy implies, just as it implies the social order of which young Donnithorne is a part. Metonymy's expansiveness depends, therefore, upon 'deletion' – upon the reader's conventional assumption of the presence in the work of what is not actually on the page, of all the details the author has chosen to exclude.[17] Jakobson argues that a different law governs poetry: that of metaphor, which works not through contiguity but through similarity, through the comparison of apparently dissimilar things. Metaphor allows the mind to juxtapose the disparate fragments of the world and reveal their hidden correspondences; to disrupt that neat progression of 'gig lamps', and explore the nature of what lies hidden between them. And modernism, as Malcolm Bradbury defines it, relies upon the metaphoric, upon:

> . . . the internal stylization of the arts, the distortion of the familiar surface of observed reality, and the disposition of artistic contents according to the logic of metaphor, form, or symbol, rather than according to a linear logic taken from story or history.[18]

Modernism as an ethos requires two things: first, the artist's imagination or memory of a stable, conventional culture; second, that culture's disruption and the artist's consequent awareness of the inadequacy of its artistic conventions to express either the multiplicity or the chaos of contemporary life. Yet in breaking with the past the modernist nevertheless relies upon it, for it provides the base from which he departs and against which he works, a set of rules to break and bend and distort.

Bradbury's account of modernism as the 'distortion of the familiar' sums up an age in which, Woolf argues, 'All human relations have shifted – those between masters and servants, husbands and wives, parents and children';[19] shifted as a new generation rebelled against late Victorian rigidity and began to ask why the given relations of society need be so given; shifted as Freud began to reveal the complexity and irrationality of the human mind, as Nietzsche suggested morality was a construct to hide man's amorality from himself. Yet in moving through that wreckage the modernist, in theory, finds a 'means of overcoming chaos'[20] through an artistic representation and contemplation of that chaos so powerful that one does not feel the lack of an external order, of that familiar 'linear logic taken from story or history'.

As David Lodge argues in *The Modes of Modern Writing*, modernism's reliance upon metaphor extends to the novel. The modernist novel will not be bound by the world as it is, but tries instead to create its own order out of chaos, to construct a meaning for a world otherwise without one. Realism had attempted to enact belief in the linear logic to which Bradbury refers. Yet the late Victorians' growing awareness of the mind's operations had helped shatter the belief in the single objective universe that linear logic required, and so modernism attempted to effect 'a complete severance'[21] between art and any externally given belief. The distortions of the modernist novel triumph over the world, announcing its inability to control the mind's free play. The past, as both Proust and Faulkner showed in radically different ways, is not always past, for the mind not only works in a linear fashion, but operates metaphorically as well. It finds correspondences between events far removed in space and time, and in doing so annihilates the distance between them. Modernism uses metaphor to extricate itself from a realism no longer adequate to experience; to give shape from within, not just to one scene or situation, but to the whole universe itself.

But if the form of the novel changed, the nature of its relation to society did not. The realistic novel's attempt to negotiate the 'antagonistic duality of soul and world' is, Goldmann writes, 'homologous' to:

> . . . the internal contradiction between individualism as a universal value produced by bourgeois society and the important and painful limitations that this society itself brought to the possibilities of the development of the individual.[22]

Woolf's insistence upon both the fragmentary nature of experience and the primacy of the individual sensibility has a similarly 'homologous' and contradictory relation to the atomized individualism of the late bourgeois society in which she grew up. Her emphasis on sensibility depends upon the leisure and security born of the long, stable prosperity of the nineteenth-century Pax Britannica of which she, like Clarissa Dalloway, was a beneficiary. Yet in their subordination of society to the free play of the individual mind, Woolf's novels not only attempt, in true atomistic fashion, to cut themselves free from the social conditions that have made them possible, but also effectively deny the antagonistic duality of soul and world that creates the interiority she so highly values.

Woolf's own mind is like that of Austen's Emma Woodhouse,

one 'lively and at ease, [that] can do with seeing nothing, and can see nothing that does not answer'.[23] Like Emma, she believes in the mind's ability to make the world respond to its desires. But while Emma's self-confidence is a delusion and the subject of Austen's ironic regard, Woolf's is genuine, and comes from the fact that she belongs to the generation she describes in 'The Leaning Tower' as having had:

> . . . when the crash came in 1914 . . . their past, their education, safe behind them, safe within them. They had the memory of a peaceful boyhood, the knowledge of a settled civilization. Even though the war cut into their lives, and ended some of them, they wrote, and still write, as if the tower were firm beneath them.[24]

The chaos around them merely confirmed the modernists in their belief that they could order it. If, as Robert Kiely writes, Woolf could not, as a modernist, see 'structures without seeing shards',[25] she nevertheless had the self-confidence that comes from 'the knowledge of a settled civilization' to believe that she could make a new structure from those shards.

Yet the situation is more complex than I've so far suggested. For as Goldmann's statement about the internal contradictions of bourgeois society suggests, the prosperity and stability that gave Woolf her extraordinary self-confidence led as well to a culture intolerant of the values in her that it helped produce. The structure of feeling from which her novels grew was concomitant with a social fragmentation that rendered her society too complex for any one mind to grasp it whole. At the turn of the century, what G. K. Chesterton called 'this strange loneliness of millions in a crowd'[26] resulted in an increasing rigidity of English social structure and mores. The stultifying manners of Galsworthy's Forsytes became not only a badge of identification worn by otherwise faceless individuals, but the type of a society in lockstep with itself. One feels this rigidification, as Martin Green writes, in both Kipling's identification of art with imperial power, and the culture's growing reliance upon cliché;[27] in the presence of the public school 'monolith';[28] above all, and on a European scale, in the diplomatic gridlock that led to the Great War. And in confronting this complex of forces the liberal sensibility of both author and character had to struggle for the moral freedom that earlier novelists had taken for granted.

Yet as Wells wrote in 1911, 'while we live in a period of tightening and extending social organisation, we live also in a period of adventurous and insurgent thought'.[29] Woolf's aesthetic carries that insurgency into the 1920s. Her work makes a declaration of the soul's independence from the world that is necessitated by the very power the world had come to possess, and is in that typical of the modernist novel. 'Compare', Raymond Williams writes:

> . . . the final 'settlement' chapter in early Victorian English novels – e.g., Gaskell's *Mary Barton* – and the final 'breakaway' chapter in English novels between 1910–1940 – e.g., Lawrence's *Sons and Lovers*.[30]

Or Lily Briscoe's final stroke of the brush in Woolf's *To the Lighthouse* (1927), which both orders her world and liberates her from it; or Joyce's decision, however ironic, to allow the form of *A Portrait of the Artist as a Young Man* to echo Stephen's growing self-absorption by turning the end of the novel into a diary in which the reader is left alone with Stephen's isolated soul. Such characters can exist as free individuals only by declaring their independence of the society that had first sponsored the idea of that freedom. As the nineteenth-century novel concentrated upon gentlemen and ladies, whose position both demands and makes possible a settlement with their society, so the modernists take the artist as the type of the modern hero, the character most able to break away and for whom breaking away is most essential.

With the modernists the novel as a genre fulfils the promise of the 'adventure of interiority' by transforming that interiority into the world itself, as part of a pan-European effort to create an alternative world through the power of art alone. Yet if in subordinating the world to the soul, if in using metaphor to reveal the 'concealed totality of life', the genre does reach the goal toward which Lukacs says the nineteenth-century novel strives, it does so only by denying the 'antagonistic duality of soul and world' upon which the form depends, at precisely that moment when the promises of liberalism have made that duality most keenly and painfully felt. The modernist novel succeeds by destroying the terms upon which its achievements depend.

Yet to the young writers of the late 1920s that artistic apocalypse did not signal anything like the 'death' of the novel later critics have taken it to be. To them the modernist revolution did not so much work out what José Ortega y Gassett called the novel's 'quarry' as blow open any number of once 'narrow and concealed veins';[31] new areas of experience to explore, and new styles through which to explore them. Even the young Evelyn Waugh, not yet a reactionary, admired Joyce and Lawrence extravagantly.[32] But in considering the second generation's first novels, one is, nevertheless, startled by how little they owe to their modernist predecessors beyond a general sense of concentration upon form; so little, in fact, that those novels seem to pose the question of Robert Frost's ovenbird: 'what to make of a diminished thing?'[33]

It is a diminishing above all of the creative spirit. Anthony Powell came down from Oxford with what he calls the 'ambition . . . of every reasonably literate young man of the period; vague intention to write a novel myself one of these days'.[34] At first one takes his remark as a sign of the genre's continuing vitality. Then one feels troubled by the difference between Powell's consideration of the novel as an accoutrement of civilized life, and Lawrence's sense of the high creative mission that the 'one bright book of life' demands. The novelists of Powell's generation are on the one hand almost entirely without the modernist's sense of innovation as both an adventure and a necessity, and on the other lack the expansiveness of traditional realism. They neither return to tradition nor break with it, and so seem hesitant, claustrophobic, constrained by their material: by gentility in Elizabeth Bowen's *The Hotel* (1927), or by the battle against it in Christopher Isherwood's *All the Conspirators* (1928); by the earnestness with which the writer engages his character's problems in Graham Greene's *The Man Within* (1929), or Henry Green's *Blindness* (1926). Even the structure of such buoyant comic novels as Waugh's *Decline and Fall* (1928) and Powell's *Afternoon Men* (1931) seems brittle and circumscribed. Each novel's last scene duplicates its first one, and this circular structure suggests that nothing has changed, that the novel's world has made no movement since the book began. Such a novel works according to a linear logic that takes one nowhere, and so becomes a metaphor for the life the novelist describes. The part these novelists describe *is* the whole, the shard the structure, so that the novel's metonymy is frustrated and its form stands as a metaphor for itself.

Such novels cannot offer the modernist prospect of unifying the world's fragments. Indeed the absence of that unification suggests a crucial difference between these novelists and their immediate predecessors. *Decline and Fall* has no 'breakaway' scene, no liberation of the soul from the world. Instead, Waugh's protagonist Paul Pennyfeather welcomes his return to the constraints within which he lived at the start of the novel, for the experience of freedom Waugh describes in the novel's middle chapters has only brought him into jail. Francis Andrews in Greene's *The Man Within* can only break away at the cost of his own life, and Arthur Zouch in Powell's third novel, *From a View to a Death* (1933), dies while out fox-hunting in the attempt to climb above his middle-class origins. Henry Green does end *Blindness* with what appears to be a 'breakaway'. His blind protagonist John Haye emerges from an epileptic seizure into a new sense of his own happiness and independence – and yet he cannot escape his loss of sight. Yet that sense is not a 'breakaway' but a 'settlement', a reconciliation to his blindness. Green was a far more consciously experimental novelist than any of his contemporaries. He continues the modernist tradition both in the linguistic innovations of *Living* (1929) and *Party Going* (1939), and in his later attempts to see what the novel genre can do without, omitting plot resolutions in *Concluding* (1948) and narrative commentary in the dialogue-novels *Nothing* (1950) and *Doting* (1952). Nevertheless he shares with his contemporaries a sense of the soul's inability to reshape the world that distinguishes their work from the work of their modernist predecessors.

But, in the years after Woolf had proclaimed:

. . . if a writer were a free man and not a slave, if he could write what he chose, not what he must, if he could base his work upon his own feeling and not upon convention, there would be no plot, no comedy, no tragedy, no love interest or catastrophe in the accepted style, and perhaps not a single button sewn on as the Bond Street tailors would have it . . .[35]

why did the second generation renounce the freedom newly won for them, and return, in constructing their early novels in particular, to that 'linear logic taken from story or history', as if life were indeed 'a series of gig lamps symmetrically arranged'? Why, as Graham Greene noted with approval, did his contemporaries submit themselves, 'after twenty years of subjectivity . . . to the old dictatorship, to the detached and objective treatment'?[36] Why did his generation do so little to explore the 'narrow and concealed veins' its predecessors had so newly blown open? Perhaps the answer to those generations is a simple one. Woolf's aesthetic was for her immediate successors already *passé*, even as she wrote *The Waves* (1931). The questions with which both the British modernists and most subsequent criticism of the novel deal are not the central issues for the novelists of the second generation. They do not emphasize the soul, the interior life, at the expense of the world. Their theme is instead the failure to achieve a satisfactory relationship between individual consciousness and objective reality in a society, and with an art, suspicious of the value, the relevance, and even the existence of the interior life itself.

It might be best, therefore, to approach the second generation through a brief consideration of two less radical modernists, Ford Madox Ford and E. M. Forster. Both Ford and Forster believe in the value of individual experience, yet neither of them treats character 'in itself', as Woolf demanded the novelist should. To them, character can never be 'in itself', for their subject lies in the conflict between an embattled liberalism and historical events that do not greatly value the individual. For Ford in *Parade's End* (1924–8), the Great War and the administrative monoliths it creates swallow Christopher Tietjens precisely because his great talents give the lie to them. In Forster's *A Passage to India* (1924), imperialism precludes the possibility of friendship between Englishman and Indian. Those writers know, precisely because they deal with some large historical event, how little the individual soul can either resist or ignore the world through which it moves. Their work, in which one finds a liberalism that has not yet pursued its implications to the point of dissolution, suggests why modernism did not destroy the novel. The Pax Britannica ended. History did not let the novel die, for in reasserting its power over individual lives, not merely in terms of social convention, but in a brutal, bloody, and obvious way, it restored the novel's traditional subject, the relation of the soul to the world.

The French Revolution, Lukacs asserts, made history for the first time a '*mass experience* . . . on a European scale'.[37] The Great War made it so for a second time. To the writers with whom I am concerned, it provided, as Waugh wrote in 1930:

> . . . the atmosphere of their adolescence. Darkened streets, food rations, the impending dread of the War Office telegram, hysterical outbursts of hate and sentiment, untrustworthy sour-

ces of information and the consequent rumours and scares; these were the circumstances which war-time children observed as universal and presumed to be normal.[38]

Not 'normal', but 'presumed to be'; and one notes the contrast with the sense of war as an interruption to normal life that Lawrence provides in a story like 'England, My England'. Waugh's generation was not old enough to fight in the Great War, but it could neither escape the facts of current history, nor rely upon the sense of security created by what Woolf calls 'the knowledge of a settled society'. For after the war, and as a result of its horrors, England entered a period in which, as Orwell argued in 'Inside the Whale' (1940):

. . . so far as the younger generation was concerned, the official beliefs were dissolving like sandcastles . . . by 1930 there was no activity, except perhaps scientific research, the arts and left-wing politics, that a thinking person could believe in. The debunking of western civilization had reached its climax and 'disillusionment' was immensely widespread. Who now could take it for granted to go through life in the ordinary middle-class way, as a soldier, a clergyman, a stockbroker, an Indian Civil Servant or what not? And how many of the values by which our grandfathers lived could now be taken seriously? Patriotism, religion, the Empire, the family, the sanctity of marriage, the Old School tie, birth, breeding, honour, discipline – anyone of ordinary education could turn the whole lot of them inside out in three minutes.[39]

– a sense summed up in the title of Robert Graves' 1929 memoir, *Goodbye to All That*,[40] to the public school, to gentility, to war, to England itself. History was in consequence revealed as what Lukacs calls 'an uninterrupted process of changes'.[41] Indeed the sheer fact of change itself stands to the writers of the second generation as imperialism did to Forster. It serves as a reminder of the power of the world over individual experience, even when, like Agatha Runcible in Waugh's *Vile Bodies*, one falls in love with that power, whose pace one cannot control and in whose innovations one delights. Agatha wants not just the racing-car whose crash leads to her death, but life itself, to go "Faster. Faster" – and as if in reply, the novel careers toward the war with which it ends.[42]

The writers of Waugh's generation must work, Woolf argues, 'under the influence of change, under the threat of war'.[43] Or with the memory of one Great War and facing the prospect of another; and under the influence of the Russian Revolution, the first Labour government in 1923, and the General Strike of 1926; the cinema, birth control, and jazz; Freud and Einstein; Picasso and modernism in general; and later, the Depression and the rise of fascism. So 'the tower of middle-class birth and expensive education', from which the artists of her own generation had regarded society began to lean, and:

> Directly we feel that a tower leans we become acutely conscious that we are upon a tower. All [these] writers too are acutely tower conscious; conscious of their middle-class birth; of their expensive educations. Then when we come to the top of the tower how strange the view looks – not altogether upside down, but slanting, sidelong.[44]

Such a writer must be 'acutely conscious' of the way in which his background has shaped his vision. He cannot persuade himself that he looks 'at the whole of life', and though conscious of the distortions his position causes, can do nothing about them. He is instead filled with the sense of his own impotence before history, of his inability to control his own circumstances, that seems the exact opposite of the confidence enjoyed by Woolf's own generation.

The writer of the second generation, then, must ask how to turn that incapacity into artistic capital, must search for a technique that will enable him to use his position upon that tower. For technique, as Graham Greene writes, is above all a way of:

> . . . evading the personally impossible, of disguising a deficiency . . . [hiding] the traces of the botched line.
>
> The consciousness of what he cannot do – and it is sometimes something so apparently simple that a more popular writer never gives it a thought – is a mark of the good novelist . . . (There is irony, of course, in the fact that the technique an original writer used to cover his personal difficulties will later be taken over by other writers who may not share his difficulties and who believe that his value has lain in his method.)[45]

Greene's concluding parenthesis suggests the reason why his generation did not, on the whole, work in the paths suggested by the modernists. The second generation lacked what Woolf calls 'the knowledge of a settled civilization', upon which modernism depended. A society in which 'the official beliefs were dissolving like sandcastles' was too unstable for innovation on a large scale; what could one press against, or break away from? Modernism addressed a different set of historical circumstances from the one these writers faced, and they were in general shrewd enough to realize that they could not treat modernist technique as a sort of cookbook for fiction, flipping through the pages for recipes. For the second generation the most influential section of *Ulysses* would seem to be not 'Circe' or 'Sirens' or 'Penelope', but the linguistically conservative 'Wandering Rocks', a montage of nineteen brief scenes happening simultaneously all around Dublin. Or does the quick cutting of Waugh and Greene owe more to D. W. Griffith?

The second generation's creative difficulties seem, once more, far closer to Forster's, who wrote in *Howards End* (1910):

> We are not concerned with the very poor. They are unthinkable, and only to be approached by the statistician or the poet. This story deals with gentlefolk, or with those who are obliged to pretend that they are gentlefolk.[46]

Forster's novels are marked by a purposeful modesty born of his consciousness that he cannot pretend to deal with 'the whole of life' but can only represent one small part of human experience. He is the first major English novelist to take as his subject the limitations of gentility; as such he now seems perhaps the most influential of all twentieth-century English novelists. In reading a novel such as *A Room With a View*, one is so constantly aware of all Forster has excluded that what he includes seems, not insignificant, but stifled and strained; a constriction of range, the liabilities of which Forster escapes only through admitting his own inability to make the full metonymic extension the genre had traditionally required. Yet Forster's decision to write out of such a partial and fragmentary vision was by no means inevitable for a novelist of his generation. It was a choice, a means of evading a deficiency; in Forster's case, perhaps his reticence about his own homosexuality, which made him aware that he could not claim to see life whole in a novel that excluded it

For the second generation, however, Forster's choice became an inevitability. The writers of that generation laboured under the belief that everything important had happened already, not just in the arts, but in British history itself. The great subject of the decade in which they began to write was, for example, unavailable to them. They were just too young to deal directly with the Great War and, as Waugh writes, 'were often reproachfully reminded, particularly by the college servants, of how impoverished and subdued we were in comparison with those great men'[47] who had fought, men just a few years older, but whose experience of the trenches nevertheless made them members of another generation. Nor could these writers pretend to the social range of Lawrence, who had made the journey from the coal mines to the country houses those mines supported. The fact that they came from the professional, public-school and university-educated class meant that they were subject to the limitations of that class's increasing homogenization; and in particular to the suburbanization, both physical and intellectual, of middle-class English life, which denied the young novelist the range of social experience once available to George Eliot in the countryside, or Dickens in the city.[48] The narrator of Isherwood's Berlin novels may climb or plunge in exploring the social hierarchy of that European city, but the characters in his English books, such as *The Memorial* (1932), come exclusively from his own class. Insofar as it dealt with English material, the social range of the novel shrank. Its characters tended, in comparison with those in a book like *Adam Bede*, to come from a single social group, and those novels, like Henry Green's *Living*, in which they did not, were seen by their first readers as exceptions.

That constriction of social range is symptomatic of other, more individual limitations which I will explore in the chapters to come. The writer of this generation had to find a way to deal with the imaginative restrictions of his age and sensibility without falling prey to them. In *Enemies of Promise* (1938) Cyril Connolly sketches a dialectical relationship between the 'mandarin' prose of high modernism, and the 'vernacular' of his own generation. The mandarin style, he argues, works through an 'inflation either of language or imagination or of both',[49] an inflation that creates a world of boundless possibility. The vernacular, a stylistic reaction against the extremities of modernism, relies upon a corresponding deflation of language, a 'dumb-ox' style that is for the younger generation 'the only way to escape from Chelsea's Apes of God and Bloomsbury's Sacred Geese'.[50] The terms 'dumb-ox' and 'Apes of God' come from Wyndham Lewis, who in *Men Without Art* (1934), Connolly writes, 'attacked Hemingway for being a "dumb ox", for choosing stupid inarticulate heroes who are the passive victims of circumstance rather than active and intelligent masters of their fate'.[51] But Lewis's criticism of Hemingway is marked by an historical awareness that Connolly misses. For Lewis, Hemingway's use of a 'dumb-ox' hero is a way to confront not just his modernist predecessors, but the quality of his society as a whole. His work stands, Lewis argues, as the 'typical art'[52] of its period, the art of a man 'shell-shocked'[53] by the bombardment of modern civilization, the art of:

> . . . the 'folk', of the masses, who are the cannon-fodder, the cattle outside the slaughter-house, serenely chewing the cud – *of those to whom things are done*, in contrast to those who have executive will and intelligence.[54]

Such work shares in the devaluation of, and refusal to believe in, any grand emotion that Paul Fussell argues is consequent on the Great War.[55] Hemingway drains his prose of explicit emotion to present a world without the spiritual possibilities that mandarin prose implies, a world in which his characters are not, and cannot be, in control of their own experience. Yet he does not triumph over the poverty of the world he describes, as Lewis does, but writes in the first person, as one 'of those to whom things are done'. His world contains no mandarins. He exempts no one from the bombardment, but instead uses the emotional anorexia of his style to create a sense of individual powerlessness before the large motions of history.

Such as age, Lewis writes, demands that the writer adopt what he calls 'the Great With-Out'.[56] Modern civilization, which has made men into things, requires that a writer treat his characters not subjectively, through an examination of the interior life, but objectively, through a report – often in excruciating detail – of the character's outward appearance and machine-like actions. And the characteristic art of that civilization, Lewis writes in *The Wild Body* (1927), must of necessity be comic, for one has no choice but to laugh at the sight of 'a *thing* behaving like a person',[57] the thing to which modern society has reduced 'those to whom things are done'. Such a 'wild body' stumbles about as if it were alive, but actually operates according to a set of complicated mechanical laws, which the artist's 'non-moral'[58] satire must expose; non-moral because it purports not to pass judgement but merely to provide an objective description of the 'rhythmic scheme'[59] by which such bodies operate.

Lewis's conception of the comic will be particularly important in considering both Powell and Waugh. He describes his characters from without, and in doing so emphasizes the volition that they are without, the soul's impotence before the world. The four novelists with whom I am concerned stand between Lewis and Hemingway. They all describe what Lewis calls the 'shell-shocked man', but they also suffer from a form of shell-shock themselves. Yet they remain suspicious of the pity that Hemingway evokes, suggesting instead that in a world of cannon-fodder, in a world that glorifies the machine and has seen that glorification triumphant in the trenches, the subjective life and all the emotions that pertain to it have become not just inaccessible, as they are for Nick Adams in 'Big Two-Hearted River', but irrelevant.

It was, perhaps, a sense of the world for which their education had prepared them. Waugh's description of the 'atmosphere' the Great War created does in some ways correspond to the 'normal' childhood of a boy from the professional classes – to what Orwell describes in 'Such, Such Were the Joys', as the 'irrational terrors and lunatic misunderstandings'[60] of boarding school life. 'The best reason I have for opposing Fascism', Auden wrote in 1934, 'is that at school I lived in a Fascist state.'[61] Both Waugh in *Decline and Fall* and Greene in *It's a Battlefield* (1934) drew a comparison, only half-jokingly, between the elaborate regimentation of a public school and that of a prison. Such an education fosters what Martin Green describes as a set of 'aristo-military' Kiplingesque values that affront 'the humanist belief that individual fulfilment is the ultimate moral criterion. Kipling says that individual lives exist to be used up in the service of social causes.'[62] At public schools boys were not valued as individuals, but to the degree that they could fit some pre-existing position in the school's communal life: prefect, member of the Eleven, fag, sixth former, new boy, and so on. In his first term at Lancing, Waugh found that the school's complicated etiquette allowed him to talk only to other new boys. Since he started in May, that meant there was just one other boy to whom he could speak. Such schools made boys into roles, treated them and encouraged them to treat others as if they could be defined entirely by the objective world.

All four of the writers I am concerned with went to public schools. None of them fit comfortably within the games-playing hierarchy they found there, and so despite their sense of their own individuality and perhaps of their own gifts, they played insignificant roles in the school monolith. Yet they all remain firmly within the English Establishment and so both partake of, and rebel against, their society's devaluation of individual experience. They face certain problems as writers not in spite of, but because of, their education, for they are too much a part of their society to have the incentive fully to break away from it, and are crippled because they cannot. Yet that very fact is precisely what makes their work homologous not only to the experience of their social group, but to that of England itself – is what makes them the most representative of mid twentieth-century English novelists. The Great War made their experience, which had always been characteristic of the public-school monolith, homologous to that of English society as a whole. A Maxim gun does not, after all, care about the individuality of its victims; neither does the ever 'faster, faster' force of historical change itself. The writers with whom I deal cannot declare their independence from Woolf's 'leaning tower' but remain committed to the 'slanting, sidelong' view it offers, for they write as members of a ruling class, of a ruling nation, slowly becoming aware that it is losing both its function and its position, that all it has left is an irretrievable past. Their sense of the power of the world over the soul not only gives formal expression to the English ruling class's half-conscious crisis of confidence after the Great War, but also, and more importantly, provides a foreshadowing of Britain's long slide from global power after the Second World War. Their collective project has two stages. In the early years of their careers they demonstrate the irrelevance or even the nonexistence of the soul in the world the trenches have left them. Beginning around the start of the Second World War, however, they attempt through the search for an adequate style to find some means of restoring value to the subjective life; a way of maintaining the importance, the credibility and the sensibility of individual experience in an increasingly depersonalized world.

In doing so these novelists attempt to restore the 'saving power of the imagination'[63] that was, Martin Green argues, a casualty of their education. Lewis's modernist confidence enables him to believe that his own 'executive will and intelligence' will allow him to triumph over the world of 'cannon-fodder'. His successors have no such faith. In *Labels* Waugh describes his first sight of a Mediterranean landmark like this:

> I do not think I shall ever forget the sight of Etna at sunset; the mountain almost invisible in a blur of pastel grey, glowing on the top and then repeating its shape, as though reflected, in a wisp of grey smoke, with the whole horizon behind radiant with pink light, fading gently into a grey pastel sky. Nothing I have ever seen in Art or Nature was quite so revolting.[64]

The passage is symptomatic of the way in which Waugh and his contemporaries attempted to see through the pieties of English society; in that, if in little else, they were indeed the children of the modernist attack upon convention. Yet they cannot summon the modernists' sense of belief in their own powers. For while his undercutting of the tourist's standard romantic vision does suggest the impossibility of believing in such emotions, Waugh cannot offer an alternative to that romanticism; can only negate the clichés of his culture rather than transcend them. The writer who has some sustaining belief feels himself capable of that transcendence, capable of explaining the world; is marked, as Lawrence was, by a willingness to assert his mastery over the life his art describes. The early fiction of Waugh's generation is, in contrast, marked by the suspicion of all beliefs that the style of his description of Etna shows, so chary of emotion, of grand language, of ideals. Graham Greene even makes a point of not allowing his protagonists to believe in their own courage.

Yet what, Orwell writes, 'do you achieve, after all, by getting rid of such primal things as patriotism and religion? You have not necessarily got rid of the need for *something to believe in*.'[65] The writers Samuel Hynes calls the 'Auden generation' found that belief in left-wing politics, to which they were drawn, in part, for the security its certainties afforded. Waugh and Graham Greene built their later work around their Catholicism. But their early novels, like those of Powell and Henry Green, are marked by the same consciousness of their own lack of conviction that Corelli Barnett has argued characterized British foreign policy between the wars – a politics and a style that, operating out of a sense of its own ineffectiveness, attempts to postpone crisis, the need to make decisions or assertions.[66] Yet England itself had what Waugh described as a 'Churchillian Renaissance',[67] a rebirth of the national will to fight; so too these writers began to search for a style, began that Yeatsian quarrel with themselves that would enable them to evade their own limitations.

The question, then, becomes one of method, of technique, that 'consciousness of what one cannot do'. How best to capture that impotence, without making the art itself incomplete? The novelist must build into the work a sense of its own limitations, so that the book suggests what it has excluded, and why. So Waugh in *Vile Bodies* (1930) ignores his characters' interior lives. Yet rather than let us assume that they have been conventionally deleted, like the muddy lanes of Arthur Donnithorne's trip, Waugh implies that what he does not present does not exist, and the novel's power grows from an awareness of its own purposeful lacunae. The difficulty of such work is that so little seems actually to be present within the novel. How can a work that depends, as Michael North writes of Connolly, upon a 'confession of failure contained within its own stylistic refutation'[68] be something other than trivial? If fiction is traditonally metonymic, a digressive attempt to make the part stand for the whole, then how should one evaluate a novel like *Vile Bodies*, in which the part Waugh chooses to represent essentially denies the existence of the whole? Yet if the novel is also a search for the 'concealed totality of life', such a denial does allow *Vile Bodies* to make a criticism of life that fulfils Lukacs' criterion for the genre by showing 'polemically the impossibility of achieving' that goal.

Nevertheless, the question of the scale of that generation's achievement remains, and in a way that Lukacs' own changing use of the word 'totality' suggests. As he moves from the Hegelian idealism of his early work to the Marxist materialism of *History and Class Consciousness* (1923), Lukacs begins to use the word as a sociological and political equivalent of Jakobson's strictly linguistic term 'metonymy'. The emphasis of his work on fiction changes accordingly. In *The Historical Novel* he describes the genre not as an account of the 'antagonistic duality of soul and world', but as an attempt 'to evoke the totality of the process of social development . . . [its] essential aim . . . is the representation of the way society moves', through a revelation of the social and economic laws of the society the novel describes.[69] Lukacs argues, however, that the 'incommensurability' of the world's 'detail' makes totalization as impossible in this sense of the word as in his earlier use of it. The novel must, rather, employ a group of 'typical' characters to provide the 'impression of an entire society in movement'.[70] Totalization depends, then, upon the realistic novel's essential metonymy – the metonymy which *Vile Bodies* refuses to provide. Granted that, Waugh's novel succeeds on its own terms. Are those terms enough to produce great art? Do they tell us enough about the society from which the novel comes? For one does, after all, make that metonymic extension even with an essentially metaphoric novel like *Mrs Dalloway*; judges it, at least in part, according to how much about its society it manages to include and imply and hold in a sustained artistic order.

Graham Greene writes that the novelist's 'career is an effort to illustrate his private world in terms of the public world we all share', an attempt that is itself an effort to negotiate the gap between the soul and the world.[71] Terry Eagleton describes his version of totalization in similar terms, as a process of extending 'the materials of a directly personal response to the quality of a whole society . . . into confidently public and representative terms.'[72] Do the novelists I consider make that extension? Are the terms in which they describe their own position on the leaning tower large enough to encompass that of English society as a whole?

One could endlessly qualify the argument I've made in this chapter; indeed, the chapters that follow attempt to provide both those qualifications and a set of answers to the questions that Eagleton's terms provoke. Having concentrated here on what these novelists have in common, upon their generation's structure of feeling, I shall in the succeeding chapters deal primarily with what distinguishes them from each other, with their individual attempts to resolve the formal problems they face. And I shall begin with what one inevitably thinks of as the 'case' of Henry Green, whose creative difficulties provide a parable of the situation of the novelist in his generation.

2

Henry Green
(1905–1973)

I

Henry Green's early novels *Living* (1929) and *Party Going* (1939) stand as the most ambitious fiction any writer of his generation produced before the Second World War. None of his contemporaries had Green's ability to describe the social forces that separate class from class. None of them had such a fine ear for both dialogue and dialect. None had the breadth of imaginative sympathy that enabled him to capture what his friend and best critic V. S. Pritchett calls 'the inner language and landscape' in which people 'lead their real lives'.[1] In the first half of his career Green used that sympathy primarily in an attempt to understand the lives of men and women from classes other than his own. *Living* was not only the first book in which any member of his class and generation tried to imagine the lives of the English working class, but the best – the novel in which the working-class characters are the least conventionalized, the most highly individualized. It is the first attempt any of the writers I am concerned with made at a totalizing picture of the way their society moved.

Green's early novels are stylistically ambitious as well, in a way that seems less characteristic of his own generation than of its modernist predecessors. His prose demands to be read as slowly and as carefully as Woolf's or Meredith's. He strains the limits of control as they do – and in fact was published by the Hogarth Press. Here he describes Amabel, the rich and exotic beauty around whom he builds *Party Going*:

In her silence and in seeming unapproachable, although he realized it might be studied, and Alex admired her so much he was almost jealous of her, it seemed to him she was not unlike ground so high, so remote, it had never been broken and that her outward beauty lay in that if any man had marked her with

21

intimacy as one treads on snow, then that trace which would be left could not fail to invest him, whoever he might be, with some part of those unvulgar heights so covered, not so much of that last field of snow before any summit as of a high memory unvisited, and kept.   (463)

Green's prose demands, for the sake of simple comprehension, far more of the reader's attention than do Waugh's or Graham Greene's fluid colloquial styles. He is what Philip Toynbee describes as a 'terrorist' of language, one of those who 'confront their language as a wrestler confronts his adversary, knowing that they must twist it and turn it, squeeze it into strange shapes and make it cry aloud, before they can finally bring it to the boards'.[2] His interpolations force one to linger over this sentence's syntactic complications, to rise to its challenge, as Alex does in turning the emotions with which he apprehends Amabel's epiphanic beauty into a precise yet nevertheless enigmatic romantic image. The sentence trembles through its motion, almost pulsing before one's eyes, transforming this woman, whom the rest of Green's narrative reveals as egocentrically petty, into something like a goddess.

Green had, in both *Living* and *Party Going*, almost every gift a novelist requires. He had the linguistic resources, the knowledge of a wide range of life, the interest in connecting the lives of his characters to those of the nation as a whole, even the ability to summon the belief in the importance of subjective experience that his contemporaries lacked. He had every gift but one – the ability to discipline his talents into a coherent whole. Green wrote under a pseudonym, working under his real name of Henry Yorke in his father's manufacturing firm by day, and on his books at night. That dichotomy both grew from and reinforced what his schoolfriend Anthony Powell describes as 'the almost overpowering sense of being divided in two' from which Green suffered all his life.[3] And his novels turn, accordingly, upon a whole set of Lukacsian 'antagonistic dualities' – upon the tension between the world and his characters' distorted imagination of it; between two social classes; between the public themes posed by his examination of social class, and his interest in his characters' 'inner language and landscape', in what he called the 'true life' which was for him separate from any consideration of politics.[4] Of those antagonistic dualities, however, the most important is that between Green's formal aspirations for his prose – aspirations inseparable, perhaps, from his sense of the true life – and the range of life that prose attempts to contain.

Those aspirations led Green to adopt an aesthetic that conflicts with and finally overwhelms the social expansiveness to which the novel traditionally aspires, and towards which his own early fiction had looked as well. In his 1940 autobiography, *Pack My Bag*, Green describes his years at Eton without once mentioning the place by name. For prose, he writes, ought to be:

> . . . a gathering web of insinuations which go further than names however shared can ever go. Prose should be a long intimacy between strangers with no direct appeal to what both may have known. It should slowly appeal to feelings unexpressed, it should in the end draw tears out of stone, and feelings are not bounded by the associations common to place names or to persons with whom the reader is unexpectedly familiar. (88)

We have all gone to school; few of us have gone to Eton. Because of that, Green argues, proper names, which can only 'distract' (88) the reader with thoughts of his own relation to them, defeat the writer's attempt to evoke the 'common, that is universal remembered feelings' (33) that he needs to create that 'long intimacy between strangers'. Green's model is, accordingly, the traveller C. M. Doughty, whose *Travels in Arabia Deserta* (1888) is filled with place-names that are at once evocative and yet absolutely without specific 'associations' for an English reader. Green admires Doughty's prose because it seems so perfectly 'an expression of his personality', and of his personality alone, a prose pure and without context, removed from all history and tradition, so exotic that 'if the dates were not available it would be hard to say when' he wrote.[5]

Such is Green's aspiration as well – to create a prose so pure as to be abstracted from history itself. In trying to evade the temptation of those 'associations', his work became what he called an 'advanced attempt to break up the old-fashioned type of novel',[6] by seeing what the novel could do without. 'The more you leave out,' he told Terry Southern in his *Paris Review* interview, 'the more you highlight what you leave in.'[7] And so he eliminates not just the place-names in *Pack My Bag*, but also tries, in *Living*, to remove the definite article from his prose. In *Concluding* (1948) he cuts out plot resolutions to help quicken one's sense of the richness of he calls 'life itself at last', (*Pack My Bag*, 246) divorced from the meanings such resolutions might impose upon it. He is a minimalist novelist whose books over the course of his career offer fewer and fewer 'associations', whose forms grow ever more spare, until in the dialogue novels *Nothing* (1950) and *Doting* (1952) he separates human speech from its context to evoke the enormous ambiguity and suggestive power of even the simplest statements. Most novelists depend, in contrast, upon the 'associations' he shuns, through which, Green claimed, the writer 'intrudes like a Greek chorus to underline his meaning'.[8] He himself emphasizes, not 'meaning' but the range of possible meanings. His novels, Frank Kermode writes, both invite 'structuration and strongly [question] the notion of definitive structures . . . [he] accepts and exploits the pluralities that arise'[9] from the variety of ways in which a world without 'associations' can be experienced.

And yet the notation of social class on which his early novels depend offers precisely the sorts of 'associations' Green wanted to avoid, the surest way of all through which a writer can underline his meaning. Green's ambitions were finally all of one kind. They were to use his style as a means, not to describe the way his society moved, but to map the 'inner language and landscape' of his individual characters' lives, the relation – or lack of it – of their souls to the world. But he could never quite achieve the stylistic breakaway he wanted, for he could not free himself from his interest in those 'associations', not even in the attenuated form of his late novels, whose extremity stands as both a sign of his position on Woolf's leaning tower and of his desire to escape it. When applied to *Living* and *Party Going*, then, Kermode's statement takes on another meaning. For they are themselves flawed by their lack of definitive structure, novels in which Green hasn't brought the association-ridden material with which he works into equilibrium with his stylistic ambitions, in which the social issues he examines aren't fully integrated with his wrestle with his language, his attempt to evoke the 'true life'. Green's career turns upon his gradual abandoning of such material, as if he could only deal with that 'almost overpowering sense of being divided in two' by denying half the interest his early novels contain. His contemporaries searched throughout their careers for a style that would allow them to describe an ever-wider range of experience. They grew into the ambition that Green assumed from the start. But as their imaginative worlds grew larger, his seemed to shrink, to dwindle.

Waugh began his career with novels whose comedy fits the terms of Wyndham Lewis's Great With-Out; Green ended his that way. His work in the second half of the 1940s – *Loving* (1945), *Back* (1946) and *Concluding* – does combine a formal perfection with a glimmer of the national life, but it lacks the breadth to which *Living* and *Party Going* had aspired, and Green did not in any case maintain that equilibrium for long. Powell writes that Green's sense of a divided self and his attempts to combat it 'corroded'[10] his nervous system and made him virtually incapable of writing after the publication of *Doting* in 1952, when he was only forty-seven. And it is in that inability to hold the two sides of his sensibility together, to make one ambition out of several, that Green seems to me both the most elusive writer of his generation, and the most emblematic of its position on the leaning tower.

II

Green's first novel, *Blindness*, is in many ways derivative – derivative, that is, for an advanced young aesthete of 1926, who had learned all the recipes the modernist cookbook had to offer about the shift from one Jamesian centre of consciousness to another. Green began the novel at Eton, and it was published in 1926, shortly before he turned twenty-one. It is, Pritchett argues, a 'book of striking pages rather than a sound whole'.[11] And it succeeds least of all in its main purpose: to present a portrait of the young artist John Haye, working through his sufferings to the point at which he can begin to create. Michael North describes the novel as an example of what he calls the 'literature of debility' typical of its period.[12] Such novels turn on their protagonists' impotence in the face of ordinary life, and are as indicative of the second generation's sense of their relation to the world as is the modernists' characteristic reliance on an artist's successful breakaway. John Haye's debility is, of course, a physical one, the blindness of the novel's title, but North extends the phrase to cover the nervous breakdown of Philip Lindsay in Isherwood's *All the Conspirators*, and my later chapters suggest it might with equal justice apply to the protagonists of both Powell's and Graham Greene's early novels, and even to the naiveté of Paul Pennyfeather in Waugh's *Decline and Fall*.

Green's later work draws upon a similar debility, and one of which he had personal experience, using the deafness from which he began to suffer in his thirties to create a richly comic picture of the isolated soul's inability to control the world. John Haye's blindness has a less complex role to play. It merely provides the disability he must conventionally overcome, which he does through an acceptance of what he calls the "fineness" in his life "being as it is" (470). Late in the novel John persuades his mother to leave their country house for London, where he believes he can begin to write, and where one Sunday morning he hears church bells that make him remember his days at school:

> Those bells, everything, brought them jostling back in one's mind. But there had been something different about the bells, they had left him trembling, and when he passed a hand over his chair he was surprised at how stolid and unaltered the plush remained, for he was certain that the wild peal of them had made a great difference, their vibration had loosed and freed everything, until even the noise of the streets became invigorating. He felt a stirring inside him; it was true, they had made a difference, he felt it, and in a minute something was going to happen. He waited, taut, in the chair. (502)

Through that memory John comes to an awareness of the extraordinary ability he has, despite his blindness, to experience the life of the senses. And what is 'going to happen' to him next is an epileptic fit. In the moment before it hits him John feels joy like that of his favourite writer Dostoevsky's Prince Myshkin, a joy whose power both frightens and reassures him, reassures him with its promise that 'the mist which lay between him and the world would be lifted . . . he would know all, why he was blind, why life had been so to him . . . how wonderful to rise on this love' (502).

Green's style carries always the sense of human possibility absent from the 'shell-shocked' prose of his contemporaries. Yet taking this passage in tandem with his description of Amabel in *Party Going* makes one realize that that possibility lies not in any direct apprehension of the world itself, but in the character's imaginative transformation of it – not in sensation but in the imagination of sensation. As the modernists tried to create an alternative world through art, so Alex creates his own Amabel to replace the one the world has given him. His vision of her depends upon an imagination of what he thinks he sees in her so powerful that it almost paralyses him, overwhelms him, as John is overwhelmed here. *Blindness* suggests both the rewards and the dangers of the interior life, of John's having to live in and through his imagination. His seizure forcibly reminds him of his own limitations, which his new awareness of his imaginative powers had made him think he might transcend. For John cannot escape his blindness, his essential isolation. No act of the imagination can enable him to do that, can fully transform the world to fit the requirements of his soul. Green uses modernist techniques to invert the central assumptions of modernism; the prose in which John is described may be mandarin, but he nevertheless remains one of 'those to whom things are done'.

For Green has no faith in the mind's ability to re-order 'the myriad impressions of an ordinary day', in Clarissa Dalloway's ability to impose her soul upon the world and so triumph over it. Instead he insists upon what North describes as the individual sensibility's 'utter irrelevance and . . . complete helplessness in the world of fact'.[13] North argues, in fact, that for Green there is 'no necessary opposition between the self and the outside world'[14] because the world of fact is so powerful as to make the self something like a shell-shocked automaton whose responses are 'contrived largely from outside materials'.[15] But Green's characters seem both absolutely open to the world and absolutely isolated from it. Alex may transform Amabel into that memorable image, but her beauty there is highlighted by what's been left out, the account of the way she manipulates the novel's other characters that Green elsewhere provides. Alex sees only a part of her, but takes that part for the whole, and while he is aware of his metonymy's limitation, Green's other characters are rarely so lucky. They remain overwhelmed by their sensations, by what they think they see and feel and hear in the world around them, unable to establish an adequate relation between the soul and the world; 'encrusted', as Pritchett writes, 'in something like a private culture'[16] from whose expressionistic 'distortion[s] of observed reality' their problems grow. Green's characters are nearly all like *Mrs Dalloway*'s mad Septimus Smith. In such a world one can only make the commonsense admission that, as Charles Addinsell says in *Doting*, "There's very little anyone can do about things" (266). For as Annabel Paynton says in the same novel, "One has got to go on living" (293) – and go on living in an objective world to which that soul's very individuality makes it extraneous.

In posing the issue of John's possible isolation in the 'inner language' for which his blindness is a trope, Green's first novel prefigures the concerns of his later books. But it also provides an example of the dichotomy between Green's formal concerns and his interest in social class. For the book's triumph lies not in its portrait of the young artist, but in this sketch of John's mother:

> She struggled into the brown jumper and before the looking glass put in the fox-head pin. There was old Pinch on the herbaceous border doing nothing already. She had never seen him about so early, it was really extraordinary. She looked a long time at Ralph in his photograph, but he was absolutely the same. His smile said nothing, gave her no advice, but only waited to be told what to do, just as he had been obeying the photographer then. He would have had more in common with the boy perhaps, would have been able to talk to him of pig-sticking out in India in the old 10th days.   (382)

Green based Mrs Haye upon his own mother, whom he describes in *Pack My Bag* as making the gardener bowl mangel wurzels across the lawn so that she could practise her shooting on them. And this portrait of her suggests that Green's eye for social class – for the details of his own class in particular – is as sharp as Forster's or as Waugh's, an eye capable, in Pritchett's words, of making 'a whole fox-hunting society [come] to life', its assumptions and the reasons for them completely understood.[17]

That eye was, however, a gift that Green's aesthetic made him distrust, and *Party Going* suggests both the terms in which he sees social class and the way he backs away from them. At the start of the novel, the descent of a thick fog strands Green's main characters in a railway station at rush hour, and prevents them from leaving on the trip they've planned to the South of France. At first they form part of the crowd gathered in the station concourse, whose numbers are each moment swelled by the arrival of more commuters from the Underground, insulated from the 'swarming ponds of humanity' around them only by their huge barricades of luggage (395). But that luggage is not protection enough. The party-goers retreat into the station hotel, and the management, frightened of the crush, then locks the hotel doors behind them. From their rooms Green's characters look down into the station concourse at what they take to be a roiling crowd, whose anonymity they contrast to their own well-cultivated supposed individuality. And yet the uniformity of the hotel's rooms, Green suggests, creates an anonymity of its own that effectively denies the party-goers' claims to be different in kind from those below them.

The two groups, those in the hotel and the crowd in the concourse, sundered halves of the same body, remain for the duration of the fog isolated from and opposed to one another. But in *Party Going* their opposition is only temporary, an accident of the fog. As such the relations between them merely provide an allegory of the stratification and polarization of English life in the 1930s, rather than a full analysis of that life itself. Those in the crowd don't appear to think themselves exploited by their exclusion from the comforts of the hotel bar. In fact they don't even think of themselves as a crowd at all, for:

> . . . being in it, how was it possible for them to view themselves as part of that vast assembly, for even when they had tried singing they had heard only those next them . . . and soon they did not agree about songs, that section would be going on while another sang one of their own.   (395)

Given Green's insistence on the crowd as a collection of individuals, and not a class, those locked doors can have only a symbolic effect. Though the opposition Green establishes between the two groups dominates the novel, it finally poses far less of a critique of English social structure than it first appears to. Green wrote in *Pack My Bag* that the social differences between people are 'occasioned by money, in other words . . . accidental' (244). But this novel's division between people, which depends on who happened to be inside the hotel when the doors were locked, is far more accidental than most.

It was, perhaps, an 'accident' of biography that drew Green to such concerns at all. He grew up in Gloucestershire, where his parents had a country house near a village in which there was, as in *Adam Bede*, a free and courteous intercourse between the classes. In consequence, Green had as a child 'the knowledge of a settled civilization', of a traditional community that the other writers of his generation craved. Then, in 1917, when Green was twelve, his parents made their house into a convalescent home for wounded officers:

The effect of this on a child of my class was to open before his feet those narrow, deep and echoing gulfs which must be bridged, narrow because after all they were officers, deep because in most cases they had as civilians to come over that rope bridge over that gorge across which intercourse is had on the one side by saying 'sir' and on the other 'my good man'. That is to say I began to learn the half-tones of class, or, if not to learn because I was too young, to see enough to recognize the echoes later when I came to hear them.   (68)

But as his conception of *Party Going's* crowd suggests, Green attached little political content to his description of those gulfs. His account of the crowd's lack of political consciousness is not a criticism of it, but rather of those who expect that consciousness to be there; implicitly, of those who, like Valentine Cunningham, hear a political echo in the 'Party' of the title.[18] Green's novels may deal with social class, but they are not about it; far less so, for example, than Isherwood's *All the Conspirators*, in which the main characters all come from the public-school class, feel stifled by it, and revolt against it.

The accidents of biography gave Green an interest in social class and the equipment with which to deal with it. Another such accident made *Living* possible. Green frames the novel around the relations between the owners and workers of a Birmingham foundry, but his concern lies almost entirely with the workers, and he allows the factory-owning Dupret family to vanish entirely from the last quarter of the novel. Most of Green's contemporaries write about the working class as a species of alien, even when interested in its political salvation. But Green's father actually owned a Birmingham factory, and because of this, Walter Allen writes, he:

. . . started his novelist's career with one great advantage over his middle-class contemporaries: as the boss's son . . . he could move, as it were, up and down the social scale as he pleased. In order to write about working class lives, as in 'The Nowaks', Isherwood had to go to Berlin; but Green could go to Birmingham.[19]

Green left Oxford to spend two years working on the factory floor before joining the company's management in London. And he used his observations of the men around him to write about their lives in a novel that, Waugh said in one of its first reviews, 'has no political or sociological axe to grind'.[20]

Nevertheless, the conjunction of *Living*'s date and subject-matter does require one briefly to examine its politics, for that subject did give Green what Allen calls 'honorary membership of a movement in writing to which he never truly belonged',[21] in what Samuel Hynes has called the 'Auden generation'. *Living*'s working-class characters have an acute consciousness of class, an awareness of the gulf that separates them from the Duprets, and of the specific ways in which the factory's management mistreats them. In a conversation between two of the book's minor characters, for example, Mr Bentley says to Mr Eames:

"It's wicked, that's what it is. And look at that feller Whitacre. 'E was 30/- short in his money when they sent it to 'im so 'e writes to 'em about it and by the next post they tell 'im they're done with 'im and 'e can go tramp over England looking for another job. 'E wrote for 'is money again what 'e'd earned by labour but didn't get an answer. Is that straight?" (238)

But Mr Bentley simply concludes that "It's downright wicked" (239) and then, since he's standing in Mr Eames' allotment garden, praises the fine new crop of apples. For all their consciousness of class, *Living*'s characters don't have much class-consciousness. Gripes remain gripes and nothing more. Mr Bentley does not see Whitacre's dismissal as part of a pattern about which something might be done, as he would in a more self-consciously proletarian novel. Instead he accepts things as they are, good apples and the evening air as well as injustice. When young Mr Dupret decides to sack all those employees within six months of the age at which their pensions will begin, the old iron moulder Craigan, the book's moral centre, is at first 'bitter'. But 'when fully he saw that his working days were done he thought it was right he should be discharged, being an old man like he was' (339–40). Craigan dedicates himself to stasis. He believes not only that things cannot be changed, but that they should not, and even says he would not educate a child above its father's station.

Green's membership in the Auden generation is honorary at best. *Living* is the work of a man who never had to learn, as Auden did, that 'poetry makes nothing happen'.[22] One can read English literature of the late 1930s, a decade after *Living*'s publication, as a chronicle of the artist's growing awareness of his impotence, *as* an artist, to affect the course of political events. Green assumed that impotence from the start of his career; perhaps the difference between his daytime career as an industrialist and his writing helped convince him of it. In fact the novel discourages change, as Craigan's words suggest, and to read it one must accept, despite the smokescreen the combination of its subject and historical context creates, that the 'true life' in it lies outside of politics.

Living's revolutionary quality lies, rather, in its prose. This is the way it begins:

> Bridesley, Birmingham
> Two o'clock. Thousands came back from dinner along streets.
> "What we want is go, push," said works manager to son of Mr. Dupret. "What I say to them is – let's get on with it, let's get the stuff out."
> Thousands came back to factories they worked in from their dinners.
> "I'm always at them but they know me. They know I'm a father and mother to them. If they're in trouble they've but to come to me. And they turn out beautiful work, beautiful work. I'd do anything for them and they know it."
> Noise of lathes working began again in this factory. Hundreds went along road outside, men and girls. Some turned in to Dupret factory.   (207)

In *The Tell-Tale Article* G. Rostrevor Hamilton argues that modern poets, Auden in particular, use the definite article to point to the known, the familiar.[23] Green's omission of that article, then, suggests the unknown and mysterious. His prose makes 'no direct appeal' to the reader, offers none of the conventional landmarks by which one customarily steers. A. Kingsley Weatherhead writes that in this 'bald prose the objects presented are more solid while the relationship between them is weakened'.[24] Such prose 'highlights' what Green leaves in – the nouns themselves, cut free from the 'associations' that, by relating them to previously known experience, the definite article would provide. Green uses words as if each one were new, as if man had just learned how to name his world but had not yet learned what meaning it held. His terrorization, his dislocation, of language makes each word stand out like bumps on a page of braille, an admission wrung from a most intractable material. Through this imagistic grating of noun upon noun, uncushioned by any sense of the relationship between them, the prose attempts to create the illusion of having no narrator, and so to persuade one that it presents 'life itself at last', independent of the conventions of representation, a life both richly mysterious and meaningful. Yet nothing is more mannered than deliberate novelty. Green's assault upon conventional prose in *Living* seems precious in comparison with the easily worn exoticism of his later work. Its style not only seems to 'squeeze' language, in Toynbee's words, but to strangle it. But after the novel's opening pages Green does allow his prose to relax into a description of the subject his title suggests, and the novel is best served by attending to that, rather than to the purposeful difficulty of its style.

Two-thirds of the way through the novel the factory worker Bert Jones is given a job to do on his lathe, the correct performance of which will lead to his promotion. Bert completes its first easy stages, and then pauses:

> If Mr. Jones did not want to go on those others watching him, and the foreman, made it into confession of failure to draw back. Also, he realized now, what he had not thought of before, that he had indeed begun – bit of metal he was using was scored now, partly used, and if he gave up they might not be able to bring it in for some other job. Also he might never have the chance again and suddenly it seemed so desirable to him that "I'll have a try," he said in mind and threw belt of his lathe over into gear.
>
> Now the job, revolving so many turns each second, now it had a stillness more beautiful than when actually it had been still. On the small surface of it was sheen of light still and quiet, for noise of his lathe could not be heard above noise of other lathes working about him. And pace of events bearing on his life quickened so that for two moments their speed had appearances of stillness. Also the foreman and others that were looking on openly by now, had now his appearance and features. He said in mind he had to go on and do the job right. He paused before it, tool in his hand and it might be the sense of power he had and which he felt for the first time, to make waster of that bit of steel or a good job out of it, it might be that kept him still undecided.   (334–5)

Bert has to decide whether or not to take charge of his own life, and hence the present contains his future. His co-workers urge him on; so too does the fact that he has unconsciously, inevitably begun. The past crowds one along, and 'the pace of events' quickens. Yet Bert is so absorbed by that 'sheen of light still and quiet' that time seems to stop, and the men around him take on his own features. For in his almost sexual awareness of his work Bert has here cut himself off from the world, caught by a 'beautiful stillness' that makes him think he can remake that world in his own image.

And then Green stops the scene, leaving Bert paralysed, even after he decides to 'have a try', by his apprehension of the work's beauty, isolated in a moment of indecision. Green's prose is as completely alive to sensation as Pater's, and Bert's appreciation of the job revolving on the lathe provides the occasion for one of *Living*'s most finely composed passages. It is a flutter of feeling, a fountain of sensation that, like Alex's vision of Amabel in *Party Going*, threatens to drown both the reader and the character who experiences it; an experience so overwhelming that it seems to deny Bert the 'executive will and intelligence' he needs to go on with the job. Yet what choice, after all, does Bert have in confronting the fact of that bit of metal? The job has begun, the bit of metal is 'scored . . . partly used'. The world does not wait until the soul is ready for it. Bert cannot choose not to begin; to step back from the job, to refuse to try it, is to fail far more completely than if his hand slipped in attempting it. Bert can take up the job, can leave the 'inner language and landscape' that has captured him here, and accept the need to 'go on living' in the world, along with the possibility of failure – or he can refuse to live and face the certainty of that failure.

For all his ability to evoke a character's experience of sensation, Green prefers those moments in which his characters step away from their frighteningly rich inner lives and turn to action, in which through an unreflecting enjoyment of beer and football and talk and work, they step fully and completely into the process of living. The life with which Green most concerns himself is that of Lily Gates. She wants to escape the drab anonymity of her life in Birmingham, keeping house for her father and old Craigan, and so plans to marry Bert Jones and emigrate to Canada with him, via Liverpool. Yet in her flight Lily learns that 'she didn't want to walk anyplace where she hadn't walked before' (349). The strangeness of Liverpool at night paralyses her, as that bit of metal on the lathe had paralysed Bert:

> Street was dark. Miss Gates felt something in the street looking
> out, looking out then it was gone. Then it was back again. Where
> was Bert, had he gone? She looked up quickly but of course he
> was there. But street was dark. She got much more frightened
> and was rigid with it for two moments. Again something looked
> and was gone. And again. She felt no, after looking up to see if
> Bert was there she wouldn't look up again to see what that was.
> There it was. She had to look. No she wouldn't. She had to, so
> she looked. It was watchlight from the lighthouse, it stroked
> over sky and was gone. With great pang she wondered what
> that was doing there. Then she decided that was what came
> from looking up. She would not look up again. They began
> walking again. She was blank, blank. Again it came along the
> sky.   (360)

In his last article, 'For Jenny with Affection from Henry Green',
Green writes 'Love your wife, love your cat, and stay perfectly
quiet, if possible not to leave the house. Because on the street
if you are sixty danger threatens.'[25] Yet even in that almost
schizophrenic essay Green recognizes that the horrors of Belgravia
exist far more in his mind than in actuality. So too do those of
Liverpool for Lily Gates. Her shell-shocked imagination of the
world of fact is so powerful as to make her 'blank, blank', to deny
her a self. Yet it is, after all, only a lighthouse that scares
her, however mysterious it seems at first. Lily's imagination of
catastrophe, her fear that this risky trip will end badly, creates that
catastrophe; spreads it across the sky so that the lighthouse
becomes an expression of her terror. It so freezes her soul that she
can't explain what she's frightened of; and Bert is in turn frozen
by his apprehension of her own seemingly meaningless panic. His
nerve fails and he abandons her at a tram stop, the first step on
her trip back to the unlovely familiarity of Birmingham. Yet *Living*
doesn't allow one to conclude that Lily's subsequent life will be
barren, in any sense of the word. For Green brings her to an
understanding of Craigan's position, an acceptance of the need 'to
go on living' whatever one's circumstances. And that acceptance,
Green suggests, can open one to the possibility of the sudden joy,
however transitory, that even the smallest moment can carry; a
joy like that Lily finds, in the novel's last paragraphs, at the sight

of a neighbour's new baby playing with a pigeon that has lighted on its pram.

Living's final concerns, then, lie not in an examination of social class but in its exploration of what Green takes to be 'common, that is universal remembered feelings' such as the ones that baby evokes. Yet while granting Green his conception of the 'true life', one must nevertheless question him on his own terms, on the novel's inability to fill the shape its opening pages imply. *Living* at first suggests a panorama, in which no one subject or group of characters dominates, a streamlined industrial *Middlemarch* that will counterpoint the lives of the factory workers and their families with those of the Duprets, and that in doing so will link the lives of two classes whom modern society ensures meet only at the workplace. But Green allows that counterpoint to fall out of the novel. *Living* shrinks to an account of Lily's situation without managing to make that situation embody the novel's larger world. For despite his interest in such essentially political issues as class and money, Green's concern lies finally in the private life alone, in his characters' attempts to move between their 'inner landscape' and 'the world of fact' to which that landscape is finally irrelevant. He does not in *Living* match that landscape to the social issues the novel raises, and so the writer seemingly most able to transcend his generation's position on Woolf's leaning tower nevertheless succumbs to it, in the form of the structural debility that the dominance of Lily's trip over the novel's second half produces. Despite its ambitions of style and subject, despite its many moving and powerful passages, *Living* is not finally as successful as a less ambitious novel, such as Powell's *Afternoon Men*, because it carries no awareness of the range within which it finally settles.

Party Going does at first carry through on the broad promise of its predecessor's public themes. It provides an elaboration of one of *Living*'s subplots, the way in which the 'accident' of the Dupret's money isolates them from the world of sensation and from each other. Green uses his first sentence to suggest the emotional consequences that isolation engenders: 'Fog was so dense', he writes, 'bird that had been disturbed went flat into a balustrade and slowly fell, dead, at her feet' (384). In *Blindness* Green had made birds sing 'in little cascades of friendliness' at the moment when John Haye realizes 'how good the world was' (447); in *Living*, Lily's sight of that baby playing with a pigeon awakens her to the desperate joy she feels at the end of the novel.

Birds figure in all Green's books, providing for him an image of life itself, breathing, flying, dying, living, a register of the emotional quality or tone of life at any given moment in his novels. *Party Going*'s first sentence is rather clumsy in comparison with the multivalence with which Green employs such imagery in his later books. Nevertheless it does set the tone of a novel that can be read as an allegory about the spiritual paralysis of an English upper class, kept by its possessions from the vitality of ordinary men and women.

Green uses a kiss to establish the difference between the party-goers and what they see as the undifferentiated masses below them:

> For when Angela had kissed Mr. Adams she had not wanted him to stay, it had been no more than a peck, but now she had seen more of their party she wished she had kissed him harder, and she was beginning to blame him. He had been extremely tiresome and he had deserved it when she had sent him off. But she felt now that she had never deserved it when he had gone.
>
> As for Julia she had kissed Max to keep him sweet so to speak, and so, in one way, had Miss Crevey kissed her young man. But what lay behind Julia's peck was this three weeks they both had in front of them, it would never do to start too fast and furious. Angela had no such motive because Mr. Adams was not coming with them.   (446)

For these characters a kiss is not a part of the sensual life, but something whose cost must be carefully weighed against the value of whatever they hope to buy with it. In the station concourse, however, people take a frank and generous delight in the sensual world. "Will you give us a kiss, darling?" (472) Julia's servant Thompson asks a girl in the crowd. And she does, without a thought beyond the moment, and runs away when she hears someone else call her name. Yet despite – or perhaps because of – the encounter's casual quality, her gesture has far more of what Thompson calls 'fellow feeling' (473) than does anything that happens in the hotel rooms above, the 'fellow feeling' that Alex realizes he and his friends have sacrificed through their absorption in 'what it is to be rich' (493).

Love for the party-goers is not a matter of giving and sharing but only of taking, a way to make the world fit the shape of their own desires, and so feed what Pritchett calls the 'inexhaustible wells of human egoism'[26] in which Green's characters isolate themselves. But then, having set up what he calls the 'malign comedy' (453) of this Audenesque allegory, Green shrugs it aside. The party-goers' train is announced, and:

> . . . it seemed to Julia, it was most like that afternoon when Miss Fellowes had said let's take the child to a matinee, when she had never yet gone to the theatre, it was so wonderful to see Max planning as he must be doing, to keep Amabel occupied with someone for herself. So like when you were small and they brought children over to play with you and you wanted to play on your own then someone, as they hardly ever did, came along and took them off so you could do what you wanted. And as she hoped this party would be, if she could get a hold of Max, it would be as though she could take him back into her life from where it had started and show it to him for them to share in a much more exciting thing of their own, artichokes, pigeons and all, she thought and laughed aloud.   (528)

While admitting the continued presence of Julia's manipulative self-interest, Green nevertheless steps away into her joy at the world opening before her, at the chance she has to take Max 'back into her life from where it had started', into the rich memories of the childhood she wants him to share. And her anticipation of the future redeems her, for through it Green suggests that his characters' lives may not be so impoverished after all. Their problem may simply be that a few hours locked in a hotel, with nothing to do and their departure uncertain, has made them get on each other's nerves. "Where's that wretched husband of mine, why doesn't he do something?" Claire Hignam asks. And Evelyn Henderson, the most sensible one in the group (as well as the poorest) answers, "But surely that's just it . . . There's nothing to do" (471). Yet Claire won't accept that. She refuses to recognize the moment for what it is, one in which nothing can be done, as Bert Jones had been incapable of recognizing his moment over the lathe as one in which something had to be done, and so she lives in a hellish boredom that such an acceptance might help her escape.

Party Going, like *Living*, is not finally about politics or social class, but about the dangers of expecting the world to conform to one's desires. Yet if *Living*'s concluding turn toward Lily's private horrors mars it, *Party Going*'s similar turn keeps it from being as rigidly deterministic an attack upon the English ruling class as at first it appears to be. Green employs the entire weight of the 1930s iconography that Hynes describes in *The Auden Generation* to establish the terms that allow one to read the novel as a description of the condition of England. But while Green uses that iconography, he finally steps away from it, like Prufrock claiming, "That is not what I meant at all."[27] Claire's expectations that the world will conform to her desires is of course a function of her upper-middle-class complacency. But those expectations are not specific to either her sex or her class, and insofar as Green's political allegory makes them appear so, it is reductive – too contingent on the accident of the fog to justify the lessons he seems to draw from it. If Green had rested there, if the train had not come and the hotel doors had remained locked, one would reject those lessons as cant. But *Party Going*'s public themes merely provide a scaffolding that Green discards once the building can stand on its own, devices through which he intensifies the private sources of his characters' panic, their sense of being trapped in a world they can't control. And in using public obsessions in pursuit of private ends, Green both questions the 'definitive structures' the novel's political themes suggest, and paradoxically validates its incidental generalizations about the soulless anonymity of the rich.

Yet I wonder, nevertheless, about the cost of Green's attempt to strip his novels of the 'associations' politics suggests. However much I admire Green's handling of his characters' panic, however much his concluding turn seems to save the novel from the determinism that threatens it, I still wonder if in that turn Green lost the chance to create a picture of the way his society moved whose totalizing vision would have rivalled that of Forster in *Howards End*. Yet if *Party Going* fails to provide a full presentation of the condition of late 1930s England, it has no equal as an allegory of the condition of England's novelists. It offers, in Green's inability fully to occupy both sides of his mind at once, an emblem of the diffidence with which his shell-shocked generation, encrusted in a 'private culture' of 'middle-class birth and expensive education' engaged their society. And there is something more as well. For the side of his sensibility that Green attempts to exclude remains present in the novel, in the roar of the crowd just outside the hotel window, a roar both impossible to ignore and impossible to confront. And that very impossibility makes *Party Going* more fully homologous to England's nervous frenzy of the years around Munich than it appears, in the end, to be.

III

It was the last time he would attempt such a comprehensive vision. As his contemporaries were preparing for what I have called the 'Churchillian Renaissance' through which they sought to evade the limitations of their period; as Waugh and Graham Greene began their exploration of the relation between religion and the novel; as Powell began his preparations for the grand style of *A Dance to the Music of Time*, Green chose to accept his own limitations, and to work in an increasingly narrow range. Yet in the process he exchanged a troubled and fragmentary expansiveness for a purification of formal vision that produced one great artistic triumph. One third of the way through Green's fifth novel, *Loving* (1945), the butler Charley Raunce follows the sound of a gramophone to Kinalty Castle's shut-up ballroom, where he finds the housemaids Edith and Kate:

> . . . wheeling wheeling in each other's arms heedless at the far end where they had drawn up one of the white blinds. Above from a rather low ceiling five great chandeliers swept one after the other almost to the waxed parquet floor reflecting in their hundred thousand drops the single sparkle of distant day, again and again red velvet panelled walls, and two girls, minute in purple, dancing multiplied to eternity in these trembling pears of glass. (65)

Green's prose grows magnificent to describe a magnificent scene. Here he brings to fruition silly Julia's sense in *Party Going* of hanging on the edge of possibility, makes it a present reality in which the senses are quickened and multiplied and exalted. Most of *Loving*'s prose has the compression of *Living*'s – although a characteristic sentence such as 'Came a man's laugh' (18) has a confidently terse elegance that Green could not summon in the earlier work. Yet as Kinalty Castle is littered with ornate tables and chairs and 'malachite vases, filled with daffodils, which stood on tall pedestals of gold naked male children without wings' (23), so too Green's prose here carries what Giorgio Melchiori describes as 'unexpected flourishes of feeling, fanciful word-pictures departing from his more restrained style in the same way as a complicated stucco scroll will suddenly break out of the quiet and balanced form of an arch or balustrade in a seventeenth century building'.[28] Melchiori's description characterizes the body of Green's work. But in *Loving*, which describes life in an Irish castle during the Second World War, those flourishes are more fantastic, more daring in their form and in the sensual richness they suggest, than in any of his other books.

But Edith and Kate are unconscious of their beauty here, and Raunce refuses to pay attention to it, even though he does eventually fall in love with Edith. "You're daft", he calls out to them (65), and turns off the waltz to which they've been dancing, refusing to recognize the beauty before him. *Loving* provides a comic re-examination of Lily Gates' and Bert Jones' problem: of the difficulty of finding an accommodation between the objective world and one's subjective experience of it. And that re-examination clarifies one's sense of Green's treatment of that 'antagonistic duality' as a whole. For by the time he wrote *Loving* Green had begun to suffer from the deafness that marked his later life, and his description of that deafness suggests both the impossibility of finding that accommodation, and provides an example of its consequences. 'The very deaf', Green told Terry Southern:

. . . hear the most astonishing things all round them which have not in fact been said. This enlivens my replies until, through mishearing, a new level of communication is reached. My characters misunderstand each other more than people do in real life, yet they do so less than I.[29]

That same interview had just provided a rich example of Green's mishearing. Southern asked him to respond to the charge that his novels were too subtle for most readers:

GREEN: I don't follow. *Suttee*, as I understand it, is the suicide – now forbidden – of a Hindu wife on her husband's flaming bier. I don't want my wife to do that when my time comes – and with great respect, as I know her, she won't.
INTERVIEWER: I'm sorry, you misheard me; I said 'subtle' – that

the message was too subtle.
GREEN: Oh, *subtle*. How dull!!³⁰

And of course it would be. Inaccuracy carries an excitement and a sense of possibility that simple direct communication lacks. Green's knowledge of his own deafness makes him aware that the interpretation he places on the life around him has no necessary relation to the actual facts of that life. The world itself does not actually offer the sensations one feels – the lighthouse that frightens Lily is only that, nothing more – and hence one has got to learn to ignore them. Yet while admitting the self-destructive powers of the soul, Green delights in the possibilities of misperception, at the opportunities it affords for the soul to transform the world, to make 'life itself' richer and more meaningful than it actually is. It is not, after all, Edith and Kate whose beauty stirs us in the passage I've quoted above, so much as their image multiplied and fragmented and transfigured by the 'thousand drops' of the crystals through which Green reveals them. One might argue that Green had to go deaf, that doing so provided a justification for the sense of isolation within one's own experience upon which the climactic moments of his fiction had always depended.

But Green's awareness of his own deafness makes him able to laugh at his own mistakes in a way impossible for those who believe in some necessary link between the soul and the world. *Loving*'s characters do believe in that link, and can therefore be thrown into a nervous frenzy by the extraordinary menace they find in the most mundane events. So too can Lily Gates, but Green reveals her mind in the act of perceiving that lighthouse, and so communicates both the cause and the quality of her fears. In *Loving*, however, his interest lies in the comedy and not the terror of misperception. He writes from Lewis's 'Great With-Out', excluding his characters' interior lives in a way that both prefigures his dialogue novels *Nothing* and *Doting*, and makes their actions comically out of proportion to the events that appear to cause them. Take, for example, the scene in which an insurance investigator, whose recent dental work makes him lisp, visits Kinalty to look into the claim for a lost ring that its owner, Mrs Tennant, has made upon his company. Edith has found the ring, and then lost it again – and so Raunce attempts to forestall the investigation by denying that anything at all has happened:

"You're the butler?"

"What's that got to do with you? It's you we're talkin' about. Who're you?"

Edith broke in again.

"He's come about the insurance."

"Nobody asked you," her Charley said sharp but with a soft glance in her direction. "You don't know nothin'," he added.

"Know nothing? . . . Mark what I'm thaying now, I never inthinuated thith young lady knew anything . . . Don't try and be thmart with me. You'll find it don't work."

"I wouldn't know what you're refurring' to."

"The ring . . . The thaffire cluthter my company inthured on . . . Mithith Tennant thent for me to come over before she got back."

"Mrs. Tennant's coming back?" Raunce cried.

"Tho I'm led to understand."

"Then thank God for that," Raunce said relieved . . . "She can clear a whole lot up, Mrs. Tennant can. But if she don't all I'll say is she can have my notice. Arriving down 'ere to bully the girls, then treating me like I was a criminal."   (137–8)

How much better to say, 'No, the ring hasn't been found' – and how much less interesting for *Loving*'s readers. Raunce's determination to deny everything throws him into a self-created confusion, in which he draws the most outrageous inferences from the most ordinary events. After the insurance investigator leaves, for example, Raunce learns from his business card that the man represents the Irish Regina Assurance Company – and takes the company's initials as a sign that the investigator is really a scout for the IRA, planning an attack upon the castle in concert with an invading Germany army.

Raunce has earlier spoken of "saving a cartridge" each for Edith and Kate in case of a German invasion, and Green feels compelled to add, 'utterly serious he was' (94) – which only increases one's laughter at the way his inner landscape is out of joint with the objective world. *Loving*'s style has no room for the interior life, which – as at a public school – has been made irrelevant to the way one moves through the world, the roles one has to adopt. Yet Green nevertheless makes his readers aware of the parts of life that his style cannot accommodate, of the way in which the novel's characters are indeed 'utterly serious' to themselves, unaware of the comedy their actions create. Periodically, for example, he makes one character discover another in tears that he leaves unexplained, the surface indication of interior difficulties whose ambiguities he does not chart. Where Waugh's novels depend upon his fear that there's nothing beneath what he calls the 'knockabout farce of people's outward behaviour',[31] Green's are marked by the sense that what lies beneath that farce is too rich and mysterious for any revelation of it to be adequate. Here he highlights not what he leaves in, but what he excludes, draws attention to the metonymy his art cannot provide with a reticence that suggests the soul's estrangement from the world far more completely than he could by examining his character's actual hopes and fears.

"Life's not easy" (176), Edith says, and because of that, as Raunce writes to his mother, "It's hard to know what to do best" (111). But one has got nevertheless "to go on living", and for Green life's difficulties must be faced rather than avoided. Raunce, however, continues to remind the other servants of how lucky they are to be in Ireland, free from the bombings and with plenty to eat, rather than in their native England. He refuses to accept responsibility for his own life, and to face the implications of being English in the early 1940s. And yet to love is for Green to find fulfilment at hand; it is to live completely in the moment with all that means. For *Loving* implies that Raunce's desire for the good things of the present, for the active dream of loving Edith, requires an acceptance of the present's difficulty as well. He must, however, be goaded into that acceptance. His protégé, the pantry boy Albert, leaves Kinalty for England, where he will enlist. Almost simultaneously Raunce gets a letter from his mother in which she accuses him of "'iding . . . away in this neutral country" (197). Then one day Edith takes him outside to see Mrs Tennant's flock of pigeons, and he proposes to her. After she accepts, she:

> . . . began to feed the peacocks. They came forward until they had her surrounded. Then a company of doves flew down on the seat to be fed. They settled all over her. And their fluttering disturbed Raunce who reopened his eyes. What he saw then he watched so that it could be guessed that he was in pain with his great delight. For what with the peacocks bowing at her purple skirts, the white doves nodding on her shoulders round her brilliant cheeks and her great eyes that blinked eyes of happiness, it made a picture.

"Edie," he appealed soft, probably not daring to move or speak too sharp for fear he might disturb it all. Yet he used exactly that tone Mr. Eldon had employed at the last when calling his Ellen. "Edie," he moaned.

The next day Raunce and Edith left without a word of warning. Over in England they were married and lived happily ever after. (203–4)

And the novel ends. Yet Mr Eldon, the old butler whom Raunce has replaced, didn't have his Ellen at his deathbed, and calls her name in vain. Raunce's Edith stands before him. By ending the novel with an epiphany that is also a beginning, Green implies that it is just possible to make such a moment endure.

In eloping, Raunce accepts the way in which "life's not easy", and in doing so can at last apprehend Edith's beauty, as he could not when he saw her 'wheeling wheeling' in the castle's ballroom. *Loving*'s world is too small for totalization; nothing like a presentation of the way an entire society moves is at issue in it, as it seems to be in *Living* or *Party Going*. Instead, it makes a more modest and tentative assertion of patriotism, an examination of the point at which love of family shades over into love of country, whose success lies in the way it suggests such major issues through a concentration upon everyday mishaps, such as Raunce's confusion over the insurance investigator's visit. *Loving*'s public themes are not a shell or scaffolding, but a skin that grows directly from the novel's deepest themes. Rather than totalization it offers a perfection of form unmatched by any of Green's other novels. For in finding that point at which one form of love shades over into another, Green finds a way to triumph, however briefly, over his 'almost overpowering sense of being divided in two'.

Loving is dominated by what it excludes – as much by the war and all its 'associations' as by the interior lives of its characters. For both the war and the interior life remain a void within the novel, which Green's setting and style allow him to skirt while making us aware that he skirts them. In that, the novel stands as perhaps the purest example of the second generation's art of exclusion. The writers of Green's generation frustrate the novel's traditional metonymy in order to suggest the impossibility of seeing life steadily and seeing it whole. In doing so they attempt to avoid the problems of the leaning tower by acknowledging them. If in his early fiction Green had imposed public themes upon his attempt to render his characters' 'inner language and landscape', in *Loving* he allows those themes to grow from that landscape itself. And he would repeat that triumph, albeit on a smaller scale, with *Back* and *Concluding*; emblematic portraits of his country that nevertheless avoid the 'associations' of names and dates and places one usually finds in novels about the condition of England.

Yet if one remembers Graham Greene's definition of technique as 'a means of evading the personally impossible, of disguising a deficiency', one begins to see the more individual roots from which *Loving*'s style grows. The physical and emotional terrors of the Blitz, during which Green worked as a fireman and faced the nightly possibility of being blown off a roof by a bomb, increased what Powell has described as the inner corrosion of Green's nerves. The world seemed on those nights to confirm the terrors Lily Gates had found in it. When in the late 1950s he contemplated writing a sequel to *Pack My Bag*, Green thought of skipping his war experiences entirely, summing them up in this single sentence: '. . . now comes the period of the 1939–1945 war, which has been described repeatedly and from as many perspectives and people as it can well be handled from, so I shall say nothing about it.'[32] At the same time he found himself incapable of completing a commissioned book on London during the Blitz. 'As he worked on the book', John Russell writes, 'the fear grew in him that he would be unable to tackle the fire sections again. The fear was substantiated . . .'[33] Green could not bring himself to face those fires one more time. He had nightmares and tried to fight them off, Russell says, through a morbid exaggeration that attempted to transform his fears into comedy. So long as *Loving* remains on the surface and deals with a lost ring, one can laugh at the characters' fears by minimizing their cause. But the novel's characters take those fears very seriously indeed. Green's refusal to enter their minds keeps the reader from having to feel with any immediacy the ways in which "Life's not easy" – and so keeps Green himself from having to describe those ways; provides a way to subdue the turmoil of the interior life into form, without having to confront that life directly.

The novels Green wrote both before and after *Loving*, *Caught* (1943) and *Back* (1946) respectively, attempt to deal with the 'inner language and landscape' Green skirts in *Loving*. Both novels are dominated by their protagonists' memories of having lost a loved one, a loss they must learn to balance against the need "to go on living", in a world whose war-created chaos matches their own 'interior tumult'.[34] In *Caught*, Green spreads the interior life of the fireman Richard Roe across the night sky of wartime London, turning the Blitz's 'greedy extravagance of fire' (48) into an objectification of the personal hell that grows from Roe's inability to accept his wife's death. His experiences in the Blitz prove both purgative and restorative, but Green does not provide a close treatment of Roe's inner life. He relies instead on the war to suggest it. And Roe himself remains a shadowy figure within the novel, until after the flames have cauterized his interior wounds, making him able, in the fine account of a burning London with which the novel concludes, to describe his own experience.

Back seems *Caught*'s mirror-image. It collapses the war's insanity into that of the 'shell-shock case' (109) Charley Summers, a repatriated prisoner-of-war, who has lost a leg to a German trap that he thinks of as 'the gun beneath a rose' (3). Charley can neither forget that trap nor bring himself to talk about it. Similarly, he can neither accept nor forget the death of his early love, Rose. When he meets her look-alike illegitimate half-sister Nancy, of whose existence he had not previously known, the novel turns into a comedy of misperception – like Raunce's game with the ring, or Green's own variations on the word 'subtle'. Charley insists that Rose never died. Instead, he claims in a sequence in which laughter deflects the threat of nightmare, she changed the colour of her hair, disguised her handwriting, and became a bigamous tart – and his job is to rescue her. Yet Charley's perceptions seem anything but an abnormality in an otherwise sanely objective world. Green makes his conclusions seem logical by describing the world so completely from Charley's point of view that those conclusions, however ludicrous, seem to grow directly from the phenomena he confronts. Green's fundamental 'sense of being divided in two' creates a sense of the normality of such 'irrational terrors and lunatic misunderstandings' that provides a perfect instrument for describing a war. For in war the objective world does correspond to the 'inner . . . landscape' of Green's characters, no matter how distorted that landscape may be.

The difficulty comes after the war. Nancy's face is for Charley a living memory with which he must learn to live. He must learn to admit the past and yet manage to live in the present. In Nancy Charley finds the salvation of common sense that, as Eudora Welty says, offers him 'a partial settlement with life'.[35] At the end of the novel, with a marriage planned between them, Charley kneels:

> . . . by the bed, having under his eyes the great, the overwhelm-
> ing sight of the woman he loved, for the first time without her
> clothes. And because the lamp was lit, the pink shade seemed
> to spill a light of roses over her in all their summer colours, her
> hands that lay along her legs were red, her stomach gold, her
> breasts the color of cream roses, and her neck white roses for
> the bride. She had shut her eyes to let him have his fill, but it
> was too much, for he burst into tears again, he buried his face
> in her side just below the ribs, and bawled like a child. "Rose,"
> he called out, not knowing he did so, "Rose."
> "There", Nancy said, "there", pressed his head with her
> hands. His tears wetted her. The salt water ran down between
> her legs. And she knew what she had taken on. It was no more
> or less, really, than she had expected.   (246–7)

And as he melts at Nancy's side, admitting the pain of the past in
the balm of the present, Charley also begins to make his recovery,
a recovery not without problems for Nancy, but one which she
nevertheless accepts. *Back* suggests that one's nightmares can't be
allowed to get in the way of the rest of life, and yet admits that
the soul's essential isolation from the world ensures that they will
anyway. In its portrait of a character, and through him of a society,
slowly feeling his way toward a normality he will never quite
attain, it is to me the most moving of Green's novels.

Back opens out with the exhilaration of the war's end to embrace
possibility. Given its title and theme, some of the 'associations'
Green customarily tries to eschew are inevitable in it – its title even
lies dangerously close to that Greek Chorus through which most
writers 'underline' their meaning. By the time Green published
Concluding, the country's atmosphere had so changed that, as J. B.
Priestley wrote, the English no longer seemed to live:

> . . . in a world of neat plots, but in a foggy atmosphere of
> prejudices and cross purposes, silly rumours, tragic blunders.
> . . . We are deafened and bedevilled now by people who believe
> in enormous elaborate plots. Like most public men, I have
> had from time to time long letters from unhappy victims of
> persecution mania, giving me in bewildering detail their accounts
> of fantastic conspiracies, sometimes involving hundreds of

people, to kidnap or murder them. I find the same hysterical tone, the same nightmare atmosphere, in much writing and talking, these days.[36]

Priestley's comment suggests the degree to which *Concluding* is a novel of its time, of the year in which Orwell wrote *1984*. It describes a single day in a socialist state of the future, and is set at a country estate now converted to a school that trains girls to be efficient state servants. Green's protagonist, the retired scientist Mr Rock, has a life interest in a cottage on the estate, which he shares with his granddaughter Elizabeth. The school's principals want the cottage for the school, and concoct an 'enormous elaborate plot' to get it. And the day itself begins with the mysterious disappearance of two schoolgirls, allowing Green to fill the novel with rumours of the sex and violence that the school presumes has caused their disappearance. Such rumours both invite 'structuration', as Kermode says, and make one suspicious of the very idea that there is anything to structure at all. What relation do the plots those characters try to impose on the life around them actually bear to that life? In *Concluding* one can't tell, for its own plot remains as 'foggy' – and deliberately so – as the ones its characters create. At the end of the novel, for example, one of the missing schoolgirls remains missing, her fate unresolved, enigmatic.

Priestley's words, then, describe not the world in which either actual Englishmen or Green's characters live, but the one in which they think they live. Green has used his technique, that way of disguising a deficiency, to make *Concluding* suggest the condition of England and yet also to avoid the structural difficulties that the more explicit 'associations' of his early novels had created. What interests him is not the condition of England as that condition might be defined in the newspaper headlines, but the country's fears and fantasies, its imaginations of 'fantastic conspiracies' that may not in fact exist. Yet because England's fears seem in themselves imaginary, Green can dispense with the actual conditions from which those fears grow, and concentrate instead upon their imaginary nature itself, upon the sense of the world that produces them. At the end of the novel, Rock walks home through a darkened forest from the school, whose annual dance he has just attended. An ordinary night-time walk – and yet a walk into the unknown as well, for he has just consented to his granddaughter's union with the economics teacher Sebastian Birt, whose ascendancy suggests his own death. But Green presents the terrors of that unknown as laughable ones, tricks the schoolgirls have prepared for Rock and his pets, Ted the goose and Daisy the pig:

> The old man maintained outraged silence. He was oppressed by the dark, by the next dirty trick that might be played.
> He did not have long to wait.
> When they were in the centre of the second pool of moonlight, which was let through by a break in trees, and Daisy skirted this, keeping to black shade, Mr. Rock heard Ted his goose, burst into sharp cries of alarm not sixty yards in front. He halted dead.
> Next there was a rush out there towards him, a rising string of honks like an old fashioned bicycle, and the goose, which had never flown before, came noisily by at speed six foot off the ground, while Daisy grunted. The granddaughter stepped to one side. But the old man knelt, trembling.
> He feared a collision.
> Then Ted was gone. (252)

Rock can in general contemplate his own death 'with disinterest'. But at night its inevitability scares him, and a simple walk through a forest becomes a nightmare that makes his voice quaver. He faces the unknown on his knees and alone – trembling in frightened and solitary expectation of he knows not what. But nothing happens. *Concluding* is a caricature of a threatening world. The night's terrors, like the rumours on which Green's characters thrive, exist in the mind and in the mind alone. Rock's fears may be real, but their cause is not; they are the products of his own misperceptions.

Concluding, like *Back*, implies that while one has nothing to fear from life, one fears it just the same. In doing so the novel suggests the dangers of the soul's inevitable isolation from the world. The imagination of sensation can carry the grains of nightmare. Rock is as paralysed in the forest as Lily Gates was by that Liverpudlian lighthouse, and with as little reason. *Concluding* contains Green's last attempt to chart his characters' inner landscape. Rock lives completely and happily in the present; even after his fears in the forest, he admits that 'On the whole he was well satisfied with his day' (254). Yet that satisfaction requires that he surrender the soul to the world. Rock lives by forgetting the past, by forgetting all that has made him what he is, by avoiding the memories that might make him sad at the limitations of old age. He fills his days instead with thoughts of food, of simple continued existence in a present that is its own justification. *Concluding* seems, in fact, to offer a prefiguration of Beckett's conclusion to *The Unnameable*, 'you must go on, I can't go on, I'll go on',[37] an assertion of the value of life itself, at whatever cost. Rock does not remember the scientific theory that made him famous. By the time he wrote *Concluding* Green had trained himself to forget his own books. Both men live by sacrificing what has made their life possible; can only maintain their mastery of their own experience by admitting the ways they are mastered by it. John Updike writes that 'A vision so clear', so sure in the knowledge of what it must do without, 'can be withering. It takes great natural health to sustain a life without illusions'.[38] Green did not have that health, and in *Concluding* one senses his strain.

IV

In his last novels, *Nothing* and *Doting*, Green makes a retreat into an even more constricted world. He writes in them from Lewis's 'Great With-Out', and the rigid objectivity of his style excludes not only the richness of social detail on which his early novels had depended, but also the possibility of the interior life and its consequent dangers. Green deals in these novels with the relationship of middle age to the sexual life, building them almost entirely around conversations between men and women of his own class and their children. I've chosen the following passage from *Doting* to provide an example of their manner:

"Now have you been all right in yourself, lately?"

"Thank you, Arthur, I'm fairly well, I suppose."

"I mean you aren't in the middle of your change of life without knowing, are you?"

She opened her eyes very wide, looked away from him, and drew herself apart.

"Arthur," she said, in a low voice, "are you insane?"

"I only wondered, my dear?"

"Why do you do this to me?" she whispered.

"My dear darling, what am I doing?"

"You know I'm not!"

"Well, you've got to face things, Di. It will happen some day and I thought this may have started, that's all."

"But why, Arthur, is all I ask?"

"Because you're so peculiar about this whole business."

"How peculiar, when I'm naturally upset for you if your young mistress who has been trying to ensnare the one friend I still have starts him off with another girl? What would you feel if you were me?"   (316)

But Green has no intention of letting one know how Diana Middleton feels in herself, let alone how her husband Arthur would feel if he were her. His whole point, in fact, is that Arthur can't be his wife. He cannot know the nature of her experience, the lay of her inner landscape, but only the ways she acts and speaks and moves through the objective world. 'Do we know, in life, what other people are really like?' Green wrote in 1950. 'I very much doubt it. We certainly do not know what other people are thinking and feeling. How then can the novelist be so sure?'[39] To preserve the illusion of life, Diana's question must go unanswered, even by the narrator, free of the 'associations' that might define its meaning, the associations that Green's own commentary or descriptive prose would provide. Green throws the act of interpretation upon the reader himself. He makes us encounter these characters as we do the people we meet in real life, about whom, he writes, 'we seldom learn directly; except in disaster, life is oblique in its impact on people'. And that obliqueness ensures that 'we learn almost everything in life from what is done after a great deal of talk'.[40]

One learns about other people only from their speech, that manifestation of the soul in the world, that 'strange frail feeler', as Pritchett calls it, that is nevertheless the only way people have to 'make contact with each other'.[41] Yet because we cannot be sure of 'what other people are thinking and feeling', for Green our understanding of their motivations is necessarily flawed. We misinterpret them by mishearing the intentions that lie behind their words. Sometimes we mishear their words themselves, as Green did with Southern's word 'subtle', substituting words that we find more interesting – or perhaps just more convenient in terms of our own desires. As Lily Gates experiences not the

lighthouse itself but only her perception of the lighthouse, so
Nothing and *Doting* explore the slippage of meaning created by our
imperfect understanding of other people's speech. And indeed
Green suggests that that imperfection is not in our understanding
alone, but in speech, in language itself. As with Lily and the
lighthouse, there is no direct connection between language and
the things it describes, for speech is most characterized by the
imprecision with which it refers – or fails to refer – to a particular
thought or state of mind.

Yet Green's characters misinterpret each other not only because
language is imperfect, but because they know the way it is
imperfect, and can therefore twist each other's meanings to their
own advantage, can wilfully misinterpret each other, or even deny
that their words mean what in fact they meant them to mean.
Updike notes that in these novels Green writes about 'the *Party
Going* class of people, now grown middle-aged',[42] and they are best
approached in terms of *Party Going*'s 'malign comedy', of Julia's
carefully calculated kisses. *Nothing* seems to me more successful
than *Doting*. The widowed Jane Weatherby's son Philip has become
engaged to Mary Pomfret, the daughter of his mother's similarly
widowed old lover, John Pomfret. But Philip's sexual maturity
threatens Jane's own power of sexual attraction. "I know children
must marry someday bless them," she says, "but we do have the
right to ask what is to become of our own lives." (115) What should
she do? Is her life over? Should she step aside for the next
generation? Out of her fear of middle-age she drops a hint that
John Pomfret might be Philip's father as well as Mary's. She wraps
her children and friends around the 'inexhaustible wells' of her
own ego – and gets away with it because she so fully understands
and exploits the ambiguity of the banalities in which the novel's
characters converse. We never learn who, in fact, Philip's father
is. Green's abstention from authorial comment will not allow him
to tell us, and Jane herself leaves the question just unresolved
enough to break up the engagement. She then lures John Pomfret
back to herself, a willing victim for the spider's web of her own
self-regard.

Doting, in which Green divides that egoism more or less equally
between its five major characters, seems lighthearted in comparison, but its mechanism is the same and calls for no independent
commentary. Such novels suggest that the only way in which one
can impose the soul upon the world is to be aware of the gap

between them. But one has, nevertheless, to ask if in life people do mishear each other in the way Green suggests. Whole scenes in these novels pass in which the only words not contained within quotation marks are the brief notations of time and place with which the scene begins, scenes in which Green's dialogue reaches a level of artistry marked by the degree to which all art seems to be absent from it. His dialogue here does not depend upon any verbal tricks or attempts to represent a regional accent, as it does in *Living*. Instead he writes without any inflection whatsoever, so much so that his dialogue seems to prefigure Harold Pinter's, letting the reader's own voice find the places where commas ought to be, but aren't. A good actor can read the same line in a dozen ways – and the simpler the line is, the more ways there are in which it can be read, the more ways in which Green's characters can misunderstand it. Yet such dialogue, Norman Page writes:

> . . . places a burden on speech which it does not have to carry in real life, where meaning is supplemented, reinforced or qualified by gesture, facial expression, vocal tone, etc.[43]

In cutting words free from the things that in life determine their referents, Green unintentionally suggests the need for the context-creating associations that his own narrative commentary could supply. Jane Weatherby's words can't mean whatever she wants them to. By allowing his dialogue to be taken in so many different ways, Green makes it more ambiguous, more enigmatic than life itself. And however fascinating that effect makes these novels as texts to deconstruct, it nevertheless runs directly counter to Green's sense of what he wanted to do in them.

Each of them contains only a few set-pieces of the descriptive prose that seems so remarkable in Green's other books, and those deal not with the characters' emotional states or even their physical appearance, but with the look of a room or with actions performed upon a stage. In *Doting* a juggler in the nightclub at which the novel opens:

> . . . started with three billiard balls. He flung one up and caught it. He flung it up again then sent a second ball to chase the first. In no time he had three, fountaining from out his hands. And he did not stop at that. He introduced, he insinuated one at a time, one more after another, and threw the exact inches higher

each time to give six, seven balls room until, to no applause, he had a dozen chasing themselves up then down into his lazy seeming hands, each ball so precisely placed that it could be thought to follow grooves in violet air . . . miracles of skill . . . no less than the balancing of a brilliant ivory ball on the juggler's chin, then a pint beer mug on top of that ball at the exact angle needed to cheat gravity, and at last the second ivory sphere which this man placed from a stick, on cue, to top all on the mug's handle – the ball supporting a pint pot, then the pint pot a second ball until, unnoticed by our party, the man removed his chin and these separate objects fell, balls of ivory each to a hand, and the mug to the toe of his patent leather shoe where he let it hang and shine to a faint look of surprise, the artist.   (175–6)

The juggler's unnoticed artistry seems a match for Green's own seemingly artless dialogue. His prose here is enlivened with the sense of fun that grows from the improbability of any juggler's act, and the 'grooves in violet air' his own prose sketches seem no smaller 'miracles of skill' than the juggler's own. Yet however satisfying the passage is in itself, it suggests the dissatisfaction I feel with these last novels. The juggler enacts a miracle of pure form, in which one can make what one will of the patterns his props have woven in the air. He holds those props in suspension, playing them off against each other, until the last moment, when he lets them drop, catching them with perfect control. *Nothing* and *Doting* aspire to the condition of the juggling act. They are beautifully and seamlessly made things, but however much we enjoy watching a juggler, we do not feel the tears that Green once wanted to 'draw . . . out of stone' start at the sight of a pint pot balancing on a patent leather shoe. These novels, unlike *Loving*, have no room for tears, for deep feeling of any kind. Their form is a willed avoidance of emotion.

It is as if Green is so aware of the fragility of his vision that he does not even peep over the edge of the leaning tower to see the unsteady world around him. Having shed the 'associations' of class and place upon which his early novels depended, Green in these final books continues that dwindling of range by shedding his concentration upon the 'inner language and landscape' of his characters' lives. In writing *Nothing* and *Doting* Green deals with his fundamental sense of being 'divided in two' by denying that

one has access to any life but the objective one. Perhaps the gap
between the soul and the world had simply grown too large for
him – perhaps he could no longer attempt to bring them into
equilibrium, even by way of dramatizing their incommensurability,
as he had with Rock's midnight vigil. *Nothing* and *Doting* are the
products of a vision so divided that it must dispense with half its
self, with the fears and terrors that Green's imagination of sensation
creates. Their formal desperation stands as the achievement of a
will determined to find a technique for dealing with the obstacles
its own sensibility presents. But Green could not continue to
exclude those difficulties – could neither exclude them nor confront
them. *Doting* was published in 1952, and though Green lived until
1973, he did not write another book.

The central problem in dealing with Henry Green's career is that
of the books he did not write. Why, after publishing seven novels
in thirteen years, from *Party-Going* in 1939 to *Doting* in 1952, and
at a time when critics were justifiably claiming that he was the
most innovative novelist then working in England – why did Green
stop? What happened? He did not stop writing. He wrote what
he described to Southern as 'a very funny three-act play'[44] which
no one would produce, and which has not been published. He
tried that second volume of memoirs, that book on London during
the Blitz – and could not finish them. And as the 1950s wore on,
he found that he could no longer write dialogue. 'A writer's
ear needs refurbishment',[45] Green told Russell, and his growing
deafness precluded that. Even though he based some of his richest
comedy on the ways in which people fail to communicate with
each other, he could not achieve those effects using memory alone.

Green's imagination was drawn, as early as his account of Lily
Gates' night-time walk, to a sense of the terror people find in the
everyday world, which as a writer he could not do without and
yet which his memories of the war made him increasingly unable
to face. As a man he had to continue to face those fears. Evelyn
Waugh describes him in 1958 as having 'some sort of spasm, seizure, or collapse', after a luncheon party at Rose Macaulay's.[46] The
ex-fireman had climbed up on her roof to look at a malfunctioning
cistern, and his position had too forcibly reminded him of his war-
time experiences. He retired from business in 1959, already an old
man though only in his mid-fifties, and in that year told Anthony
Powell that he thought his death was near. But he had fourteen
years left, which he spent almost entirely in his Belgravia house,

increasingly isolated from the world whose sensations he had so splendidly described.

One feels a loss in all this. Yet in some sense there was nothing left for Green to write. *Nothing* and *Doting* are the *reductio ad finitum* of the aesthetic he sketched in *Pack My Bag*, novels that so fully explore the implications of Green's earlier work as to make further writing impossible. Green's career seems complete. It arcs smoothly from *Blindness* to *Doting*, the bulk of that work being done in a decade of marvellous fecundity. There are no failures of sensibility among his nine novels. He was not perhaps a strong man. Yet the man's weakness grew directly from the novelist's main strength. His work depends upon an ability to imagine the soul's frightening isolation from the world of fact, an ability that carried within it the seeds of that work's premature conclusion.

3

Anthony Powell
(1905–   )

I

Near the end of his first novel, *Afternoon Men* (1931), Anthony Powell describes an argument between Hector Barlow and Raymond Pringle over Pringle's girlfriend Harriet Twining, whom he has discovered sitting in the dark, 'a bit dishevelled' (173), with Barlow. Powell presents the scene through the eyes of the novel's protagonist, William Atwater, who recognizes, toward the argument's end, that 'It was one of those situations when it did not make much difference whether you were in the right or in the wrong, if regarded purely from the point of view of development.' (176) Time moves on in any case, without any regard for right or wrong, providing the impartial observer – or the novelist – with new developments to be observed and described. The next morning Pringle writes a suicide note, and goes off to drown himself. But as he swims out to sea he changes his mind, and lets a fishing boat pick him up. His rescue obviates the guilt Barlow had felt upon discovering the note, and cuts the chain of consequences Harriet's flirtation had threatened.

That rescue suggests, moreover, that the actions of Powell's characters have no moral consequences. The particular way an incident develops does not matter. All that matters is that it does develop, one moment leading into another, and another, a 'series of gig lamps symmetrically arranged' to which moral considerations are irrelevant. Forster writes in *Aspects of the Novel* that the traditional novel is built around the difference between 'the life in time and the life by values'.[1] But Atwater's sense of the 'point of view of development' has no room for the 'life by values'. He cares only for the 'life in time', for the world and not the soul. And Powell himself shares his point of view in a way suggested by his early critic G. U. Ellis, who writes that Powell maintains a 'complete objectivity of approach to his characters', which allows him to describe a series of 'alternate forms of experience, none of which is more preferable than any other.'[2] *Afternoon Men* grows out of a fascination with an incident's development, with the shape a situation takes over time, so great as to make any consideration of an event in terms of the 'life by values' seem unnecessary. Yet that fascination also entails a suspicion of the moral certainty implicit in the attempt to interpret a situation according to the life by values. It suggests an awareness that one's own point of view is only that, so that Powell's 'objectivity" is both an attempt to avoid the limitations of the 'slanting, sidelong' view of the world that Woolf's leaning tower imposes upon him, and a sign of them.

Powell maintains throughout his career that commitment to 'the point of view of development', to which the 'life by values' is relevant only insofar as it is contingent upon and conditioned by the revelations of time itself. But that point of view is itself capable of development. "Nothing in life is planned – or everything is", the narrator Nicholas Jenkins says in *The Acceptance World* (1955), the third book of the twelve-volume *roman fleuve*, *A Dance to the Music of Time* (1951–75), on which Powell's reputation must rest. '. . . Every step is ultimately the corollary of the step before; the consequence of being the kind of person one chances to be.' (70) Yet Powell himself initially seems to be two very different persons. He is first the author, in the 1930s, of five short and brittle comedies whose spare prose seems a model of the 'vernacular' that his Eton contemporary Cyril Connolly called characteristic of the period. And he is also the author, after the Second World War, of the *Dance*, an enormously long novel whose leisurely and complex periods might with equal accuracy be termed 'mandarin'. The two sets of books hardly seem to be the products of the same imagination, and yet Powell himself avers that his method hasn't really changed as much as it might seem. 'Wasn't it all there in *Afternoon Men*?'[3]

To Powell the essential man, whether author or character, remains the same. The critic James Tucker complains that in middle age Jenkins still judges Kenneth Widmerpool, around whom Powell structures the *Dance*, by the same superficial standards he employed when they were at school together.[4] And yet Jenkins' conception of Widmerpool grows increasingly complicated with each volume. New aspects of his character come into prominence; others, once apparently dominant, become unimportant. "Truth" is "unveiled by Time" (18) – the title of a small statue the dancer

Norman Chandler sells to the painter Edgar Deacon in the novel's fifth volume, *Casanova's Chinese Restaurant* (1960). As Jenkins watches Widmerpool over the fifty years that separate the action of the *Dance's* first volume, *A Question of Upbringing* (1951) from its last, *Hearing Secret Harmonies* (1975), he sees time strip away the peculiarities of the moment to reveal the essential man. But Widmerpool's essence remains the same from first to last. The endless and elaborate qualifications with which Jenkins describes others' behaviour are not, as Tucker would have it, an attempt to make first impressions stick, but a way of locating what gave rise to that first impression. *A Dance to the Music of Time* uses memory to extend the aesthetic principle on which *Afternoon Men* depends, to make 'the point of view of development' capable of describing not just a furtive clinch in the dark, but the quality of a whole life. And yet in doing so, Powell's triumph lies, not merely in his extension of that principle, but in the way that extension so tests that point of view as to be brought up sharply by an acute awareness of its own limitations, by the subjective 'life by values' with which it cannot deal.

II

In *Afternoon Men* Powell describes the mutual seduction of Atwater and Lola as a:

> . . . vast Heath Robinson mechanism, dually controlled by them and lumbering gloomily down vistas of triteness. With a sort of heavy-fisted dexterity the mutually adapted motions of each of them became synchronised, until the unavoidable anti-climax was at hand. Later they dined at a restaurant quite near the flat.
>
> (83)

That 'anti-climax', as Powell's metaphor suggests, seems infinitely replicable so long as one possesses the 'heavy-fisted dexterity' necessary to operate its controls. Powell's 'Heath Robinson mechanism' seems analogous to Wyndham Lewis's idea in *The Wild Body* (1928) that the artist should treat people as the constituent parts of a social machine, 'a hotel or fishing boat, for instance, the complexity of [whose] rhythmic scheme is so great that it passes as open and untrammelled life'.[5] Lewis describes such an art as 'non-moral' satire;[6] non-moral because it does not pass judgement, but merely provides an objective description of the mechanical basis of life – a description that in itself makes a moral judgement of just the sort Lewis pretends to avoid.

Yet while Powell admired Lewis's work, his account of this 'brooding edifice of seduction' serves as much to distinguish his work from Lewis's as it does to link them.[7] In Lewis's schema laughter depends on the sight of a '*thing* behaving like a person'.[8] Such a wild body acts as if it had thoughts and feelings, but really operates according to a set of complicated mechanical laws; a process that renders all human action intrinsically comic. Powell's 'Heath Robinson mechanism', in contrast, does not control his characters' actions but is instead 'dually controlled by them'. It may predict and objectify their motions, but does not rob them of the volition required to turn the machine on in the first place. For Powell, people can be understood by analogy to the workings of a machine, both here and in what he calls the 'the formal dance' (*The Acceptance World*, 69–70) of his later work, but they are not in themselves machines.

Powell's own non-moral approach has a grace and economy that Lewis entirely lacks. His sentence about the 'point of view of development', for example, accomplishes what Lewis requires whole chapters in *The Wild Body* to explain, for his method depends not on a harangue, but on the style of his prose. At the first of the series of parties of which *Afternoon Men* consists, for example, Atwater finds that:

> It was becoming difficult to reach the table with the bottle and glasses on it. When Atwater arrived at it there were no clean glasses so he took one that had a red drink in it and washed it out with soda water. Then he went back across the room. It took some minutes to get anywhere near the sofa. Waiting to pass people he watched the girl on the sofa. She was wearing rather unlikely clothes and he thought he had seen her before somewhere. She might have been an art student, perhaps, brought along unexpectedly. Her general tendency was to resemble an early John drawing, but she had adapted this style to the exigencies of the fashion of the moment. The ensemble was not strikingly apt. He gave her the drink.   (19)

The prose makes no stylistic or tonal distinction between a sentence such as 'The ensemble was not strikingly apt' and one such as 'He gave her the drink'. They have the same status within the paragraph, are both structurally statements of fact. Yet in most novels the first statement would be one of opinion, probably held by Atwater; an opinion moreover, that would characterize him as much as it does Lola, 'the girl on the sofa'. Powell makes it a 'fact' by omitting the expected qualifier, 'he thought', so that we can't tell who holds this opinion – character, narrator, or both. It becomes, in consequence, a disembodied objective statement on the same order as 'He gave her the drink.' This pretense of objectivity allows Powell to make such bald and authoritative statements as 'her general tendency was to resemble an early John drawing', over which an ordinary, 'responsible' narrator might hesitate. That sentence seems evaluative and even dismissive, but it's neither, for the 'general tendency' is linguistically indistinguishable from the facts the paragraph provides about Atwater's temporal progress across the room, his 'taking some minutes to get anywhere near the sofa'. Lola may 'resemble an early John drawing' but that description remains a simple fact without any value attached to it one way or another.

Ellis argues that Powell presents 'experience as it really seems to people at the time of its experience, without regard to what pattern it may assume in retrospect',[9] experience in which, because the passage of time has not provided a pattern for it, fact and opinion do seem indistinguishable. Powell writes *Afternoon Men* from the point of view of an observer so bombarded by details as to become the literary equivalent of Wyndham Lewis's shell-shocked man. The creeping barrage of detail is so relentless, the succession of one shell after another so swift, as to make the pattern behind them insensible. For experience in *Afternoon Men*, as Bernard Bergonzi writes, is cut into 'countless disparate units'[10] that may be connected but are in no way subordinated to each other. "There's no doubt there's money to be made there," one character says about the City. But then he adds "And money to be lost", presenting the alternatives as if there were no choice to make between them (126). Powell reports absurdities with the same laconic objectivity as the order of a drink, blurring the relation of one event to another, of cause and effect. "Have some cake," Barlow says, "It's rather stale" (50) – as if that were reason to take a piece.

Given such fragmentation, one can't tell whether any one of

life's 'countless disparate units' is right or wrong; all one can do is watch the way it develops. Yet if nothing is any better than anything else, then nothing is worth taking any trouble over. Early in the novel Atwater sits in a bar with an itinerant journalist named Fotheringham, who drunkenly complains:

"We just go on and on and on and on and on."
"We do."
"We sit here when we might be doing great things, you and I."
"Might we? . . ."
"Every minute the precious seconds flit by. The hour strikes. Every moment we get a little nearer to our appointed doom . . .'
"Try not to think about it."

And Fotheringham bursts into a lament over the emptiness of:

". . . this mad, chaotic armageddon, this frenzied, febrile striving which we, you and I, know life to be; and when we come at last to those grey, eerie, and terrible waste lands of hopeless despair . . . that drink and debt and women and too much smoking and not taking enough exercise and all the thousand hopeless, useless, wearying and never to be sufficiently regretted pleasures of our almost worse than futile lives inevitably lead us to . . ."
(60–2)

All that is certain, in the uncertain, unsteady world of the leaning tower, is that life goes 'on and on and on'. Yet in this parody of 'The Waste Land' Fotheringham's sense of futility doesn't spring from anything like a world crisis, but from the simple fact that man's subjection to that 'life in time' estranges him from the 'life by values'. Fotheringham has no fragments to shore against his ruins, no memory of a settled civilization to help him make sense of his experience. His speech gestures toward that part of life the novel excludes, the metonymy Powell does not provide, toward the 'life by values' that the numbing power of the 'life in time' precludes. Life just goes on, yielding nothing except the confusion he laments, and the futility of that leads Powell's characters to the brink of that wasteland of 'hopeless despair', the brink over which the novel's every scene, party after smoke-filled nightclub after claustrophobic room, conspires to push them. Yet one cannot take this passage as a simple condemnation of the novel's world. For Powell uses Atwater's affectless responses to suggest the impossibility of fighting against it, and in doing so offers a way of surviving in the world of the leaning tower. Atwater coaxes Fotheringham along, tells him what he wants to hear, bends to fit the shape of his conversation as he bends to fit that of all the novel's other characters. He shies away from Fotheringham's implied question – 'What does it all mean?' – not because he disagrees with Fotheringham's perceptions of the world, but only because he disagrees with his attitude toward those perceptions. "Try not to think about it", Atwater says, and if he had the energy he would tell him that 'What you say is true, but please, let's not bother. Life is impermanent, so are social relations, but we've always known that and can't in any case do anything about it.'

"Men do treat women badly," Atwater later tells Lola, whom he is treating badly, so that the general case excuses the specific one. (121) He tries to start an affair with Susan Nunnery, but after several meetings she tells him, "I mean you know it couldn't be what's known as a success." (142) And even though Powell provides no explanation of why it "couldn't be what's known as a success", both Atwater and the reader agree with her. No matter what the characters do or say, 'material things [force] themselves forward' (43), undermining their attempts to make any moment, thing, or person, count more than any other. To such characters, permanent personal relations are impossible, casual sex is the norm, and women are but expensive and bothersome sexual baubles. Powell's style fills the novel with a cotton wadding that cushions people, events, and even sentences from each other in order to desribe a world made of boredom, in which the sheer passage of time makes all effort pointless. It is therefore useless to rage, as Fotheringham does, against life's problems. One had much better just accept them, as Atwater does, with what V. S. Pritchett calls Powell's characteristic 'stolid native melancholy'.[11] The novel's characters are, as its epigraph from Robert Burton's *The Anatomy of Melancholy* suggests, 'a company of giddy heads, afternoon men', driven so mad that they are 'for fear ready to make way with themselves'. Yet that epigraph is simply a description of them, not an objection to them. They *are* mad. Nothing can change that, and so while Powell accepts Fotheringham's premises, he denies his conclusions.

In a world where all effort seems futile, what remains is precisely that which Fotheringham most bemoans: the fact that one just ones 'on and on and on'. What remains is the 'creep' of the barrage of experience, the progression of time itself. Powell writes that:

> Lola woke up a little. She said:
> "Do you live near here"   (3)

Powell's omission of the question mark after Lola's line of dialogue reinforces one's sense of a world in which all statements are neutral. More crucial, however, is the colon with which he links these two brief paragraphs, for it offers an emblem of *Afternoon Men* as a whole, a mark of time's implacable urge forward, its inability to pause. Yet while that progression drives Fotheringham to despair, it also provides the sole principle through which one can order a fragmented and otherwise insensible experience. For in a world without values, one has no choice but to depend upon chronology, 'that series of gig lamps symmetrically arranged' with which Woolf said modern fiction would *not* be concerned.

At the end of the novel, Powell's characters prepare to leave the seedy nightclub at which the book opened, for a party presumably identical to the one they'd attended in the novel's first chapters. Nothing has changed except the characters' sexual arrangements; both Lola and Harriet have now attached themselves to other men. No 'conclusion' in the conventional sense has been reached, but the reader's comparison of the novel's beginning with its end, his awareness of their similarities and dissimilarities, does organize the experience with which Powell deals, implying that this fragment of what one assumes life ought to be is all his characters actually have. And yet the novel's circular construction provides its own justification. It makes one see the novel's action from the point of view of development, so that its ending is neither right nor wrong, in any moral sense, but simply appropriate, the proper 'corollary' to the chain of circumstances that has preceeded it. In that appropriateness, *Afternoon Men*'s conclusion suggests, in Lukacs' words, the 'impossibility of achieving [its] necessary object', the sense of purpose for which Fotheringham longs. The novel takes that character's claim that life just goes 'on and on and on' at face value, admits the fearsome and unending equality of events, and yet by concentrating on 'the point of view of development', twists that sense so radically as to give one a way to enjoy it.

Yet to enjoy that point of view requires something like the attitude

with which Atwater's sometimes girlfriend, Susan Nunnery, enters
a room:

> She paused and looked round at everyone . . . as if she were all
> at once amused and surprised and at the same time disappointed.
> It was as if it had been just what she had expected and yet it
> had come as a shock to her when she saw what human beings
> were really like. (23)

Powell's description foreshadows James Hall's description of Jenkins in the *Dance* as encountering life as 'a series of small shocks
to be met with slightly raised eyebrows and the instantaneous
question of how it all fits'.[12] Susan has the ability to be surprised
by the way things develop even though they may be just what she
had expected, and that surprise provides a defence against the
boredom, and the consequent melancholy, that underlies the world
of the novel. Her quietly amused acceptance of whatever happens,
however disappointing, does mean that she cannot attempt to be
someone of what Lewis describes as 'executive will and intelligence'. Indeed *Afternoon Men*'s central doubt of what Kingsley
Amis calls the 'validity of effort'[13] gives the novel an extreme
version of the passivity before experience which troubles Amis
about Powell's later work. Yet the novel shows as well that
some effort, like Fotheringham's, can be destructive; and that an
abstention, like Susan's, from the attempt to control experience can
offer a limited and yet sustaining point of view. *Afternoon Men*
makes an attempt to combat melancholia through a systematic
awareness of the life in time that produces that same melancholia.
In its near-exclusive concern with the effects of that life, rather
than the life by values, it is the most original first novel written in
England between the wars.

The plot of *Afternoon Men* turns on the romantic and professional
machinations of a loosely-connected group of painters and Bohemian hangers-on. In subject it is a variation on what Connolly called
the generic plot of the period's literature, 'The Clever Young Man
and the Dirty Deal',[14] but it lacks the self-pity so characteristic of
other examples of the genre, such as Huxley's *Chrome Yellow* (1921),
or Connolly's own *The Rock Pool* (1935). Powell's young men are
clever and may at times believe they have received a dirty deal.
But their creator's interest lies in their actions rather than their
feelings, and his mercilessly sure descriptions of the ways in which

they manipulate each other over the price of a drink makes pity – or indeed any emotion – absolutely irrelevant. Pringle and the others fade, however, beside Powell's cleverest young man, the social-climbing painter Arthur Zouch, in his third novel, *From a View to a Death* (1933). There Powell purges the essential sadness of *Afternoon Men* through a more rigorous application of the objectivity that can create that sadness. He writes the entire novel out of the same unillusioned surprise at what 'human beings [are] really like' with which Susan Nunnery enters a room, remains so busy observing the oddity of human behaviour that he has neither the need nor the time to pause over questions like Fotheringham's.

From a View to a Death describes Zouch's will to power, his attempt to impose himself upon other people in order to make them fit the shape of his own desires; a subject to which Powell will return throughout his career. But the stakes in this novel have risen from the drinks that Pringle and Barlow try to cadge from one another in *Afternoon Men*. The novel's action is controlled by the fact that its two chief combatants aren't social equals, but men of different ages and classes. Zouch has come to Passenger Court at the invitation of Mary Passenger, whose money and social position he wants to marry. Her father, the landowner Vernon Passenger, opposes the match. In the combat between them:

> Mr. Passenger took every possible advantage that accrued to him on account of his age, position, and the fact that he was host, while in return Zouch presumed on his own standing as guest, allowed himself considerable latitude of behaviour on account of his profession, and extracted the utmost from his status as Young Man. He did all this only when necessary as a retaliatory measure, but, as Mr. Passenger disliked *prima facie* all guests brought to the house by his daughters, Zouch found that in self-defence he was compelled to call up his reserves quite often. (38–9)

Powell has, as Arthur Mizener writes, an 'almost anthropological'[15] interest in those drawn to power, that produces the near clinical objectivity of the prose in which he describes this combat. Passenger hates country life, but is nevertheless the embodiment of an old order whose only remaining power is that it controls something other people want. Zouch wants that country life badly enough to abandon the 'conventional unconventionality' of his role, including his beard, 'provided that something better [is] offered in exchange' (144). Yet Zouch has only been able to enter the house because he's an artist, and therefore doesn't bore Mary, with her intellectual pretensions, as her usual Guards officer escorts do. He can only react to his situation as 'the kind of person' he is, not as the one he would be. He does get engaged to Mary, but he remains a counterfeit artist who uses his art for social advantage, and in pursuit of that advantage becomes a counterfeit fox hunter as well. On his first morning out his horse throws him, and he breaks his neck. Even the 'superman' (6) Zouch imagines himself to be cannot impose his will upon the numbingly inert world of Passenger Court. Zouch has attempted to pass himself off as a "crack rider", but as the local innkeeper says, "Is it likely he'd have been a crack rider? With a beard?" (207). One laughs at the prejudice, and yet in this case it's absolutely correct, for the particular artistic pose his beard sums up has prevented Zouch from acquiring the skills he would need to move into the Passenger's life.

Robert Morris has said that in this novel, the 'unfittest' survive.[16] Yet it does not matter whether power should by rights belong to people like Zouch rather than to people like Passenger; does not matter who is right or who is wrong. Only Powell's description of the combat of the will matters, a description to which moral questions are irrelevant because they cannot affect the outcome. Zouch's death is but the logical end of the developments the novel describes; inevitable, a consequence of both he and Passenger being the sort of persons they are. And the cold delight with which the point of view of development makes one view his battle with Passenger keeps the painter's death from carrying any moral or emotional weight whatsoever.

It is, in fact, impossible to 'like' any of the characters in Powell's first four novels, however much one enjoys watching them perform. The limitation of Powell's early novels lies in their inability to make the reader care deeply about the life they describe, about the 'life in time' divorced from the 'life by values'. Powell's second novel, *Venusberg* (1932), and his fourth, *Agents and Patients* (1936), are particularly marked by that limitation, and the failings of the latter in particular indicate the range of issues with which Powell's style can and cannot deal. He sets part of *Agents and Patients* in a comic version of the Berlin nightclub world, just before Hitler came to power, that Christopher Isherwood had written about the previous year in *Mr Norris Changes Trains* (1935):

Two brownshirts were selling papers in the street when they
went outside. Maltravers said:
   "Heil Hitler."
   "Heil Hitler" said the brownshirts.
   "They'll be coming into power soon," Maltravers said. "Just
as well to be on the right side of them."   (136)

Fifteen pages later Powell introduces a bumptious waiter named
Adolf, who on his night off insists that "I'm not a waiter tonight.
I'm a gentleman" (151), and uses the crook of his walking stick to
trip other waiters. But one can't consider Hitler from the 'point of
view of development'. It obviously did matter what happened, in
ways long apparent by the time of the novel's publication. Powell's
style operates best in describing a society in which one can depend
upon a certain basic level of comfort and freedom, in describing
the lives of the English upper-middle classes. But such a style
cannot encompass Hitler, and the irresponsibility of Powell's
presentation of him as a comic triviality suggests the dangers of a
style to which the 'life by values' is irrelevant.

Agents and Patients takes as its theme the debilitations of the will
to power; a theme, given its setting, about which it seems naive.
To that will Powell opposes not the positive counter-example
of any single character within the book, but his own stylistic
commitment to the 'point of view of development', a commitment
that, in its unconcern with the specific way an incident turns out,
precludes any imposition of the will. Yet that style is so unobtrusive,
so muted and bland, that it seems impotent beside the giddy-
headed energy of the characters contained within it. The crucial
move in Powell's career, then, was his decision to write his fifth
novel, *What's Become of Waring* (1939), in the first person. For
Waring's style is not just that of the book, but that of a character
within the book, and its nameless narrator's even-handed discussion of the novel's other characters does provide an explicit
alternative to the longing for power that infects them.

With *Waring*, moreover, the life of Powell's protagonist begins,
as it will in the *Dance*, to approach the circumstances of his own.
Powell was born in 1905, the only child of an Army officer and his
wife, a barrister's daughter. After Eton and Oxford he began in
1926 to work for the publishing firm of Duckworth, and in 1934
he married Lady Violet Pakenham, a daughter of the 5th Earl of
Longford. The life of Powell's narrator in *Waring* seems a fictional

version of Powell's own as a young unmarried man in London: not yet in love, working for a publisher, beginning to write (here, a book on Stendhal), and moving, with a diffident fascination, through a social life that includes both seances and weddings at the Guards Chapel. *Waring's* narrator remains a shadowy figure in the novel, only an observer of, rather than a participant in, the novel's actions; less a character than a structuring device. Yet the sheer fact of his presence does have one major consequence, for it allows Powell to establish the web of chance but recurrent meetings between the members of a finite group of characters that will so mark the *Dance*. His earlier novels employ such coincidences but do not depend upon them. In *Venusberg* the commerical traveller Count Bobel makes several appearances in unlikely situations; so, in *From a View to a Death*, does the journalist Fischbein. Yet coincidence in those novels is precisely that. In *Waring*, however, the narrator's involvement in the novel's action allows the odd coincidence, the stray bit of gossip, to cluster, to become a pattern that will enable Powell's characters to answer the question the novel's title poses.

What *Waring* lacks is a sense of history. Though the narrator tells his story in the past tense, Powell binds him by the requirements of the present, so that he describes the novel's action 'without regard to the pattern it may assume in retrospect'. The narrator doesn't attempt to understand his experience, to comprehend the novel's web of coincidences, but allows them to remain a simple string of discrete accidents, of 'countless disparate units'. It seems in reading as if the pattern behind those 'units' lies latent in the novel, available to the reader but not to the narrator and perhaps not to the author either. What Powell requires to turn *What's Become of Waring* into *A Dance to the Music of Time* is memory, the internal residue of the life in time, that by matching one event against another reveals the truths that experience 'as it really seems . . . at the time' is too fragmented to convey.

III

What's Become of Waring, published shortly before the war broke out in 1939, seems clearly a transitional novel, the work of a professional novelist who feels he can use the present volume to test out themes and techniques he will develop later. During the war itself, Powell lacked the inner peace he felt he needed to work, and wrote nothing. He joined the Army and served, first in the Welch Regiment, in which his father had built his own military career, and then as a liaison officer between the British Army and the general staffs of the European allies. Immediately after the war he wrote a biography of the seventeenth-century antiquarian John Aubrey (1948), and finally returned to fiction with *A Question of Upbringing*, the first of the *Dance's* twelve volumes, in 1951. In his memoirs Powell notes that for a writer of his period the term 'novel' had come to mean a narrative of about eighty thousand words. He felt confined by that length and yet characteristically felt unable to violate the convention that dictated it. At the same time he worried that because 'certain specific types and happenings haunt every . . . novelist's imagination,' thereby limiting his range, he might have difficulties continuing to produce. Since completing *Waring* he had, in consequence, been considering:

. . . the possibility of writing a novel composed of a fairly large number of volumes. A long sequence seemed to offer . . . release from the re-engagement every year or so of the same actors and extras hanging about for employment at the stage door of one's creative fantasy. Instead of sacking the lot at the end of a brief run – with the moral certainty that at least one or two of the more tenacious will be back again seeking a job . . . the production itself might be extended, the actors made to work longer and harder . . . The eighty-thousand word fetters would not be entirely struck off, if normal process of commercial publication were accepted . . . but [that] might have advantages in checking too diffuse a pattern, by imposing a series of shorter sections each more or less complete in itself.[17]

Some of Powell's 'actors and extras' had in fact already proved 'tenacious'. Pringle and Barlow from *Afternoon Men* had reappeared in *Agents and Patients* as Chipcase and Maltravers, and Atwater had metamorphosed into the nameless narrator of *Waring*. Yet if Powell conceived the *Dance* out of his fear that he might dry up, one should nevertheless see his decision historically as well. For in deciding to write such a multi-volume work, Powell took up the characteristic strategy that English novelists in this century, and after the Second World War in particular, have adopted in dealing with 'big' subjects – with the war, for example, or with the end of the British empire. Ford Madox Ford began the trend with his tetralogy *Parade's End*, on which Waugh modelled his own *Sword of Honour* trilogy; and one has besides Olivia Manning's *Balkan* and *Levant* trilogies, Paul Scott's *Raj Quartet*, Anthony Burgess's *The Long Day Wanes*, and Doris Lessing's *Children of Violence*.

Such a multi-volume form gave the novelist a way to slip out of what Powell calls 'eighty-thousand word fetters' dictated by the economics of twentieth-century publishing without having to sacrifice the scope that their subjects warranted. One could, perhaps, consider it a variation on the serialization that helped lend such size and breadth to the Victorian novel, albeit one whose instalments came in hardback at intervals of several years, rather than bound in paper and monthly. Powell's own work has a more oblique relation to large historical events than do most of these novels, for it is chiefly concerned with the motions of private rather than public life; even the war trilogy contained within it shies away from anything like the battle pieces one finds in Waugh, or the historical exposition of Scott. But he exploits the technical advantages that form offers to their fullest, and in doing so tacitly accepted V. S. Pritchett's 1947 call in 'The Future of Fiction' for his contemporaries to eschew the pedestrian technical perfection of their early works, and to risk the *longueurs* that had disfigured both the nineteenth century and the modernist novel against the chance to write a masterpiece.[18]

Longueurs the *Dance* certainly has. James Tucker writes that its jokes tend to get lost in their own 'fat',[19] and Marvin Mudrick's description of it as a 'maddening catalog of trivia'[20] does in places ring true. Yet 'with all novelists the reader has to put up with something',[21] as Powell writes of Balzac's vulgarity, and the rewards the *Dance* offers, like those of *La Comédie Humaine* itself, far exceed the punishments it inflicts. Powell's embrace of Pritchett's challenge does, however, appear paradoxical, for he seems by far the most modest novelist of his period, the least assertive, the most open about the limitations of his art. The *Dance* depends, in fact, on Nicholas Jenkins' admission of his inability fully to understand the lives of the men and women around him. Jenkins' every statement remains tentative, qualified by his awareness that his point of view is only that, an individual perspective that cannot in the age of the leaning tower be considered a definitive reading of the events he describes. And yet despite that modesty *A Dance to the Music of Time* is the most ambitious and adventurous work any novelist of Powell's generation undertook after the Second World War, a novel that paradoxically transcends the limitations of the leaning tower by accepting their insuperability.

One must before proceeding dispose of a nagging critical issue. The *Dance* chronicles the relations of over a period of fifty years between the novelist Nicholas Jenkins, whose sensibility and career are confessedly based on Powell's own, and a large group of friends, relatives, colleagues, and acquaintances. Because Powell works by exploring Jenkins' memory, and because the novel fills many volumes, he is often considered and dismissed as an English and lesser Proust, a derivative novelist who merely repeats the lesson of the master. Powell's work does not, admittedly, provide the turning point in the international history of novelistic form that Proust's does. Nevertheless, the 'Proustian fallacy'[22] places a naively modernist emphasis on innovation at the expense of acknowledging the lessons that writers have always learned from their predecessors. I prefer to distinguish between the two novelists. Powell's interest lies in 'Truth Unveiled by Time'; Proust's in 'The Past Recaptured'. To Proust, memory makes the past live in the Bergsonian flux of one's present experience, so that, as in Woolf, the world exists insofar as it lives in the soul. Powell lacks that modernist confidence in the soul's ability to reshape the world. He wants only to comprehend an objective world whose operations seem incomprehensible, and so requires not memory's attempt to bend the world to the soul, so much as the sheer passage of time, of which that memory is an indication. 'Truth' is Unveiled by Time – by the world and not the soul. Powell uses memory because he needs it to suggest the pattern to Jenkins' experience, but that pattern lies, the novel hypothesizes, not in Jenkins' subjective ordering of events, but in the objective world itself.

In the process, however, memory serves another function. Jenkins' sustained attempt to comprehend the way the present rewrites the past becomes a means to stave off the melancholy created by the inconsequentiality of life's 'countless disparate units'. Yet that sense of *ennui* comes not from Proust so much as from Proust's own sources in Stendhal and Balzac. Powell is steeped, far more than the other English writers of his generation, in the nineteenth-century European novel – and not just in the French but in the Russian novel as well. One finds in him, for example, traces of both Lermontov and Dostoevsky, writers whose protagonists, as Irving Howe writes, suffer 'from *acedia*, that torpor of the spirit,'[23] from which Jenkins in *Temporary Kings* says he suffers himself. One would, I suspect, find more to say by examining their influence on Powell than by concentrating upon Proust. But this is not a study of influence, and in any case the essence of Powell's aesthetic antedates the seeming incorporation of Proust into his work. *A Dance to the Music of Time* is *Afternoon Men* enriched by a memory that creates what Pritchett calls a reconsideration,[24] and hence a fuller understanding, of that 'company of giddy heads'.

The *Dance* is a novel of education, the story of the process through which Jenkins has become the 'kind of person' capable of telling that story. Powell presents that process through the series of memories Jenkins summons once the 'formal dance' of his life appears to be complete, in the few weeks that lie between the last two scenes of the novel's last volume, *Hearing Secret Harmonies*. Leaving a London art gallery just after learning of the death of Kenneth Widmerpool, to whom his life has been bound by a series of apparently chance meetings, Jenkins sees a group of road menders 'gathering round their fire bucket' (251). The sight sparks the meditation with which Powell had opened *A Question of Upbringing* twenty-five years before:

The men at work at the corner of the street had made a kind of camp for themselves, where, marked out by tripods hung with red hurricane-lamps, an abyss in the road led down to a network of subterranean drainpipes. Gathered round the bucket of coke that burned in front of the shelter, several figures were swinging arms against bodies and rubbing hands together with large, pantomimic gestures: like comedians giving formal expression to the concept of extreme cold. One of them, a spare fellow in blue overalls, taller than the rest, with a jocular demeanour and long, pointed nose like that of a Shakespearean clown, suddenly stepped forward, and as if performing a rite, cast some substance – apparently the remains of two kippers, loosely wrapped in newspaper – on the bright coals of the fire, causing flames to leap fiercely upward, smoke curling about in eddies of the north-east wind. As the dark fumes floated above the houses, snow began to fall gently from a dull sky, each flake giving a small hiss as it reached the bucket. The flames died down again; and the men, as if required observances were for the moment at an end, all turned away from the fire, lowering themselves laboriously into the pit, or withdrawing to the shadows of their tarpaulin shelter. The grey, undecided flakes continued to come down, though not heavily, while a harsh odour, bitter and gaseous, penetrated the air. The day was drawing in. (5)

Powell's imagination, as Arthur Mizener notes, is essentially pictorial.[25] Jenkins describes this scene as if he were an art critic, casting every imputation, every assignation of meaning, as a speculation on a physical attitude, for he can only know these 'figures' from the outside, from their 'large, pantomimic gestures'. To Lewis in *The Wild Body* all men must be necessarily comic because 'they are all *things*, or physical bodies, behaving as *persons*'.[26] To Jenkins, however, the roadmenders are not finally bodies, objects in a formal composition, but men. They may be 'like comedians giving formal expression to the concept of extreme cold', and yet they are only like them. The image dissolves, the men disappear into the pit. In doing so they underline the fact that this description of them in the terms of Lewis's Great With-Out can provide only a partial understanding of them. Are they comedians? What does their ritual mean? Why have they retreated to the pit? And what do they do there? For the roles Jenkins assigns them are not, he suggests, necessarily the ones they actually play. They perform a 'rite' – that much is certain – but the 'substance' of their 'required observances' can only be inferred, is finally known only to themselves. The narrator has no real access to those parts of the roadmenders' lives that lie below the surface of the street, those parts of life that are, as he says in the novel's tenth volume, *Books to Furnish a Room* (1971), 'hidden, much more likely to be important' (115).

Orwell's description of his generation as one for whom 'the official beliefs were dissolving like sandcastles' signals a loss of faith in the organizing narratives of British culture. But where a writer like Waugh turned toward Catholicism to supply one, where Auden turned first toward Marxism and then toward Christianity, Powell takes as his theme one's inability fully to construct such an all-encompassing, explanatory narrative. The *Dance's* controlling metaphor allows for its own inability fully to explain the world, to offer some sustaining belief. Jenkins cannot make the novelist's traditional metonymic extension from the 'required observances' of human society to an understanding of the motivations behind them, cannot move from the world to the soul. He can describe only the ritual of those observances, the masks worn in this 'formal expression' of the patterns of social life. Yet the fact that the road menders will crawl into their shelter is predictable. People act in inexplicable ways that nevertheless conform to an intermittent pattern, whose implications Jenkins begins to suggest in the novel's second paragraph:

> . . . something in the physical attitudes of the men themselves as they turned from the fire, suddenly suggested Poussin's scene in which the Seasons, hand in hand and facing outward, tread in rhythm to the notes of the lyre that the winged and naked greybeard plays. The image of Time brought thoughts of mortality: of human beings, facing outward like the Seasons, moving hand in hand in intricate measure: stepping slowly, methodically, sometimes a trifle awkwardly, in evolutions that take recognisable shape: or breaking into seemingly meaningless gyrations, while partners disappear only to reappear again, once more giving pattern to the spectacle: unable to control the melody, unable, perhaps, to control the steps of the dance.   (5–6)

Human action becomes an awkward ritual, a dance now elaborately patterned, and now chaotic. Powell here provides the terms one can use to describe the parts of other people's lives that, made grotesque by their objectification, are nevertheless all that an observer can know. ' . . . something in the physical attitude of the men themselves . . . suggested Poussin's scene', the picture, now in the Wallace Collection, that in giving its title to the novel puts the general case of which the roadmenders are specific examples. Powell does, like a modernist, build his work upon a metaphor. Yet he uses the controlling image Poussin's painting suggests, not to circumvent what Malcolm Bradbury calls the 'linear logic taken from story or history', but rather to understand the operations of time's inescapable linearity. For Powell that linearity makes everyone one of 'those to whom things are done'. The dancers, he writes, cannot control the melody to which they dance, the 'intricate measure' of social life that guides them; nor, having once begun to dance, can they fully control each individual step. The past crowds them along. Each step grows not out of conscious volition, but is only a 'corollary of [the] step before', a part of the pattern behind one's developing experience that seems insensible as one lives from moment to moment. Each new marriage, job, friendship, catastrophe is only a 'consequence of being the kind of person one chances to be'. Given such premises, perhaps neither what happens in the pit nor one's reasons for going there matter very much. Perhaps, Powell suggests, the soul is irrelevant to an understanding of the world, and through that suggestion his controlling metaphor of the dance allows him to 'disguise [the] deficiency', created by that same objectification of the world he describes.

Powell's description of Poussin's painting both recalls his own account of Aubrey's conception of 'life as a picture crowded with odd figures, occupying themselves in unexpected and sometimes inexplicable pursuits',[27] and undams Jenkins' memories of his lifelong connection with Widmerpool. Those memories conclude a few weeks later in Jenkins' life with his quotation, at the end of *Hearing Secret Harmonies*, of a 'torrential passage' from Robert Burton's *Anatomy of Melancholy* that sums up the events he has recalled:

> . . . war, plagues, fires, inundations . . . a vast confusion of vows, wishes, actions . . . tidings of weddings, maskings, mummeries . . . cheating tricks, robberies, enormous villainies in all kinds, funerals . . . comical then tragical matters. (251)

Powell makes Jenkins write a book on Burton as an analogue for his own post-war work on Aubrey – which led, he says, to complaints that 'Burton is not at all a suitable alternative because Aubrey is a man of life and Burton is a man of death.'[28] Yet those are the poles between which the novel moves: between the roadmenders' posture before the fire, and their retreat to the 'pit'; between the known, or the partially known, and the unknown. One could say that the *Dance* charts the social manifestations of man's progress toward mortality. Powell uses Aubrey's sense of life, his delight in human variety, to stave off a melancholy so 'terrifyingly full-blooded'[29] as to approach Burton's own. The *Dance* grows from a stolid yet passionate need to understand the life in time, from a ceaseless and ever more complicated consideration of the point of view of development. Yet Powell combines that effort with an equally ceaseless attempt to discover just those parts of life to which his aesthetic doesn't apply. The *Dance* is in consequence marked by a sense of its own limitations so sure, and so openly ςpressed, that over the course of twelve volumes, Powell's objective description of social life paradoxically develops into a fully articulated ethical system. If, Powell argues, one pays sufficient attention to the life in time, the traditional life by values will not suffer, but flourish.

Powell's sense of the indeterminate meaning of experience 'as it seems to people at the time', gives the novel a flexibility that allows for the individual gyrations of any character within its overall framework, both in his own mind as he moves from volume to volume, and within the 'formal dance' the novel describes as well. His changing use of Kenneth Widmerpool provides an example. In *A Question of Upbringing* Powell introduces Widmerpool's name even before providing the narrator's own, and first presents Jenkins' closest friends, Charles Stringham and Peter Templer, through the comments they make about him. Powell has claimed, however, that while Widmerpool was from the start intended as an 'anchor-man' for the series, neither the degree of his importance, nor the shape of his development, were predetermined; he claims that as the novel progressed, Widmerpool's role became both more important and less predictable.[30] 'Truth' is 'Unveiled by Time', both to Jenkins and to Powell himself, whose skilful exploitation of an artistic indeterminacy homologous to that of history itself allows him to revise his earlier assessments of the world he has created. In the early volumes Widmerpool is at best an equal partner with Stringham and Templer. But by the time Powell wrote the fourth volume, *At Lady Molly's* (1957), he knew enough about his characters to allow Jenkins to recognize that Widmerpool has become the most important recurring figure in what he now regards as the 'mysterious patterned way' of life – 'a milestone on the road: perhaps it would be more apt to say that his course, as one jogged round the track, was run from time to time, however different the pace, in common with my own' (47).

Powell depends on such situations, on those moments in which Jenkins' jog 'round the track' touches the 'course' of the people with whom his life has been matched before, and in doing so provides new evidence of 'the formal dance with which human life is concerned' (*The Acceptance World*, 69–70). The question, then, becomes one of the dance's choreography, the question from which Jenkins' periodic meditations on 'human life' arise. To suggest the flavour of the novel as a whole, therefore, let me quote one of those meditations, from the second chapter of the novel's third volume, *The Acceptance World* (1955), and work out from it. Jenkins is here in his mid-twenties, has written one novel and has another in progress, and works for an art publisher. As the scene opens he sits in the lounge at the Ritz, waiting for his Oxford contemporary, the poet Mark Members. As he waits, he begins

> . . . to brood on the complexity of writing a novel about English life, a subject difficult enough to handle with authenticity even of a crudely naturalistic sort, even more to convey the inner truth of the things observed . . . Intricacies of social life make English habits unyielding to simplification, while understatement and irony – in which all classes of this island converse – upset the normal emphasis of recorded speech.
>
> How, I asked myself, could a writer attempt to describe in a novel such a young man as Mark Members, for example, possessing so much in common with myself, yet so different? How could this difference be expressed . . . [how] to capture and pin down . . . his final essence . . . into the medium of words.
>
> Any but the most crude indications of my own personality would be, I reflected, equally hard to transcribe . . . Even the bare facts had an unreal, almost satirical ring when committed to paper, say in the manner of innumerable Russian stories of the nineteenth century: 'I was born in the city of L——, the son of an infantry officer . . .' To convey much that was relevant to the reader's mind by such phrases was in this country hardly possible. Too many factors had to be taken into consideration. Understatement, too, had its own banality; for, skirting cheap romanticism, it could also encourage evasion of unpalatable facts.   (38–40)

Jenkins here poses the problem that Powell faces himself. Intimacy, he writes in *A Buyer's Market*, 'impedes all exactness of description' (202). Both writer and character feel themselves too close to English life to describe it well, are too aware of its intricacies for Jenkins to feel he can 'convey the inner truth of the things observed' with the broad strokes of those 'innumerable Russian stories'; too close to accept the simplifications that any attempt to 'pin down . . . [its] essence . . . into the medium of words' seems to impose. Too many competing 'factors [have] to be taken into consideration' (*Books do Furnish a Room*, 115). After an incident in *A Buyer's Market*, which I shall discuss below, Jenkins describes Widmerpool as "Rather the sort of man people pour sugar on." (81) – as, in fact, a young woman has just done. But when Bertha Conyers in *At Lady Molly's* asks Jenkins what Widmerpool is 'like' (73) he has to fumble for an answer, 'since I saw no way of giving a simple reply to a subject so complicated as Widmerpool's character' (77). For by that time Jenkins knows too much about Widmerpool to allow himself that earlier blunt statement, and must content himself with a more general meditation on his 'oddness'. How then to write? Precision is impossible, simplification is unsatisfactory, and understatement, which lies between the two, can 'encourage evasion of unpalatable facts' – as it had, for example, in *Agents and Patients*. Powell's answer is to make an admission of his narrator's difficulty in steering between a multitude of 'facts' and that sense of the 'inner truth of the things observed'. Jenkins knows himself, and therefore knows how little he knows for sure.

Jenkins' musings in *The Acceptance World* come to an end when a group of South Americans sitting across the room get up 'in a body, and with a good deal of talking and shrill laughter' (40), leave the lounge. Their clamour makes him emerge from his reverie to encounter a series of events whose 'complexity' suggests again the difficulty of writing about English life. He looks up to see 'several familiar faces' (40) scattered around the room, and a minute later his schoolfriend Peter Templer appears. Templer is now a stockbroker who 'liked his friends to be rich . . . relatively dissipated in their private lives [and] to possess no social ambitions whatever'. He has an equal abhorrence of both the 'bohemian' and the 'smart' (44–5), but one of his sisters has married a peer and Jenkins has earlier met Templer's new wife Mona at a bohemian party – in the company of Mark Members. After Mona arrives with her husband's sister, Jean Duport, Templer invites Jenkins to join them for dinner and then to come home with them for the weekend. As a teenager Jenkins had had a crush on Jean; that night he begins the affair with her that will dominate the rest of the volume. The next day Templer's brother-in-law Jimmy Stripling comes for lunch, bringing with him – to Jenkins' surprise – the fortune-teller, Myra Erdleigh, to whom Jenkins' Uncle Giles had introduced him in this volume's first chapter. She had told his fortune then, and he had dismissed her generalities; but she had, he now recalls, predicted he would have an affair with a woman whose description matches Jean's. Mona insists on inviting Nick's friend, the leftist critic J. G. Quiggin, to lunch as well. The meal is not a success – but it does spark off an affair between Quiggin and Mona that will wreck the Templers' marriage.

'Afterwards', Jenkins muses in the passage from which I've taken some of the phrases on which my argument depends:

> . . . that dinner in the Grill seemed to partake of the nature of a ritual feast, a rite from which the four of us emerged to take up new positions in the formal dance with which human life is concerned. At the time, its charm seemed to reside in a difference from the usual run of things. Certainly the chief attraction of the projected visit would be absence of all previous plan. But, in a sense, nothing in life is planned – or everything is – because in the dance every step is ultimately the corollary of the step before; the consequence of being the kind of person one chances to be.   (69–70)

The sequence provides a microcosm of the type of life the novel describes. Several characters from different parts of Jenkins' life come together, apparently by chance, and their collision forges a new chain of events, whose consequences will only become clear as time reveals the pattern hidden in experience. But such meetings also unveil the truth, clear up mysteries from Jenkins' past. He now, for example, knows what Mrs Erdleigh's predictions for him meant. But he won't fully understand the laws governing his affair with Jean until two chance meetings several years and several volumes later.

The actions Powell describes are not, however, synonymous with the lives of his characters, not even with Jenkins' own life. He deals only with those moments at which events conspire to make his characters 'take up new positions'. For this reason the criticism that Powell's narrative relies on coincidence beyond 'the limits of tolerable likelihood'[31] is irrelevant. The *Dance* is premised upon coincidence. It describes just those restricted areas of, and moments in, life in which coincidence operates. The *Dance* is not about Jenkins' life as a whole, but only about those parts of it that fit either the objective terms of the novel's opening paragraphs, or those of his reflections on that dinner in the Ritz Grill. Hence Powell's abbreviated description of Jenkins' life after the Second World War. For in retiring to the country to write, in the years between the events described in *Books Do Furnish a Room* and

Temporary Kings, Jenkins effectively removes himself for years at a time from that part of life most like a 'formal dance'.

Those epistemologically enforced restrictions, through which Jenkins polemically shows, in Lukacs' words, 'the impossibility of achieving [his] necessary object', both justify and create the difficulty he has in concentrating the necessarily subjective 'final essence' of other people in words. His meditation at the Ritz stands as a type for the novel as a whole, an attempt, which he knows can be only a partial success, to find a style that will let him address that difficulty. One turns back, then, to a passage early in *A Question of Upbringing*, in which Jenkins considers his Uncle Giles, who:

> . . . had been relegated by most of the people who knew him at all well to that limbo where nothing is expected of a person, and where more than usually outrageous actions are approached, at least conversationally, as if they constituted a series of practical jokes, more or less enjoyable, according to where responsibility for clearing up matters might fall. The curious thing about persons regarding whom society has taken this largely self-defensive measure is that the existence of the individual himself reaches a pitch when nothing he does can ever be accepted as serious. If he commits suicide, or murder, only the grotesque aspects of the event dominate the circumstances; on the whole, avoidance of such major issues being an integral part of such a condition. My uncle was a good example of the action of this law; though naturally I did not in those days see him with anything like this clearness of vision.   (19–20)

In *Faces in My Time* Powell quotes with approval Nietzsche's observation that 'the individual when closely examined is always comic',[32] a principle this portrait of Jenkins' uncle illustrates. Jenkins expects nothing of his uncle in both senses of the phrase. He finds his actions random and unpredictable, those of a 'wild body'. But he also has no faith that those actions will ever take an unambiguously positive turn. In consequence he sees Giles' life as a comedy, a 'series of practical jokes' which his family has agreed to consider from 'the point of view of development'. Powell's conception of Uncle Giles provides a model for Jenkins' consideration of the novel's other characters as a whole. To regard all characters as if they were Uncle Giles is to turn life's dance into a comedy, but Jenkins couples that comic awareness to a sense of its limitations. Nothing much happens to Uncle Giles beyond financial or sexual embarrassment. Jenkins' comic appreciation of his uncle depends, as he realizes, upon Giles' continued 'avoidance of . . . major issues', on the avoidance of any passion so strong that one cannot regard it 'at least conversationally', as a joke. His life must avoid the issues into which Powell has blundered in *Agents and Patients*. And to the degree that the *Dance* remains a comic novel, both Giles' life and the lives of those for whom he is a type do so avoid them.

To see his uncle in this way does, however, require that Jenkins sacrifice the 'canons of behaviour' (*A Question of Upbringing*, 55) he has learned at his public school, which have taught him to place other people without bothering to think about what in them – or in him – makes him so place them. For if nothing can be expected from Uncle Giles then he cannot, despite what Jenkins calls his 'neat, and still slightly military appearance', be regarded as in any way conventional. 'When closely examined,' Jenkins thinks in *At Lady Molly's*, 'no sort of individual life can truly be labelled' (206) a conventional one. And in *The Valley of Bones*, his best friend, the composer Hugh Moreland, claims that "It's no more normal to be a bank-manager or a bus-conductor, than to be Baudelaire or Ghenghis Khan . . . It just happens there are more of the former types." (13) If everyone can be treated as if nothing can be expected from them, the very idea of conventional behaviour breaks down, one more of Orwell's 'official beliefs . . . dissolving like sandcastles'. For this reason the mature Jenkins – the narrator and not the schoolboy whose life the volume describes – thinks in *A Question of Upbringing* that 'It is not easy – perhaps not even desirable—to judge other people by a consistent standard.' (54) That realization enables him to see other people's actions not as right or wrong, but from 'the point of view of development', as the 'practical jokes' of a wild body. And in doing so it provides him with his first awareness of the 'life in time' from which his understanding of the 'mysterious, patterned way' of life's dance itself will grow.

The novel's first two volumes describe the process through which, in learning the necessity of that flexibility, the young Jenkins' own beliefs dissolve. He is a judgemental young man, the very opposite of the figure who describes his world to us, whose 'canons of behaviour' are rigidly and confidently held. At a debutante ball in *A Buyer's Market* he meets up with Kenneth Widmerpool, whom he still thinks of as an 'embodiment of thankless labour and unsatisfied ambition' (35), even though Widmerpool has already started to make a lot of money in the City. During supper a pretty girl named Barbara Goring refuses to dance with Widmerpool, and then tries to sprinkle a few grains of sugar on him, because he needs "some sweetening" (77). But the lid of the sugar castor falls off, and its contents cascade over him, sticking to his 'liberally greased' hair, a 'cataract' pouring through 'the space between eyes and spectacles' (77–8). The scene is one of the *Dance's* funniest set pieces, yet its aftermath is even more crucial, for it provides Jenkins with his first unsettling indication 'of how inadequate, as a rule, is one's own grasp of another's assessment of his particular role in life' (85).

As Jenkins leaves the party, Widmerpool appears at his side, and tells him that the incident has been particularly painful because Barbara:

> ". . . knows well what my feelings are for her, even though I may not have expressed them in so many words . . . "
> This disclosure was more than a little embarrassing . . . [because] I used to think that people who looked and behaved like Widmerpool had really no right to fall in love at all, far less to have any success with girls – least of all a girl like Barbara – a point of view that in due course had, generally speaking, to be revised: sometimes in mortifying circumstances. This failure to recognise Widmerpool's passion had, of course, restricted any understanding of his conduct, when, at the supper table he had appeared so irritable . . . I could now guess that, while we sat there, he had been burning in the fires of hell. (86–7)

Truth is unveiled by time, even if the amount of time that unveiling takes is as negligible as it is in this sequence. The secure assumptions with which Jenkins has started adult life are inadequate, and the rest of the evening only confirms the lesson Widmerpool has begun to teach him. The two men move on to another party which Jenkins finds far less proper and – to his surprise – far more interesting than the dance at which the evening began. Some of the men at this second party wear evening dress, but the servants do not announce the guests' names on arrival. A 'hunchback wearing a velvet smoking-jacket' (112) plays the accordion, and the marriage market of a debutante ball has become a sexual bazaar. Invitations do not seem to matter, nobody bothers to thank their hostess, guests of all ages and social classes mingle indiscriminately, and the party ends with a fight between two homosexuals after one accuses the other, a fey cabaret performer, of putting "a weapon in the hands of the puritans" (158). When at dawn Jenkins returns to his Shepherd Market flat, the subversive power of the evening's waves have begun to dissolve his conventional expectations about social life, and about himself as well; have begun to teach him that 'the kind of person [he] chances to be' is not at all what Eton has made him believe he ought to be. Or to use Woolf's metaphor rather than Orwell's, the evening has begun to make the tower of his 'middle-class birth and expensive education' lean. At the very end of the volume, at any rate, as Jenkins walks home from another unsettling evening with Widmerpool, it seems to him as if all of London's 'buildings . . . might swing slowly forward from their bases and down into complete prostration' (285).

But his lessons on that first night do not conclude with his sight of those two homosexuals tumbling down the stairs in their quarrel. In the street outside his flat he meets his Uncle Giles. They talk briefly, part, and Jenkins goes inside:

> While I undressed I reflected on the difficulty of believing in the existence of certain human beings, my uncle among them, even in the face of unquestionable evidence – indications sometimes even wanting in the case of persons for some reason more substantial to the mind – that each had dreams and desires like other men. Was it possible to take Uncle Giles seriously? And yet he was, no doubt, serious enough to himself. (167)

That last line contains Jenkins' final lesson on a night that has by this time become a new day, the beginnings of the awareness that "there's another point of view entirely" that will characterize him for the rest of the novel (*The Soldier's Art*, 216). Widmerpool's confession has already made Jenkins aware of the subjectivity of his own impressions. Now his admission of the 'difficulty of believing . . . even in the face of unquestionable evidence' that Uncle Giles, like Widmerpool, has 'dreams and desires like other men' makes him realize the full limitations of the way in which he has seen other people. For why shouldn't people like Uncle Giles or Widmerpool take themselves as seriously as Jenkins takes himself? Jenkins' awareness of his own interior life provides a warrant for believing that Uncle Giles is 'serious enough to himself', however unlikely it seems. The effect of this crucial evening is to match Jenkins' laughter with sympathy, to couple an understanding of the 'point of view of development', which Uncle Giles' very unconventionality had first made him aware of, with an admission of the ways in which events might in fact be 'right or wrong' to the individuals involved. Powell's mature style springs from his interrogation of the sensibility behind *Afternoon Men*. He describes the outward manifestations of social life, which tend 'to be brought to the level of farce even when the theme is serious enough' (*A Question of Upbringing*, 34), to chart the steps of life's dance that an observer can see and describe, if not entirely understand. But while he may have a theoretical basis for treating the actions he describes as comic, he nevertheless couples that theory to the un-Lewisian realization that some parts of life lie outside that comedy.

Yet one can still only know the interior lives of other men and women through inference. One assumes the existence of Widmerpool's pain over Barbara's performance with the sugar castor, but that pain itself remains inaccessible, unknowable. Because he is extraneous to Jenkins' consciousness, Widmerpool remains an object of sorts, a man whose soul paradoxically both controls his presence in the world, and yet is hidden by it. Powell accordingly lets Jenkins continue to consider events 'from the point of view of development' but complicates that consideration with an awareness of just how little that point of view actually tells him. He qualifies his assertions and admits his prejudices in a way that makes his prose an oddly ornate attempt at precision, at saying in just what it is that Widmerpool's innate oddness does and does not lie. Powell settles for a limited objectivity; sacrifices the conventional sense of the 'life by values' his schoolboy's official beliefs had provided him with, in order to concentrate upon the revelations of the 'life in time'. And yet much of the novel's power grows precisely from its acknowledgement of its inability to step beyond that objective linearity, to deal with the interior life, with the psychological roots of pain – from its speculations about the possibilities of 'the life by values' that its reliance upon the 'Great With-Out' precludes. Jenkins' speculations carry with them always the admission that he might be entirely wrong. Widmerpool's private life remains private. He is 'serious enough to himself', and so must be handled with a delicate respect for what the narrator does not know. But the very privacy of his inner life ensures that he finally defies definition except through a description of his life as an object.

Yet each step such a body takes in 'the formal dance with which human life is concerned' can be seen 'with justice only in relation to a much larger configuration, the vast composition of which was at present – that at least was clear – by no means even nearly completed' (271). This awareness of Time's revelations provides the crucial difference between the style of the *Dance* and that of Powell's early novels. Memory subdues the 'countless disparate units' of experience into order, and thereby staves off both Fotheringham's despair and Atwater's *ennui*. In considering Widmerpool, Jenkins can compare one moment to countless others, can ask if Widmerpool is behaving as he has habitually done, or whether a new permutation of his character must be charted. Jenkins operates empirically, by comparing sets of objective data. He can therefore bring more information to bear on any given situation than could the third-person narrators of Powell's early novels. He knows how each scene will turn out from the point of view of its final development, and can therefore provide something like a conventionally omniscient third-person narrator's account of it, yet an account that, conditioned by his generation's sense of the limitations of their own mastery of experience, is in fact extremely unconventional.

That style allows Jenkins to revise his first impressions of an incident to fit the 'Truth Unveiled by Time', so that his own opinions undergo the same process of development as do the steps of the dance itself. And Powell uses Jenkins' ability – or willingness – to change his mind to distinguish him from Widmerpool, in a way that makes his aesthetic his ethic as well. After a school reunion dinner in *The Acceptance World*, the two men join in guiding the elegant but drunken Charles Stringham home to bed. Widmerpool asks if Stringham's drinking has become habitual, and Jenkins replies:

> "I don't know. I haven't seen him for years."
> "I thought you were a close friend of his. You used to be – at school."
> "That's a long time ago."
> Widmerpool seemed aggrieved at the news that Stringham

and I no longer saw each other regularly. Once decided in his mind on a given picture of what some aspect of life was like, he objected to any modification of the design. He possessed an absolutely rigid view of human relationships.   (213–14)

Widmerpool cannot attend to the life in time, cannot allow for 'modification of the design'. He suffers from what Benjamin DeMott calls 'delusions of moral superiority'[33] that make him attempt to subordinate other people's lives and values to his own. The change in Jenkins' relation to Stringham threatens those delusions, for it implies that his importance does not enter into some parts of life. Jenkins, in contrast, knows that he himself is extraneous to most parts of other people's lives.

They get Stringham to his apartment, manage to undress him, and put him to bed. And then Stringham sobers up, and tries to get up:

> Widmerpool took a step forward. He made as if to restrain Stringham from leaving the bed, holding both his stubby hands in front of him, as if warming them before a fire . . .
>
> "Much better to stay where you are," said Widmerpool, in a voice intended to be soothing.
>
> "Nick, are you a party to this?"
>
> "Why not call it a day?"
>
> "Take my advice," said Widmerpool. "We know what is best for you."
>
> "Rubbish . . ."
>
> Once more Stringham attempted to get out of the bed. He had pushed the clothes back, when Widmerpool threw himself on top of him, holding Stringham bodily there . . .   (216)

Widmerpool speaks in the imperative, suggesting that Stringham cannot take care of himself – and in fact Stringham can't. But in forcing him to go to bed Widmerpool imposes his will upon him, not because he has Stringham's interests at heart, but for the sake of the will alone. Jenkins contents himself with a quiet word of Atwater-like advice, cast as a question that does nothing to put his friend to bed, but nevertheless maintains both a quiet attention to Stringham's interests and a reluctance to dictate his behaviour. In consequence, one has here no doubt that Jenkins' behaviour, however ineffectual, remains preferable to Widmerpool's. Widmerpool's desire for power makes him attempt to assert his will whether or not he has any business doing so, and one sense that this moral failing stems from the same egoism that makes him inattentive to the changes wrought by time.

Widmerpool's insistence on considering others only in relation to himself blinds him to the range of human experience that Jenkins' own flexibility reveals. Yet, as I've suggested, that range of experience does have sharply defined epistemological limitations. Jenkins – and hence the novel itself – can only describe the social manifestations of the soul, the show of pain in the world, but not the soul itself. The 'formal dance with which human life is concerned' can only take people as absurd, wild bodies who remain serious to themselves, and Powell imbues the novel with a melancholy awareness that that is all it can do. The real subject of *A Dance to the Music of Time* is the part of life that it doesn't quite manage to exclude, those 'hidden, much more likely to be important' areas of experience before which Jenkins' style quails. As Powell moves in *Casanova's Chinese Restaurant* through a description of the years before Munich, the essential tone of the novel as a whole becomes clear:

> Once, at least, we had been on a Ghost Railway together at some fun fair or a seaside pier; slowly climbing sheer gradients, sweeping with frenzied speed into inky depths, turning blind corners from which black, gibbering bogeys leapt to attack, rushing headlong toward iron-studded doors, threatened by imminent collision, fingered by spectral hands, moving at last with dreadful, ever increasing momentum toward a shape that lay across the line.   (220–1)

Toward the body that is inevitably one's own. And what lies beyond the 'shape . . . across the line'? In his *Paris Review* interview Powell admits to an interest in the occult, but he draws away from its claims to demonstrate that something lies beyond this world, and does not here allow Jenkins to speculate about them.[34] What controls the pattern of the dance? Jenkins does not – cannot – know for sure. Powell refuses to let him make the metonymic extension for which that 'shape . . . across the line' calls, and this conscious absence of a religious sense weaves an eerie, grim, macabre thread through the novel, its last volumes in particular. All one can do, Powell suggests, is accept the inevitability of the body across the line, the final truth unveiled by time, the end of the chain of development. For while the novel can describe the ravages of time, it can neither redress nor offer a consolation for them. Powell takes human life so far and then stops, admits his inability to proceed. In doing so his technique does not hide what Graham Greene calls 'the traces of the botched line', but draws attention to it, acknowledges the parts of life before which he retires in confusion. Powell concentrates on the 'life in time' and confesses that that concentration says little directly about the 'life by values'. He admits that Uncle Giles must be 'serious enough to himself', even though Jenkins cannot understand how. The hesitations and qualifications of Powell's style hide nothing. Its operations are as open and as honest as any in the history of the English novel, and in its admission of its own limitations *A Dance to the Music of Time* carries the moral weight of a great novel.

IV

After this lengthy consideration of the *Dance's* style, my account of the novel's other aspects must be an abbreviated one. The novel's main theme, Mizener writes,[35] is the opposition between men of will and men of imagination, an opposition that Jenkins first poses as that between Widmerpool and Stringham. As a schoolboy, Widmerpool, whose father manufactured liquid manure, is both fat and clumsy. But he is nevertheless a compulsive achiever, and as an adult uses his steamroller will to flatten everything in the way of his own material success. Stringham is the offspring of an Edwardian plutocracy glutted on South African wealth, a man with a social position to which no social function adheres. He has both great personal charm and great gifts as a mimic and a storyteller. To the young Jenkins there seems no question that Stringham has been born to win the glittering prizes his society offers. When Widmerpool triumphs over Stringham by putting him to bed at the end of *The Acceptance World*, it therefore suggests to the young Jenkins (but not to the narrator) nothing less than a 'whole social upheaval . . . Widmerpool, once so derided by all of us, had become in some way a person of authority'. Yet while the scene is a reversal, it is not, as Jenkins then imagines, 'a positively cosmic change in life's system' (218). No – only a new step in the dance, in which being the kinds of persons they are has led Stringham and Widmerpool to make a change in individual position so radical that the still-young Jenkins mistakes it for a 'social upheaval'.

Mizener himself makes the same mistake in describing the novel's world as one 'nearly transformed by Widmerpools though still haunted by Stringhams',[36] a world in which the plodding technocrat replaces the graceful aristocrat. That description implies that the *Dance* depends on a myth of decline in which, in what Waugh condemned as the 'Century of the Common Man'[37] Widmerpools replace Stringhams in positions of social power and authority. Yet no writer who works by regarding events from the point of view of development could subscribe to such a myth, for the present not only revises one's understanding of the past but is itself a 'corollary' of it. Mizener's mistake lies in seeing Powell's elaborate reconstruction of the past in terms of the sort of historical novel in which two incompatible social types stand opposed to one another, as Fergus MacIvor and the eponymous Edward Waverley do in Scott's novel, the one giving way to the other as the past makes the present. Powell does not, however, suggest that the one excludes the other, but rather suggests their continued coexistence. Widmerpool is for his period a type of the man of will, as Stringham is a type of the man of the imagination, and the change in their relative positions only indirectly reflects a larger social movement. For Stringham's problems lie not in some process of social decline, but in the more interesting historical operations through which men like him came in the first place to seem possessed of 'executive will and intelligence'.

In *A Question of Upbringing* Jenkins describes Stringham as looking 'a little like one of those stiff, sad young men . . . in Elizabethan miniatures, lively, obstinate, generous, not very happy, and quite relentless' (12). Powell's characters are as specific to their period as Stendhal's. This description seems to take Stringham out of his time, yet actually fixes him in it, in the English ruling class of 1921, when the novel opens. For the hagiography of the Great War described all its well-born dead young officers as 'Elizabethans', men who seemed to combine the imagination and the will as Sidney had. In retrospect, some of that era's chief saints – Rupert Brooke, for example – seem to have been men of imagination forced by the combination of public school rhetoric and the accident of war to trade the imagination for a simplistic heartiness, and to present themselves like men of the will. One

wonders if, had such men lived, they would have been strong
enough to call their society's bluff, or if they would have been as
incapacitated by the myth thrust upon them as Stringham is by
his role as their successor.

Bored by university, Stringham toward the end of *A Question of
Upbringing* takes a job as private secretary to the industrialist Sir
Magnus Donners, and so confirms the young Jenkins' conventional
estimation of him. Donners' other private secretary, after all, is Bill
Truscott, famous among Jenkins' generation as a future Prime
Minister – or Poet Laureate, whichever he prefers. But Stringham
has obtained his job on charm, which in the afterglow of the Great
War's idealization of those young aristocrats, dead in the trenches
before they had a chance to disappoint anyone, both Jenkins and
his society have mistaken for 'executive will and intelligence'.
Stringham is essentially unsuited for such a job, the victim of a
system that equates personal manner with professional ability, and
in any case the society Powell describes only *appears* to value him.
In actuality it both needs and rewards Widmerpool. For while
there may be something innately odd about Widmerpool, only the
young Jenkins' acceptance of the same rhetoric that's caught
Stringham makes that oddness seem incompatible with worldly
success.

Yet Stringham, educated in a system that mistakenly assumes
both that men of his particular talents are born to rule and that
their largely decorative social connections will enable them to do
so, remains as suspicious as one of Matthew Arnold's barbarians
of that alternative to the will, of the imagination he undoubtedly
has. Only in *Temporary Kings* does Jenkins come to understand
that the refusal of the life of the mind has produced Stringham's
failure and subsequent alcoholic *ennui*. There Jenkins describes the
melancholia of his own brother-in-law Dicky Umfraville, a superb
mimic who has throughout the novel been compared to Stringham,
as growing from a 'lack of professional commitment to his own
representations' (6). Stringham's failure, then, lies not in a 'positively cosmic change in life's system', but in his refusal to accept
his own imagination, to use it rather than play with it. Yet if
Stringham is the type of the man of imagination in an age when a
public school education, with its cult of athletics and amateurism,
results in what Martin Green calls a 'blighting' of creative
ambition,[38] then Jenkins is the man who has preserved his imagination despite it. For he has that 'professional commitment', can

use the imagination to create a style to provide a defence against melancholy. When army service during the Second World War keeps Jenkins from writing he suffers from an enervating boredom like Stringham's own. At the end of the war he rejoices because he can once more lose himself in the literary work that makes life bearable. It is only the undisciplined imagination, like Stringham's, that proves debilitating in the modern world, in any world. And so too, I will suggest, does the undisciplined will.

The 'complete man' (*Temporary Kings*, 80) combines both the imagination and the will, as does General Aylmer Conyers in *The Kindly Ones*, the novel's sixth volume. That volume opens with Jenkins' memory of a luncheon party his parents gave on the summer day in 1914 when news of the shots at Sarajevo reached England. After the meal, but before the news arrives, the party moves to the drawing room. Enter Billson, the Jenkins' parlour-maid, stark naked, suffering from a nervous breakdown. The room freezes, and then the General gets to his feet, takes a 'Kashmir shawl of some size and fine texture' off the piano, wraps it 'protectively round her', and leads her from the room. 'Action had been taken, will-power brought into play', Jenkins recalls, and yet the will to act is not by itself enough (63–4). The will alone would lack the delicacy Conyers' action displays, the imagination one needs to find a solution that doesn't call for Widmerpool's self-assertion. Action is not synonymous with the will, and the imagination need not be at odds with action. To act with Conyers' tact requires both.

Powell opposes Conyers' success to another scene in that volume. At the time of Munich a houseparty at Donners' Stourwater Castle acts out a series of *tableaux vivants* based on The Seven Deadly Sins. And while watching her husband perform the concept of 'Lust' with another woman, Peter Templer's second wife Betty suffers a breakdown. 'For some reason', Jenkins thinks:

> . . . my mind was carried back at that moment to Stonehurst and the Billson incident . . . here, unfortunately, was no General Conyers to take charge of the situation, to quieten Betty Templer. Certainly her husband showed no immediate sign of wanting to accept that job. (135)

Both Jenkins, who embodies the imagination, and the industrialist Donners, here the embodiment of the will, are frozen into inaction by a situation that calls for both qualities. Their impotence in confronting a situation that they cannot order to fit their own desires makes them morally indistinguishable. Both artist and industrialist have a love of pattern, of arrangement, but each has here retreated so far into that love that they cannot recognize that the imagination, or the will, should be used *for* something, that they are not ends in themselves.

Each man is in addition implicated in the creation of the scene, for Jenkins has suggested The Seven Deadly Sins as a topic, and Donners has assigned the roles, which are in each case appropriate. But neither man takes responsibility for what he has helped create, and Jenkins' own 'sin' is a particular reproach. Donners gives him 'Sloth', in which, he says, 'There are, of course, no personal implications.' (129) But there are. Another name for 'Sloth' is *'accidie'*, or spiritual torpor – "Feeling fed up with life", as Jenkins says in *Hearing Secret Harmonies* (60), in recalling the enervating indecision in which he lived in the late 1930s. It is, he says in *The Kindly Ones*, "impossible to write with Hitler about" (96), but he has not yet found anything else to do. Instead he accepts whatever happens with a dissatisfied complacency that results in his impotence at Betty Templer's breakdown. The rest of the volume details the ways in which Jenkins learns to lay the imagination aside for the necessary miseries of army life. The war will temper and confirm the lessons he draws from the scenes at both Stonehurst and Stourwater. Jenkins does not become a man of action; he is not that 'kind of person'. Rather he fuses the imagination and the will into one consistent act of style that both acknowledges the imagination's limitations and criticizes the excesses of the will. There is not much difference, finally, between the moral tact of his allowance for the ways in which Uncle Giles is serious to himself, and General Conyers' use of that Kashmir shawl.

Because he is the kind of person he chances to be, Jenkins meditates on military life, on the different ways in which it is possible to live as a soldier. Those meditations give the three volumes of the *Dance* dealing with the war a thematic unity that makes them a largely self-contained section of the novel. The model Jenkins finds most congenial is that of the French poet Alfred de Vigny. In *The Valley of Bones* (1964), the novel's seventh volume, Jenkins' friend David Penistone tells him of Vigny's argument that:

. . . the soldier is a dedicated person, a sort of monk of war . . .
those in uniform have made the great sacrifice by losing the man
in the soldier – what he calls the warrior's abnegation, his
renunciation of thought and action. Vigny says a soldier's crown
is a crown of thorns, amongst its spikes none more painful than
passive obedience . . . the army [is] a way of life in which there
is as little room for uncontrolled fervour as for sullen indifference.
The impetuous volunteer has as much to learn as the unwilling
conscript.   (115)

Vigny's conception of military service gives Jenkins an explanation
for the problems both he and the other men in his unit have had
in adapting to military life. And through that explanation Powell
makes his most explicit attempt to give the *Dance* the totalizing
quality that Lukacs describes as 'the representation of the way
society moves'. Tucker argues that because he takes nearly all his
characters from the public school and university-educated class,
Powell has almost nothing to say about 'that duller, poorer,
grubbier world most of us inhabit'.[39] Yet in his description of
Jenkins' service with the Welch regiment in *The Valley of Bones*,
Powell does attempt both to describe a range of social types not
seen in the *Dance's* earlier volumes, and to make those types
metonymic of British life as a whole. None of the men Jenkins
meets in that regiment become recurring figures in his life, with
the exception of the alcoholic Bithel, Widmerpool's comic double.
His service with them remains a bubble in his experience, separate
from the rest of his life. Yet Captain Rowland Gwatkin is a man of
imagination, a provincial banker who has become what Vigny calls
an "impetuous volunteer", his dreams of military glory fed by
reading Kipling; his subaltern Idwal Kedward is a man of will; and
Bithel, like Uncle Giles, is a man from whom nothing can be
expected, but who nevertheless remains 'serious enough to himself'. Through Jenkins' description of his regiment, Powell implies
that the terms learned at what Walter Allen describes as the
intersection of Soho and Mayfair[40] can indeed suggest the 'totality'
of British life, whose 'details' no novel, no matter how long, can
fully embrace.

But is that implication enough for Powell to extend what Eagleton
describes as 'the materials of a directly personal response to
the quality of a whole society . . . into confidently public and
representative terms?' Certainly Powell's sense of the oddity of

individual men and women, and the typology through which he describes that oddity, does transcend the parochialism Tucker finds in the *Dance*; certainly the private experience of other people remains in actual life inaccessible to an observer, no matter what his class, or theirs, may be. And yet a different sort of writer, perhaps one whose education had not depended so much upon the precise notation of social surfaces, might have an easier time imagining that private experience, might assume from the start that Uncle Giles is serious to himself, rather than have suddenly to realize it. The question that remains, and which I will defer to my consideration of the novel's last volumes, is whether or not his conception, not of individual characters, but of life as a 'formal dance' does actually provide that totalizing picture of British society.

In helping to describe the situations of the men with whom he serves, Vigny's terms also give Jenkins a point of stability from which to look at his circumstances calmly. He finds at first that Vigny's ideas help produce a 'terrible, recurrent army dejection, the sensation that no one cares a halfpenny whether you live or die.' (*The Valley of Bones*, 123) Yet it is only through the soldier's 'renunciation of thought and action' that one can lose the self in the work, achieve the sort of poise with which Susan Nunnery in *Afternoon Men* enters a room, and so escape that same dejection. Vigny's injunction to lose the man in the soldier gives Jenkins a way to avoid both slothfulness and wilfulness, and affords as well an antidote for his own futile dreams of military glory: he never even sees combat. Such a conception of military life makes Jenkins think of Sir Philip Sidney, 'who, like a monk, submitted himself to the military way of life; because he thought it right, rather than because it appealed to him' (*The Military Philosopher*, 186). And in that submission to what he thinks is right Jenkins finds, paradoxically, a way to save his own humanity.

Powell sets that model against the behaviour of those, like Widmerpool, who are drawn to military life by its promise of power; power not as the weapon with which the monks of war stand guard over society, but as an end in itself. In *The Military Philosophers*, (1968), Jenkins listens to a conversation between Colonel Widmerpool, three regular officers, and two Widmerpool-like civilians about the newly-revealed Russian massacre of the Polish officer corps in the Katyn Forest. Widmerpool offers a very proper list of political reasons why a fuss should not be started over the matter, not least of them the fact that "the Poles themselves are in a position to offer only a very modest contribution, when it comes to the question of manpower." (112) He argues:

"Just because these details are very upsetting to the Poles themselves – naturally enough, harrowing, tragic, there isn't a word for it, I don't want to underrate that for a moment – but just because of that, it's no reason to undermine the fabric of our alliances against the Axis . . ."

"Even so, you can't exactly blame them for making enquiries through the International Red Cross," the soldier insisted.

"But I do blame them," said Tompsitt. "I blame them a great deal. Their people did not act at all circumspectly. The Russians were bound to behave as they did under the circumstances."

"Certainly hard to see what explanations they could give, if they did do it," said the airman. 'Look here, old boy, we've shot these fellows of yours by accident . . .'" (111)

The two civilians join Widmerpool in treating Katyn as a political problem; the regular officers see it as a human disaster. For Widmerpool "there isn't a word for it" (111) but rather a whole list of words, which he can so glibly spew because he does not believe that the event matters except as a problem in public relations. For him the bare fact of the massacre provides its own justification; having the power to do something is the only excuse one needs to do it. In one sense Widmerpool has a better understanding of the nature of war than the regular officers do. War is about power, about the imposition of one country's will upon another. Yet in considering such an imposition as its own *raison d'être* Widmerpool loses whatever humanity he once possessed. The regular officers, like Vigny, have their eyes on means, not ends, because they themselves are but means to a political end, and so have the freedom to be shocked at the Russian action in a way that Widmerpool cannot. They know that the will must serve some purpose beyond itself, and through them, as through Jenkins, Powell demonstrates how to remain human in war despite the essential inhumanity of war itself.

Widmerpool the comic buffoon, "the sort of man people pour sugar on", was a marvellous invention, and yet Powell's treatment of him in the early volumes remains full of reservations. He never allows one to take Widmerpool as merely comic, and as the *Dance* moves through time the character becomes much more than an improbably successful oaf. For as Widmerpool attempts, at the end of *The Military Philosophers*, to parlay his war career into political power, Powell unveils the nightmare beneath the buffoon:

> "I have come to the conclusion that I enjoy power", said Widmerpool. "That is something the war has taught me. In this connexion, it has more than once occurred to me that I might like governing . . ."
> He brought his lips together, then parted them. This contortion formed a phrase, but, the words inaudible, its sense escaped me.
> "Governing whom?"
> Leaning forward and smiling, Widmerpool repeated the movement of his lips. This time, although he spoke only in a whisper, the two words were intelligible . . .
> "*Black men . . .*"   (210)

Widmerpool wants such a job not because it must be done, as Sidney went to war, but for the taste of the thing itself, to satisfy his dream of a world in which, as in the Katyn Forest, power provides the only law; a dream whose obscenity Powell suggests through the 'contortion' of his lips. Widmerpool speaks softly, with a Kurtz-like whisper, almost as if he is aware of that obscenity; but really, one suspects, out of a secret self-satisfaction that he does not much wish to share, not even with Jenkins. But Widmerpool does not go out to the Colonies. Instead he enters Parliament on the Labour side, where whatever political convictions he has seem so completely subordinated to the convenience of his will as to be entirely meretricious. He sacrifices everything and everyone to gain the power that both feeds his ego, and lays it waste. By the mid 1950s, the time of *Temporary Kings*, 'the flesh of his face [hangs] in sallow pouches' (283), not just as ageing flesh tends to sag, but as if it has been internally corroded, eaten away beneath the skin. His words to Jenkins at the end of the war trilogy betray the first slow, festering growth of that corruption, and suggest as well the novel's turn toward the ghastly farce of its last three volumes.

A Dance to the Music of Time finally deals not with what Mizener describes as the difference between Widmerpool and Stringham, but with their similarity. It shows that Widmerpool's unharnessed

will is as dangerous, as fatal, as Stringham's undisciplined imagination. The real opposition of styles in the novel is not that
between Stringham and Widmerpool, or even between Jenkins and
Widmerpool, but between Jenkins and the briefly sketched Field-
Marshal in *The Military Philosophers*, unnamed, but clearly a portrait
of Montgomery:

> . . . the Field-Marshal's outward personality offered what was
> perhaps even less usual, will-power, not so much natural, as
> developed to altogether exceptional lengths. It was an immense,
> wiry, calculated, insistent hardness . . . One felt that a great
> deal of time and trouble, even intellectual effort of its own sort,
> had gone into producing this final result . . . There was a faint
> and faraway reminder of the clergy, too; parsonic, yet not in the
> least numinous, the tone of the incumbent ruthlessly dedicated
> to his parish, rather than the hierophant celebrating divine
> mysteries. (189)

John Keegan describes Montgomery as having 'drawn from his
First World War experiences a conviction that the squandering of
life is the cardinal military sin'.[41] His words provide a gloss on
both Powell's description of Montgomery as 'parsonic', and his
account of the regular officers' reactions to the news from Katyn
Forest. The Field-Marshal has harnessed the will to a purpose
beyond itself, as Widmerpool has not. He has made it a tool capable
not only of using, but of controlling, the power at its command.
'Only sometimes', John Russell writes of the *Dance*, 'with some
people, does will-power become detrimental.'[42] Montgomery exer-
cises power not by 'imposing his personality on the public, as an
alternative to the real thing' (31), as in *Books Do Furnish a Room* the
gossipy Oxford don Sillery does, but by consciously subordinating
that personality to the service of the end he must reach. The
paradox of such subordination, as Eliot writes in 'Tradition and
the Individual Talent', is that 'only those who have personality'[43]
can desire to escape from it. The Field-Marshal's will crystallizes
the self. It makes that personality, developed step-by-step as the
need for the will increases with each new accession of command,
stand clear in its 'calculated, insistent hardness', an achievement
of style that finally parallels that with which Nicholas Jenkins
engages his altogether different world.

V

One of the compensations for growing old, Jenkins muses in *Hearing Secret Harmonies*:

> is a vantage point gained for acquiring embellishments to narratives that have been unfolding for years beside one's own, trimmings that can even appear to supply the conclusion of a given story, though finality is never certain, a dimension always possible to add.   (31)

To regard events from that 'vantage point' is to have an eye not on right or wrong, but on the 'conclusion . . . a given story' appears to reach, the way it develops. Yet while another 'dimension [is] always possible to add', any individual's comprehension of those 'narratives' is necessarily limited by the fact that one's own development stops. As the *Dance* moves towards its close Powell makes it clear that all development takes finally the same shape. 'As in musical chairs', he writes in *The Valley of Bones*, 'the piano stops suddenly, someone is left without a seat, petrified for all time in their attitude of that particular moment.' (206) Life's 'formal dance' excludes them, and rushes on. The dancers begin to drop away and in the end even the music stops, so that, as the last sentence of the novel as a whole puts it, 'Even the formal measure of the Seasons [seems] suspended in the wintry silence.' (252)

Yet what lies outside the dance? In the novel's eighth volume, *The Soldiers Art*, Jenkins thinks of war as a piece of 'theatre', a 'show' in which he has been 'cast for a walk-on part' (5–7). His choice of words does play on military jargon, but if war seems like a piece of theatre, so too does the spectacle of other peoples' lives, actions performed on a stage on which it's one's privilege, or punishment, occasionally to play a 'walk-on part'. Men and women are like actors, taking on roles that must eventually be cast aside. Yet for what? The 'show' is distressingly real. The dance of life becomes in consequence a "lamentable Tragedy mixed full of Pleasant Mirth" (279), as Moreland says in *Temporary Kings*, reading off the subtitle of an Elizabethan drama. After the war volumes, the note struck by the ghost railway at the end of *Casanova's Chinese Restaurant* begins to dominate the novel. Visiting Moreland in hospital shortly before the composer's death, Jenkins notes that their conversation was 'the last time I had, with anyone, the sort of talk we used to have together . . . [Yet] Things drawing to a close, even quite suddenly, was hardly a surprise.' (280)[44] With age, he implies in *Hearing Secret Harmonies*, one grows accustomed to death's musical chairs, accepts the 'dismantling process steadily [curtailing] members of the cast . . . in the performance that has included one's own walk-on part.' (36)

Jenkins couples his willingness to face that sad deflating truth to a growing wonder at what, if anything, lies beyond or outside the 'show' in which he's played that part. Powell makes Jenkins admit that he does not finally know what life is about, or even if the metaphor he's found to describe it is adequate. In the novel's last volumes he concentrates on marking the boundaries of the experience with which his metaphor cannot deal, and in particular the great and haunting unknown beyond the moment at which the music stops. The *Dance* records an empiricist's fascination with metaphysics and eschatology, with what he cannot know, that Powell embodies in the beautiful dead-white face of Pamela Flitton, Stringham's niece and Widmerpool's wife. Pamela speaks, Jenkins notes when he first meets her in *The Military Philosophers*, 'as if speech was a painful effort to her'. (62) She is Lewis's 'wild body' come to an unendurable life, and yet still a thing. Life to her is a burden that, both sexually insatiable and frigid, she attempts to shrug off through an endless series of ghastly copulations. "She wants it all the time", the novelist X Trapnel tells Jenkins in *Books Do Furnish a Room*, "yet doesn't want it. She goes rigid like a corpse. Every grind's a nightmare. It's all the time, and always the same." (239) 'Is this all there is to life?' every action of this female Fotheringham seems to scream, always one of 'those to whom things are done', despite her sexual aggressiveness. 'Is this all? Is it?' And she finds no answer.

Against her in both *The Military Philosophers* and *Temporary Kings*, Powell sets Uncle Giles' old friend, the fortune-teller and astrologer Myra Erdleigh. For Mrs Erdleigh the physical world leads to the realm of the soul, the 'life in time' to the 'life by values'. She sees the objective world as but the visible manifestation of a transcendent order, of the 'secret harmonies' that an adept can hear, and which imply a meaningful pattern to life's dance. In reviewing *The Kindly Ones*, Waugh wrote that Powell reveals nothing about his characters' souls.[45] But he did not live to read the last volumes, and so misses the degree to which Powell wonders if they have any. Yet Powell does not affirm the existence of a spiritual order.

Mrs Erdleigh's is but one point of view, and not necessarily more correct than Jenkins' 'own grasp of another's assessment of his particular role in life'. She cannot stop Pamela from killing herself. Jenkins stands between the two women, impartial. Yet Pamela's agony contains a frenzied version of his own melancholia. Her questions are the same as those behind his more stolid meditations, for the 'Truth Unveiled by Time' is always, in the end, a grim one. All development tends toward a point about which neither life's dance nor the novel itself can say anything. But Jenkins saves himself from Pamela's desperation by the thought that Uncle Giles remains serious to himself whether or not some controlling force exists to grant that seriousness to him. *A Dance to the Music of Time* provides, in the end, a series of lessons on how to live in the absence of religious certainty, of how to maintain the 'life by values' even though all one knows is the 'life in time'.

One must here pause to take up the question of the adequacy of Powell's conception of the world. In one sense the *Dance* fails to achieve totality precisely because of its great strength, Powell's insistence upon a description of the surface of social life. He does, admittedly, wonder what lies beneath that life, but nevertheless simplifies it by making one choose between either his own confusion at those 'intricacies of social life' or Mrs Erdleigh's insistence on a transcendent order. Yet surely the particular pattern, the particular web of coincidence he describes, depends on both the operations of social class and London's position as England's one great metropolis. Powell describes the way life appears to work, given those factors. But he does not explore the way those factors themselves shape that life, the way that an Englishman of Powell's class and generation could not merely sit in the Ritz lounge but, as Waugh wrote in *The Ordeal of Gilbert Pinfold*, go almost anywhere in the world and find that 'few throngs comprise only strangers'.[46] Such coincidences are, of course, one of the novel's 'givens'. One isn't bothered by them as such, but by Powell's refusal to explore the social and economic reasons for the general fact of such recurrences; the reasons he would need to supply to produce an authentic picture of the way his society moves.

Powell's controlling metaphor is, as Bergonzi suggests,[47] finally smaller than the life it seeks to describe. But could it be made larger without destroying the quality in it that, while dependent on a notation of British social life, is not simply less than that life, but greater than it as well? In his awareness of his own metaphor's limitations, Powell manages to show 'polemically the impossibility of achieving' any full understanding not just of British life, but of life itself. And in doing so he remains true to the life he has described by paradoxically remaining true, not to the world, but to the soul, to the confusions of old age when, as one's friends begin to die, life's pattern does seem to stop, and all one has left is memory.

The great modernists tried to find an alternative to the seeming incoherence of modern society by attempting to create the world anew through style. Powell seems more comfortable with their programme than does any other English writer of his generation, but he has no faith in art's final triumph. Style is not for him a way to recreate the world in his own image, but a defence against that world's ravages; not a way to create new verities, but a consolation in uncertainty, through which the soul can – at best – fight to a draw with the world. In that, the novel seems homologous to an age when all England has to balance against its loss of world power is style itself. Jenkins makes 'a professional commitment to his own representations' (as England has to the business of being English), in order to stave off melancholia, a renewed attention to the 'point of view of development', to the narratives that have been unfolding for years beside his own. And so one turns from the thoughts to which Pamela Flitton gives rise, and begins to follow her husband's final development.

By the end of *Books Do Furnish a Room* Widmerpool holds minor office in the Labour government; as *Temporary Kings* opens he has lost his seat in the House, and accepted a life peerage – a prize with no power attached to it, and one emblematic of the novel as a whole, since the title itself suffers the consequences of life's musical chairs. But Widmerpool's exclusion from the mainstream of power only makes him seek it elsewhere. At the time of the Burgess–Maclean spy scandal he begins to pass information from one side to another and back again, and narrowly avoids a trial for treason. In *Hearing Secret Harmonies*, after Pamela's death and a long stint at a public policy centre in the United States, Widmerpool has allied himself with the revolutionary youth of the late 1960s. At a literary awards banquet he takes the podium, without invitation, to proclaim:

"I take pride in ridiculing . . . honour, respectability, law, order, obedience, custom, rule, hierarchy, precept, regulation, all that is insidiously imposed . . . I am grateful to the author of this book – the title of which for the moment escapes me – for . . . giving me opportunity to express . . . the wrongness of the way we live, the wrongness of marriage, the wrongness of money, the wrongness of government, the wrongness of the manner we treat kids like these."   (104)

Widmerpool's speech answers Fotheringham's in *Afternoon Men*, for it exults in the absence of the traditional morality for which Fotheringham had lamented, in the absence of everything that restrains the lust for power. Yet as Jenkins thinks in *The Military Philosophers*, 'freedom from one sort of humbug merely [implies], with human beings of any epoch, thraldom to another' (232), and Widmerpool is enslaved by what he worships. He joins a cult led by the demonic ambisexual Scorpio Murtlock, and believes that the revolution the cult desires will give him power. But Murtlock is younger than Widmerpool, and stronger. He feeds off Widmerpool's will, until one winter morning, they go out for a run, and Widmerpool's will breaks free. For Powell the present replicates the past. Widmerpool pushes himself to the head of the group, ignoring Murtlock's injunction to go more slowly. Instead he shouts "I'm leading, I'm leading now" (249), as he would have, if he dared, on the solitary winter run through which Jenkins introduces him as a schoolboy in *A Question of Upbringing*; runs faster and faster, propelled by his lust to be first, until his heart cracks.

"He was never greatly interested in other people's doings" (284), Jenkins says of Widmerpool at the end of *Temporary Kings*, and in that lack of interest lies his chief failing. By subordinating other people's doings to his own, he loses an understanding of 'the point of view of development'. He has no interest in watching the pattern of events unfold, but attempts to shape that pattern to fit his own desires. Because he cannot pay attention to the 'life in time', he destroys his 'life by values'. And in sweeping all before his insistent 'I', Widmerpool ignores precisely what one finds, and values, in Jenkins – the willingness and the understanding required to see events and people as more complex than one can fully understand. For Widmerpool himself is but an ordering principle, a means toward the establishment of a system of values within the

novel, a system that finally establishes Jenkins' style not only as
the novel's chief good, but as its subject as well. As *Afternoon Men*
posited 'alternate forms of experience, none of which is more
preferable than any other', so the style of *A Dance to the Music of
Time* has the flexibility to admit that there may be other ways of
seeing things than the one it has itself adopted.

After an evening at a pub in *Books Do Furnish a Room*, Jenkins,
Pamela's current lover, the novelist X Trapnel, and the drunken
journalist Lindsay Bagshaw walk back to Trapnel's flat along the
Maida Vale Canal, in whose waters Trapnel spots a floating bundle
of paper. He catches one of the sheets on the point of his beloved
death's-head swordstick, and reads it. Bagshaw, 'tired of waiting',
calls out:

> "Is it a work of genius? Do decide one way or the other. We
> can't bear more delay . . ."
>
> Trapnel gave a kind of shudder. He swayed. Either drink had
> once more overcome him with the suddenness with which it
> had struck outside the pub, or he was acting out a scene of
> feigned horror at what he had read. Whichever it was, he really
> did look again as if about to fall into the canal. Abruptly he
> stopped playing the part, or recovered his nerve . . .
>
> Then an extraordinary thing happened. Trapnel was still
> standing by the edge of the water holding the dripping sheet of
> foolscap. Now he crushed it in his hand, and threw the ball of
> paper back into the canal. He lifted the swordstick behind his
> head, and, putting all his force into the throw, cast it as far as
> this would carry, high into the air. The stick turned and
> descended, death's-head first. A mystic arm should certainly
> have risen from the dark waters of the mere to receive it. That
> did not happen. Trapnel's Excalibur struck the flood a long way
> from the bank, disappeared for a moment, surfaced, and began
> to float downstream . . .
>
> "You'll never get your stick back, Trappy", Bagshaw said.
> "Whatever made you do it? We'll hurry on to the bridge right
> away. It might have got caught on something. There's not much
> hope."   (236–7)

The manuscript is, of course, Trapnel's own novel-in-progress,
which Pamela has thrown into the canal to signal the end of their
affair. As the scene progresses, Bagshaw, 'in spite of his feelings

about the manuscript, could not forget the stick' (238). He continues to admonish Trapnel for his foolishness, and so provides a comic control to an essentially melodramatic scene. Yet Bagshaw's reaction prevents him from seeing the scene's tragic aspect. Comedy can't deal with every situation; it entirely misses Trapnel's subjective experience. Jenkins' simultaneous awareness of both Bagshaw's point of view, and the fact that the journalist has nevertheless missed the 'lofty side' (241) of Trapnel's action, provides a microcosm of the novel as a whole, and an indication of its self-critical streak. Powell here communicates the existence of an experience whose essence is incommunicable; an experience we can only understand by remembering the way in which we are finally serious to ourselves. Jenkins' description of life's formal dance cannot take full account of the subjective life of other men and women, and Powell's final act of courage is this tacit admission that the work upon which he has spent so many years may finally miss the heart of every action it describes. And it is just that admission that beneath the novel's brocade of social detail, its rich characterization, its reflections upon human oddity – it is just that admission that makes *A Dance to the Music of Time* a great novel.

Powell has taken his quite genuine puzzlement at life and consequent unwillingness to assert his mastery over experience, and built his novel around it; taken his uncertainty, his position on the leaning tower, and turned his limitations into his strength. Yet the scaffolding he has erected, the metaphor of the dance, can only take the novel to its conclusion, when 'Even the formal measure of the seasons seemed suspended in the wintry silence' (252). Widmerpool's death implies Jenkins' own, implies his own exclusion from life's game of musical chairs, and in facing the uncertainty of that inevitability no thought of such an objective pattern can provide an adequate consolation. At that moment one prefers Myra Erdleigh's 'secret harmonies' to the 'torrential passage' from Robert Burton with which Jenkins nevertheless has the courage to close his meditation. Yet as he burns a stack of old newspapers in the late autumn air and thinks of Burton, Jenkins knows something more than he did when the sight of the roadmenders outside that art gallery sparked his train of memory. He knows how persistently inadequate his comprehension of his own experience has been – and so one allows the ambiguity of that word 'seemed'.[48]

Powell, however, is not Jenkins, despite their near-identity of sensibility. He still lives a decade and more after finishing the novel, and still suffers the consequences of being the 'kind of person' he has always been: working, that is, as hard as before. He has written his memoirs and has, surprisingly, added two more novels to his *oeuvre*. Both *Oh, How the Wheel Becomes It!* (1983) and *The Fisher King* (1986) are minor works, like subplots from the *Dance* turned into thin volumes of their own. They provide an amusing hour, but no more, and will not help his reputation. Yet neither will they hurt it, and the sheer fact of their existence attests to the power of one of the *Dance's* lessons, of the necessary commitment, if one is that 'kind of person', to the work of the imagination as a means, not merely of enhancing, but of sustaining life.

4
Graham Greene
(1904–   )

Toward the end of Graham Greene's fourth novel, *Stamboul Train* (1932), the revolutionary Richard Czinner tells a court that has already condemned him of his hopes for a "new world". Yet as Czinner speaks, he recognizes the 'tub orator' in his conventional denunciation of the state for putting "the small thief in prison [while] the big thief lives in a palace" and so becomes 'conscious of the artificiality of his words which did not bear witness to the great love and the great hate driving him on'.[1] Czinner's emotions are real. But his expression of them is trite, and his realization of that gives him an awareness of his own life, in the terms of the novel's epigraph from Santayana, as 'lyrical in its ideal essence: tragic in its fate, and comic in its existence'. And the tragedy of Czinner's own particular fate is that at the moment of his death his existence remains comic. The gap between the depth of his emotion and the artificiality of his language, between his soul and the world, makes him a Lewisian 'thing behaving like a person', whose automatic responses are no more and no less than his judges expect.

Czinner's consciousness of his own predictability does, however, allow the reader to grant him the seriousness with which he views himself. The novel's other characters are less disturbed by their own conventionality. The lesbian journalist Mabel Warren, for example, tells herself that she is 'one of those who love and remember always, who keep faith with the past in black dresses or black bands' (55–6), and her self-dramatization does little to persuade one that she's capable of either a 'great love' or a 'great hate'. Instead, this romanticization of her own emotion makes her the object of a not-quite-funny comedy that condemns her for her inability to feel in any other than a stereotyped way.

Stamboul Train describes a world that has become entirely conventional, and yet uses that predictability to give fiction a new way of looking at the world:

> "A fine spring day, my God," said the purser aloud, trying to dismiss the impression of the last few hours, the drenched deck, the smell of steam and oil and stale Bass from the bar, the shuffle of black silk, as the stewardess moved here and there carrying tin basins. He glanced up the steel shafts of the crane, to the platform and the small figure in blue dungarees turning a great wheel, and felt an unaccustomed envy. The driver up there was parted by thirty feet of mist and rain from purser, passengers, the long lit express. I can't get away from their damned faces, the purser thought, recalling the young Jew in the heavy fur coat who had complained because he had been allotted a two-berth cabin; for two God-forsaken hours, that's all.   (3)

In his autobiography, *A Sort of Life* (1971), Greene describes the influence that Percy Lubbock's *The Craft of Fiction* had on him, with its Jamesian requirement that the novelist present each scene from a particular point of view. Greene sees this scene through the purser's eyes, which move from the 'crane to the platform and the small figure in blue dungarees', but he presents the purser's consciousness entirely in terms of an objective description of what the character sees and smells and hears. The purser's thoughts translate directly into images, and Greene allows no doubt, as would Ford Madox Ford, about the accuracy of his impressions. The character becomes a medium, and one ignores him for the sake of what he sees, as if his eyes were, like Raven's in *A Gun for Sale* (1936), a pair of 'little concealed cameras' (6), sweeping the quay to establish the scene.

Such scenes remind one that Greene belongs to the first generation of novelists for whom going to the movies was a normal part of childhood experience. If Eisenstein's *Potemkin* (1925) shows the adaptation of the modernist reliance upon collage to film, then Greene's work offers an early example of the movies' influence upon literature – but not Eisenstein so much as the Hollywood style of invisible editing that developed from D. W. Griffth. As his long involvement with film, as both critic and screenwriter, might suggest, Green's work seems made for the camera in a way that this scene makes readily apparent. For it reads like a shooting script, right down to the inclusion of camera angles. The purser's thoughts provide a fictional version of a cinematic montage in which Greene cuts from image to image to create a visual texture richer than any one 'take' could produce.

In doing so, Greene both re-educates the reader's eye by teaching it to see as the camera does, the camera which, even more than language, can be used to typify a scene; and takes advantage of the novel's ability to collapse one moment into another. The effect of such 'selectively typical catalogues', as Richard Hoggart calls them, is to place 'with a certain sureness and inevitability' the surface details of life, to make us see them as part of a 'vast pattern'.[2] If Henry Green's omission of the definite article makes everything he describes individual and unique, then Graham Greene's reliance upon it – 'the smell of steam . . . the shuffle of black silk' – turns each item into an expected one. It names them and then wearily dismisses them, as if they are no more than one has expected to find. For Greene is both drawn to and appalled by convention. No one has ever written both so fondly, and so sharply, as Greene has of writers like Rider Haggard or John Buchan or Anthony Hope, matching his praise of *The Prisoner of Zenda*'s ease and excitement with a condemnation of its 'clever, brittle sentiment . . . [its] fragile, romantic, rather bogus style'.[3] Yet the same qualities mark Greene's own work. He has such a sure sense of the conventional that he can find the one familiar feature in any experience, no matter how extraordinary, and by assigning it that definite article, make the entire experience seem mundane. Yet that very facility threatens Greene's ability to represent his characters' thoughts and emotions, which can seem too readily expressed for one to believe them.

Greene succeeds most when, as with Mabel, he adopts his character's own language to reveal the limitations of the self-conceptions that language creates for them. For Czinner's problem is Greene's own. His work, Martin Green writes:

> . . . insists on the old, stale, conventional quality of his system . . . insists that we notice the shorthand and give up our illusions that experience should be more than this . . . Implicitly he is telling the reader that the number of human possibilities is so limited that all experience falls into patterns.[4]

Greene's world lacks the capacity to surprise him. He describes a society in which the 'official beliefs' have vanished, but in which no new beliefs have appeared to replace them; a world marked by what Martin Green calls England's post-Great War turn to cliché, to which this style is homologous.[5] Yet Greene's awareness of that turn keeps him from Hope's or Buchan's high-spirited enjoyment of that 'rather bogus style'. His *oeuvre* depends instead upon an attempt to bridge the gap between his sense of man's tragic fate and comic existence, an attempt to suggest deep emotion despite the artificiality of the words he uses to present it. His technique, his way of 'disguising a deficiency', lies in his reliance on conventional settings, emotions, and characters, and his simultaneous dismissal of them as only that – a world he loves but one without the soul he needs. For he is as much a romantic as Mabel. He too wants a world where Czinner's speech would be something more than that of a 'tub orator', a world that lies outside his own power to trivialize it.

II

Stamboul Train determined the world in which Greene set most of his later novels, the border country between politics and the private life, populated by drunkards and failures, show-girls and spies, charming nihilists and restless half-believers, that critics since Arthur Calder-Marshall have called 'Greeneland'.[6] Greene himself rejects that term, arguing that it eliminates the differences between his different settings. Yet he has also written that six lines from Browning's 'Bishop Blougram's Apology' could serve as an epigraph for all of his work:

> Our interest's on the dangerous edge of things.
> The honest thief, the tender murderer,
> The superstitious atheist, demirep
> Who loves and saves her soul in new French books—
> We watch while these in equilibrium keep
> The giddy line midway.[7]

And that thematic consistency is a physical one as well. Greene sets his novels in those places where the physical conditions of life provide an objective correlative to his sense of morality's 'dangerous edge'. Vietnam just before the battle of Dien Bien Phu; Haiti under the dictatorship of Papa Doc Duvalier; Brighton during a gang-war for control of the race tracks – settings in which, as R. W. B. Lewis says, 'The human situation [is] made scenic.'[8] However much such places may differ in physical detail, their 'feel' is the same; in all of them the intersection of convention with the danger of sudden death produces a sense of the banality of extremity.

'Greeneland', John Spalding writes, 'is not the original landscape . . . [but] a landscape . . . distorted as in a heat haze by the view of life projected on to it',[9] by the way Greene's own psychological landscape blankets the settings he chooses. He is not a realistic but an expressionistic writer, whose work remains subject to expressionism's chief danger. Hoggart describes his early novels as 'cartoon art', books in which the characters:

> . . . have a kind of intense nervous life which at first almost convinces but is soon seen to be breathed into them by Greene's breath, and always by his breath . . . In Greene's novels we do not 'explore experience'; we meet Graham Greene . . . [If] we find the novels up to a point arresting . . . [it is] because they are forceful, melodramatic presentations of an obsessed and imaginative personality.[10]

Hoggart argues that whenever Greene tries to present deeply felt emotion one feels the butcher's thumb of his own voice on the scale of his character's experience, so that their emotions are 'pulled out of shape, put into overbold relief'.[11] Yet while he points to a central problem in Greene's work, Hoggart nevertheless misses the degree to which Greene is aware of that weakness, and turns it into a comment on the world he describes.

The creation of that distorted landscape called Greeneland seems to me a larger achievement than that of any single one of Greene's novels, just as Hardy's Wessex transcends the books he sets there. But while *Stamboul Train* does determine the physical landscape of Greeneland, it does so without the 'obsessed and imaginative personality' that can animate it, without the distortions of Spurling's 'heat haze'. Its cleverly constructed account of a diverse group of characters brought together on a train taught Greene crucial lessons about the manipulation of subplots and the controlled use of conventional characters. But its *Grand Hotel*-style structure makes it too diffuse for any one character's situation, even Czinner's, to carry the febrile urgency of Greene's best novels, and for an example of that urgency one must turn back to his first book,

The Man Within (1929).

Greene writes in 'The Young Dickens' that 'the creative writer perceives his world once and for all in childhood and adolescence, and his whole career is an effort to illustrate his private world in terms of the great public world we all share'.[12] The statement, like most of Greene's critical writings, is as much a self-description as an account of another writer's work. "In the lost boyhood of Judas, / Christ was betrayed",[13] he quotes from A. E.'s 'Germinal', and the obsessions of his own private world are particularly Judas-like. His work is dominated by a sense of the inevitability of exile and betrayal, by his sense of the consequences of being both a student and the son of the Headmaster at Berkhamstead School.

In *A Sort of Life* Greene describes the emotional upheaval he felt when he left his parents' house, with its Edenic croquet lawn, to board in the dormitories of what was still, inevitably, home:

> . . . a changing-room smelling of sweat and stale clothes, stone stairs, worn by generations of feet, leading to a dormitory divided by pitch-pine partitions that gave inadequate privacy . . . I was a foreigner and a suspect, quite literally a hunted creature, known to have dubious associates. Was my father not the headmaster? . . . I was surrounded by the forces of the resistance and yet I couldn't join them without betraying my father . . .[14]

Even more than most public-school boys, the young Greene felt his existence determined by the role his sheer physical presence in the school assigned him – a presence that made his own emotional confusion seem as irrelevant as the thoughts of a man in the trenches. And yet Greene was in no physical danger. Cyril Connolly argues in *Enemies of Promise* that the 'experiences undergone by boys at the great public schools . . . are so intense as to dominate their lives and to arrest their development'; an argument that he calls the 'Theory of Permanent Adolescence'.[15] But the threats to the self those experiences produce, Orwell countered, are trivial ones, however intensely they may be felt, the product of a 'lukewarm bath of snobbery . . . [in which] hunger, hardship, solitude, exile, war, prison, persecution . . . [are] hardly even words'.[16] So it was for Greene. The sense of imminent danger and inevitable betrayal his school experience produced was factitious compared to the threats posed by the trenches his generation had escaped, and of which they were always aware. In using the emotions school produced in him as a basis for his fiction he had, therefore, to find a way to make them seem more than the product of an adolescent self-pity. He had to find an objective correlative for them, a world that could offer the qualities that Orwell defines as missing in his own.

His search for that world led him to set his first novel, *The Man Within* (1929), in the smuggling communities of early nineteenth-century Sussex. Greene's protagonist Francis Andrews is a 'hunted man' (14) who is also a haunted man, haunted by his memories of his father, the leader of a band of smugglers, who has died in a fight at sea. The band's new leader Carlyon has taken young Andrews from school and put him to work, with a set of crewmates who constantly match Andrews' performance against their memories of his father, and find him wanting. Andrews takes solace in self-pity, which allows him his 'favourite process' (14) of seeing himself dramatically, 'chased by harsh enemies through an uninterested world' (24). He thinks of himself, in Wyndham Lewis's terms, as one of 'those to whom things are done', as nearly all Greene's protagonists are, rather than a man of 'executive will and intelligence'. The novel's melodramatic plot involves Andrews' betrayal of his compatriots and his flight from their revenge, during which he forces a woman, Elizabeth, to give him shelter in her solitary forest cottage. As the novel progresses, the cottage becomes a moral as well as a physical refuge. There Andrews catches a glimpse of what Maurice Castle in Greene's late novel, *The Human Factor* (1978) thinks of as 'the city called Peace of Mind',[17] a vision of the quiet life he has not been allowed to have; and one that Greene, himself an exile from the garden of his own childhood, will summon for the rest of this career.

Andrews is always aware of 'the man within' him, who is, as the novel's epigraph from Sir Thomas Browne suggests, 'angry' with him; of the 'inner critic' (136) who reminds him of his own cowardice. Yet Elizabeth doesn't think him weak. She believes in the strength of the man within, and through her belief, and finally her love, he lays 'His father's . . . stubborn ghost' (220). Elizabeth believes in a God, and that enables her to believe in Andrews in a way that lets him believe in himself, to find some positive value outside the realm of his own self-pity. He dies as a result, and yet death gives his life the meaning it had lacked. It is a 'proof of sincerity', as the narrator Brown thinks in the 1966 novel *The Comedians* (253). It makes one realize what Greene calls 'the importance of the human act',[18] realize that human life does matter, that it's not what Andrews thinks of as a bundle of 'negatives' (25). In the Catholic novels of his mid-career Greene makes that importance a function of the religious sense. *The Man Within* is less specific; it's marked by the religious impulse toward transcendence, but it also suggests that a belief in anything outside the self will serve.

One senses in reading, however, that Greene has yet to grow up to the sound of his own voice, cannot yet invent an action onto which he can project his personal melodrama. The world of historical romance is too highly coloured, too distant from ordinary experience, to support Greene's schoolboy sense of a banal and ghastly quotidian, in which exile and treason are as much facts of daily life as brushing one's teeth. Nineteenth-century Sussex fools him into assenting to Andrews' 'Vague romantic longings' (170), emotions of the sort he would condemn in Mabel Warren three years later in *Stamboul Train*. Perhaps there is simply too large a gap between a smuggler and a headmaster for a young writer to span.

The novel sold well just the same, and Greene's publishers gave him a contract for three more. But Greene considers his next two novels, *The Name of Action* (1930) and *Rumour at Nightfall* (1931), to be so bad that he has never allowed them to be reprinted. Each deals with the attempts of a bored young Englishman to involve himself in other people's political struggles. In that, they seem more important as a prefiguration of Greene's own occasional work after the Second World War as a courier for various dissident groups, than they do for any study of his fiction. I agree with Greene's estimation of them. Neither novel affords him a world that can both qualify and justify his psychological predicament, and their failure made him think of abandoning novel-writing in order to support his family. *Stamboul Train* changed that. He wrote it to make money, and it did. But in writing it he also began to discover a public world through which to illustrate his private one, and for the first time revealed that crucial knowledge of the conventionality of his own material and his corresponding distrust of the very emotions in which he so wants to believe.

The book is the first of Greene's memorable thirties' thrillers, novels in which he creates a richly seen and textured physical world that offers a feel for the decade in fiction analogous to that provided by Auden's poetry. Greene's novels from the thirties describe life in what he calls the 'sinless graceless chromium world'[19] of modern civilization, whose concentration on 'the smart, the new, the chic, the cerebral'[20] does not bear witness to the emotions of which he believes men and women ought to be capable. And yet that world is created above all by Greene's own style, so that novels like *It's A Battlefield* (1934) or *England Made Me* (1935) are as much about that style as they are anything else, works in which Greene acknowledges his inability metonymically to digress from 'the artificiality of his words' to the feelings that those words represent. Greene's novels are reportorial, they have their eye on the headlines, and as a group they help create what Goldmann calls the 'collective consciousness'[21] of their period by providing one of the English novel's first, and still finest, accounts of life in an urban mass society. Demonstrations in Hyde Park, gas attack drills, strikes, traffic jams, the cinema, the delights of fast cars, Mass Observation, roadhouses, newspaper boys – Greene uses all these to suggest the cramped world of the grotesquely familiar that Kate Farrant sums up in *England Made Me* as "my Ladies Bar . . . my beastly port" (136).

Yet Kate's voice, like Greene's own, fills with love when she says that, a love for the things and surfaces of the physical world that paradoxically atrophies the very emotions that could make that world worth living in. For Greeneland's 'seedy' (*Journey Without Maps*, 224) predictability strangles its inhabitants, robbing their emotions of any validity, and Greene both pities and condemns his characters for the spiritual poverty that grows from the self-conscious conventionality of his own imagination. After a hasty and unsatisfactory coupling with the waiter Jules Briton, whose motions have been but an excuse for Jules' self-regard, the factory girl Kay Rimmer in *It's A Battlefield* thinks that 'You expected such a damned lot from love, a unique excitement, a quality of everlastingness; no value remained unshaken when love was like this' (153). Jules thinks of love in material terms, as a sexual exchange that both feeds his ego and gives Kay the means to purchase 'everything which made life worth living, the cinema, the dance hall, powder and scent and rouge and stockings' (149). But to Kay sex itself makes 'life worth living', for it provides a momentary escape – a 'mere glimpse of meaning', in Lukacs' words – from that reified world of stockings and the cinema in which Greene's style forces her to live.

If for Woolf the objects of the physical world exist only insofar as they register in the consciousness of her characters, then for

Greene his characters' interior lives exist only through their relations to those objects. Such a treatment of the interior life is of
course inescapable in film, is indeed the norm around which the
medium organizes itself. In prose fiction, however, it becomes an
implicit comment on the limitations of the world Greene describes.
It is his own version of Wyndham Lewis's 'Great With-Out', a
way to suggest the reification, indeed the non-existence, of his
characters' interior lives, and their consequent loss of human
contact. But given that, Greene asks, how can one get that sense
of 'everlastingness', of emotional depth, in which characters like
Kay must believe, into their lives and so into the novel itself? How
to cut through the conventional surfaces of the purely physical
world in which his eye so delights, and so express Czinner's 'great
love' and 'great hate'?

It's A Battlefield offers no answers to that question. Greene sees
the social problems of his period in much the same terms as do
the members of the Auden generation, but he doesn't commit
himself to political activity as they did. Instead, he takes as his
main character an assistant commissioner of police who believes
only in his craft, in reading the meaning of a beret that forms a
clue in a murder case, 'noting the texture of the wool, the pattern
of the crochet' (13). He believes his job is simply to catch criminals,
without bothering about causes or consequences, which are 'not
his business' (168). But nothing can stay 'plain' (169) in the mist of
the modern city, and one case in particular makes him think of
resigning, for its political complexities rob him of 'any conviction
that [he is] on the right side' (201–2). Perhaps, he thinks, 'Younger
men . . . might live to serve something in which they believed'
(169), but he has no hope of doing so, and his devotion to the
particularities of his craft, rather than to abstract causes, makes
him incapable of fighting for such beliefs.

Instead he wearily accepts his own impotence – and yet, at the
end of the novel:

> . . . without warning . . . all that worried him dropped away,
> like the little figures running back from the landing ground as
> an airship lands. He began to write in his small meticulous
> handwriting across the top of the Streatham report: 'What the
> officers in charge of this case have not realized is the significance
> of the prostitute's evidence that she saw Flossie Matthews

waiting on a park chair as early as 6 p.m. Taken in conjunction
with the other evidence . . .' (202)

And the novel ends. He retreats into craft, into the truth and
precision that his art requires, and Greene's characterization of
him provides an allegory of the writer's position as well. *It's A
Battlefield* suggests both the impotence that comes from a refusal to
commit oneself to a political struggle, and the advantages that
abstention offers. The assistant commissioner has an awareness of
the 'general state'[22] of the action that the novel's other more
politically committed characters lack. He can make connections
between events, things, people, can assemble them into a pattern
of significance. Yet behind that commitment to craft lies Greene's
own inability to commit himself to anything else. Neither he nor
the assistant commissioner can find a satisfactory answer for the
man within. They remain, as Terry Eagleton argues, 'desperately
bound to a quotidian world which is hated but which cannot be
changed',[23] filled with a sense of their own impotence that, in the
age of the leaning tower, bespeaks a loss of the modernist's faith
in the power of art to reshape the world.

It's A Battlefield retreats from commitment into the precise
observation of its period that is Greene's refuge from his own
romanticism. This seems particularly true of the two 'entertainments', he wrote in the second half of the decade, *A Gun for Sale*
and *The Confidential Agent*. Until the late 1960s when he abandoned
the distinction, Greene divided his work between 'novels' and
'entertainments'. 'In one's entertainments', he says:

. . . one is primarily interested in having an exciting story as in
a physical action, with just enough character to give interest to
the action, because you can't be interested in the action of a
mere dummy. In the novels I hope one is primarily interested
in the character and the action takes a minor part.[24]

To me the distinction lies between the books in which Greene
relaxes enough to let his eye enjoy the physical world, and those
in which his 'inner critic' reminds the reader of his characters'
vacancy in that world. His themes remain the same – betrayal, the
search for a refuge, the relationship between private desires and
political actions. But in the 'entertainments' those themes merely
provide part of what Waugh called the novel's 'furniture',[25] the

props one needs to make a story move, rather than its motive force.

A Gun for Sale and *The Confidential Agent* (1939) are heavily stylized thirties' morality plays, set against the prospect of a coming war, which Greene wrote in the hopes of duplicating *Stamboul Train*'s popular success. Hoggart argues that they aren't books 'whose life we can "entertain as a possibility" whilst we are reading',[26] but they are nevertheless some of Greene's most readable, and enjoyably re-readable novels. At the end of *A Gun for Sale*, Ann Crowder travels on a train that:

> . . . drew in to London over a great viaduct under which the small bright shabby streets ran off like the rays of a star with their sweet shops, their Methodist chapels, their messages chalked on the paving stones. Then it was she who thought: this is safe, and wiping the glass free from steam, she pressed her face against the pane and happily and avidly and tenderly watched . . . (186)

Greene's eye for the typical elements of his culture's urban life is as sharp as that of any modern novelist. He doesn't here suggest the limits of his absorption in physical details, but rather delights in it, in the 'small bright shabby streets' that his prose loves as much for their shabbiness as their brightness. Here he evokes the ordinary life with which this novel about political assassination has *not* been concerned, suggesting both its value and its precariousness. *The Confidential Agent* elaborates on that precariousness. Like its contemporary, Hitchcock's *The Lady Vanishes*, it views England's placidity with a mixture of contempt and wistfulness that suggests the country's unpreparedness for the melodrama of contemporary history. As an imaginative understanding of the condition of England, these novels lack the penetration of Henry Green's *Party-Going*. They have both too much, and not enough, of the caricature about them, for Greene doesn't make the stick-figure quality of his characters tell, as he does in those books he calls 'novels'.

In *A Gun for Sale*'s predecessor, *England Made Me*, Greene does, however, make an interrogation of his own style similar to that of *It's A Battlefield*. He takes as his protagonist Anthony Farrant, who is 'not young enough and not old enough; not young enough to believe in a juster world, not old enough for the country, the king, the trenches, to mean anything at all' (180). Anthony is part of that generation for whom what Orwell called the 'official beliefs' have crumbled. He can only believe in the public-school mythology that so fascinates Greene himself, and indeed his generation as a whole. But for Anthony any old school tie will do. When he meets his twin sister Kate at the start of the novel, she notices that he isn't wearing his own. "I've promoted myself", he tells her. "It's Harrow" (15).

Anthony relies on surfaces, upon charm and 'one good suit' (8), but 'behind the firm hand-clasp and the easy joke [lies] a deep nihilism' (51), the recognition, through 'a temporary break in the cloud of his self-deception' that he hasn't 'a future' (29). He recognizes his own nothingness, the way he's let the world strangle the soul with a set of conventions for which he remains unsuited. Or rather, the way Kate has strangled him. All their actions refer to their shared memory of a night when, as teenagers, they met in a barn halfway between their respective boarding schools, he 'with his school cap crumpled in his hands' (12), and she talked him out of running away. One recalls Greene's fondness for those lines from A. E.'s 'Germinal' – that 'in the lost boyhood of Judas, / Christ was betrayed'. In nearly all his novels Greene refers the psychological causes of his characters' actions back to a moment, often in childhood, whose memory both encapsulates and determines the whole course of their future lives. Such a technique may stylize the interior life, but it also lets Greene present it as the product of an objective physical moment, in a way that lets him evade the artificiality with which he presents emotion. It allows him to present Anthony as caught in a 'permanent adolescence', unable to step outside that moment in the barn.

Greene matches Anthony up against the 'sinless, graceless chromium world' of modernity in the person of Kate's lover and employer, the Swedish industrialist Eric Krogh. Kate has Krogh give her brother a job as his bodyguard, and in doing so believes that "I've undone the damage I did him when I sent him back, back from the barn to conform, to pick up the conventions, the manners of all the rest" (141). But when Anthony sees Krogh's troubleshooter, a thuggish working-class Englishman named Hall, beat up a workman he realizes that his job is not 'respectable' (115). He decides to go back to England, but before doing so discovers that Krogh has swindled his partners, and decides that his own respectability doesn't preclude blackmail. But Anthony is not, Kate says, "unscrupulous enough to be successful" (144), and he lets his plan slip too early. And even though Kate herself knows what's going to happen, she is too implicated in that 'chromium world', too much at home with 'the manners of all the rest', to warn him that Hall will kill him.

Yet while one prefers Anthony to either Krogh or Kate, one isn't troubled by his death, and in that lack of disturbance Greene finds his subject: in the inability of a world dominated by convention to support a genuine sense of outrage. Anthony cannot, even in defeat, provide an effective moral alternative to Krogh's world. He decides to leave Sweden only because Krogh's behaviour has violated his sense of respectability. But he cannot imagine that the novel's other characters have no interest in respectability; that like Hitler, Krogh believes only in power and will do anything to preserve it. The old school tie will not let Anthony entertain the possibility of his own betrayal, of a moral universe that exists outside the "Ladies Bar . . . [and] beastly port" of his own world. The strength of *England Made Me*, Greene's best early novel, grows from its demonstration of the 'impossibility of achieving [its] necessary object', from a sense of the impotence, not just of Anthony's values, but of its own.

III

Greene converted to Roman Catholicism in 1926, but did not, he writes, begin to feel an emotional attachment to his faith until 1938, when his publishers commissioned him to report on the Mexican government's persecution of the Church. But by the time he went to Mexico he had already begun, in *Brighton Rock* (1938), to let his Catholicism help shape his fiction. In retrospect one sees that Greene's early fiction is marked by an implicit awareness of the absence of religion in the world he describes, by the absence of any sustaining belief that could make men more than things. In *Brighton Rock*, however, Greene began to create characters whose consciousness includes an awareness of a spiritual world against which their actions must be judged.

Greene's idiosyncratic Catholicism in what R. W. B. Lewis has called the 'trilogy'[27] of *Brighton Rock*, *The Power and the Glory* (1940) and *The Heart of the Matter* (1949), brought him at mid-century both a critical acclaim that linked him with Malraux and Camus as an explorer of 'the human condition', and the enormous popular audience he continues to enjoy. Yet Greene's religious novels are but one phase in a long career, and after *The End of the Affair* (1951), he began to turn away from religion to a renewed absorption with politics. Given that turn, *Brighton Rock's* importance lies not so much in its religious themes *per se*, as in the consequences the sheer presence of those themes have for his later fiction. Critics argue endlessly about Greene's theology. What seems inarguable is that his use of religion in *Brighton Rock* allowed him the conviction he needed for an unironic presentation of the 'great love' and the 'great hate' that motivate his characters. That conviction did not leave his work when he turned in *The Quiet American* (1955) from religion to politics; which suggests that religion for Greene served primarily as a way to persuade himself that his characters do indeed have the emotional grandeur he wants them to have.

In his Mexican travel book, *The Lawless Roads* (1939), Greene traces the birth of his faith to his own experience, in the epigraph he takes from Newman, of a 'terrible aboriginal calamity' – his expulsion from the heaven of the family croquet lawn into the hell of boarding school. 'One began', Greene writes, 'to believe in heaven because one believed in hell', in the hell of the 'pitchpine partitions of dormitories [and] lavatories without locks' (14). The presence of evil persuaded him of the existence of good. Yet his early sense of their relation was not religious, but literary, a sense corresponding to the 'pattern' he found in Marjorie Bowen's historical romance *The Viper of Milan*, in her character:

> . . . Della Scala who . . . turned from an honesty that never paid and betrayed his friends and died dishonoured and a failure even at treachery . . . Goodness has only once found a perfect incarnation in a human body and never will again, but evil can always find a home there. Human nature is not black and white but black and grey. I read all that in *The Viper of Milan* and I looked round and I saw that it was so . . . she had given me my pattern – religion might explain it to me in other terms, but the pattern was already there – perfect evil walking the world where perfect good can never walk again.[28]

Greene requires a fictional world capable of supporting that sense of evil, of supporting the weight of a sensibility shaped by the inevitable betrayals of his childhood as the headmaster's son. Yet his eye for the conventions of the 'sinless graceless chromium world' sacrifices what in *Journey Without Maps* he calls the 'finer taste, the finer pleasure, the finer terror' (226) of the childhood in which he had perceived that 'pattern', sacrifices the intensity of that vision of good and evil. His early novels therefore describe a world that he can't take entirely seriously. The moral scope his style gives them is inadequate to his conception of what it ought to be; cannot contain the deep feeling that he knows exists, but for which he has no terms. Indeed, for all his attempt to present Czinner's 'great love' and 'great hate', Greene finally and fundamentally distrusts emotion itself. In the end, long after the 'trilogy', he turns away from emotion in *The Comedians*, with an admission of his own weakness in doing so, to recognize the priority he has always given to the visible world; even to those 'pitchpine partitions' that he both loathes and lingers over.

That suspicion of emotion seems fully in keeping with Greene's membership in a generation for whom the Great War had made all fine feeling suspect, teaching them to detect what Czinner calls the 'tub-orator's clichés' even in the things they believe. Or want to believe, for in seeing through their culture's 'official beliefs' Greene's generation did not, Orwell argues, get rid of the need for something to believe in. Greene's positing of a range of feelings that lies outside the terms he has to express them suggests how much they wanted that something. The language he must use has been made suspect, and so he needs to invent another. He must find some way set the leaning tower straight, to become what Wyndham Lewis calls a man of 'executive will and intelligence', calmly surveying the world, rather than one of 'those to whom things are done', a passive victim of the tower's 'slanting, sidelong' view.

For Greene himself that leaning tower manifests itself both in the burden he places upon his own childhood at Berkhamstead and his consciousness that his view of that childhood is a distorted one, that his own feelings place more weight on that experience than he can possibly expect it to bear. He is both endlessly absorbed by his own sensibility and incapable of believing that its development ought in itself to furnish him with material; remains too conscious of himself as a special case to take his own experience as typical. Instead, his projection of Marjorie Bowen's 'pattern' onto his life at school puts that experience into what Hoggart calls 'overbold relief'. To rectify that skewed vision, he had to take more

than that 'pattern' from Bowen. He had to take her subject-matter
as well, a violent public world of murder, assassination, and
revolution on which to project his own sensibility. Nevertheless,
he still needed a confirmation of that pattern's universality before
he could take his fictional world seriously, needed some way to
make that violent world sustain the burden of human significance
that his own style precludes.

For Greene, Catholicism set the leaning tower straight and gave
him that sense of universality. In *Brighton Rock* he makes his
characters substantial figures by allowing them to believe in another
world – to believe, unlike Anthony Farrant, that they have a future;
to believe that their actions in this world are important enough to
determine their fate in the next one. And by assuming the existence
of that other world, Greene mounts his most potent criticism of
the world of his own early work. *Brighton Rock* literally does open
over a glass of 'beastly port' in a saloon bar, a glass drunk by the
'sinless graceless chromium' world's embodiment, the middle-aged
blonde Ida Arnold. On a holiday in Brighton, Ida meets a man
named Fred Hale – who immediately gets himself murdered.
Afterwards, Ida thinks:

> Somebody had made Fred unhappy, and somebody was going
> to be made unhappy in turn. An eye for an eye. If you believed
> in God, you might leave vengeance to him, but you couldn't
> trust the One, the universal spirit. Vengeance was Ida's, just as
> much as reward was Ida's, the soft gluey mouth affixed in taxis,
> the warm handclasp in cinemas, the only reward there was. And
> vengeance and reward – they were both fun . . .   (37)

Kay Rimmer in *It's A Battlefield* uses sex to purchase 'everything
which made life worth living', yet longs for it to be something
more. But Ida has no thoughts of such 'everlastingness', and in
consequence her sex-life, Greene writes, bears 'the same relation
to passion as a peep-show' (146). For Ida doesn't believe in 'heaven
or hell' (36), in 'good and evil', but only in 'right and wrong',
in the world of conventions both observed and violated.

She begins her investigation into Fred's death in a bar, from
whose window she sees:

> . . . the Brighton she knew . . . two girls in beach pyjamas arm-
> in-arm, the buses going by to Rottingdean, a man selling papers,

a woman with a shopping basket, a boy in a shabby suit, an excursion steamer edging off from the pier, which lay long, luminous and transparent, like a shrimp in the sunlight. (72)

Ida sees nothing unusual in the street before her. But Greene has already let us know that the 'boy in a shabby suit' is Hale's murderer, the teenaged gang-leader Pinkie Brown – a boy in a shabby suit, yes, and yet also a man with a soul to save or damn. Greene concentrates in *Brighton Rock* on the spiritual world beneath the physical one, a world whose values differ radically from Ida's. Ida "couldn't burn if she tried" (113), for she is bound by the conventions of the Ladies' Bar. The Catholic Pinkie is not. He believes not in 'right and wrong' but rather in 'good and evil'. Yet like the young Greene, he believes in Heaven only because he believes in Hell, a hell whose existence seems implied by his cramped childhood in the Brighton slums, watching his parents make love across the room. Greene's success in this novel lies in 'the coupling of good and evil' (177) to criticize the worldly terms of right and wrong. He allies Pinkie with the Catholic innocent Rose, whom he marries because she's a witness to Hale's murder, and pits them both against Ida. The novel's theology is, of course, suspect. Greene implies that the existence of any given character's soul depends on his or her awareness of it, so that *Brighton Rock*'s non-Catholics are, as Orwell writes, presented as 'too ignorant to be guilty';[29] surely a 'good' Catholic would hold that Ida has a soul to save or damn whether or not she's conscious of it. Nevertheless, Pinkie's consciousness of his own capacity for damnation, and Ida's lack of it, does effectively define their capacities for moral action – of whatever kind.

In public, Pinkie glories in the prospect of his own damnation. In private, however, he hopes for a deathbed repentance and comforts himself with this childhood jingle:

> Between the stirrup and the ground
> He mercy sought and mercy found. (91)

Yet pain, as he learns when a slashing by a rival gang gives him a sense of what that fall might be like – pain robs him of 'the energy to repent' (107). But he continues to crave that 'city called Peace of Mind', a peace that for him lies in freedom from persecution and prison, a peace he vows to find it even if it means 'murdering a

world' (92). But each step he takes toward that peace drives him
further along the path to damnation – and paradoxically makes
him ever more aware of his own position, makes him realize that
'what was most evil in him needed . . . [Rose]. It couldn't get
along without goodness' (126). Increased evil brings Pinkie an
increased consciousness both of itself and of the way he has killed
'the flickers of the Christ'[30] within him.

Pinkie attempts to master the world through his own hatred of
it. He hates music because he does not understand it; it moves
him and threatens his self-containment. He loathes the idea of sex,
for it reminds him of his parent's 'frightening weekly exercise' (90),
and of the slum he's tried to leave. Yet Greene allies hatred to
love, as he does evil to good, and so suggests that this capacity for
hatred contains the possibility of its own redemption. 'Corruptio
optimi est pessima' (246), a priest tells Rose after Pinkie's death;
the worst are the corruption of the best, evil the corruption of
good, as Satan is a 'fallen angel'.[31] Pinkie's very crimes indicate
his capacity for deep emotion, and at the end of the novel he
begins to discover in himself a capacity not for hate but for love.
Toward the end of the novel, Rose asks him:

> "Last night . . . the night before . . . you didn't hate me, did
> you, for what we did?"
> He said, "No, I didn't hate you."
> . . . It was quite true – he hadn't hated her; he hadn't even
> hated the act. There had been a kind of pleasure, a kind of
> pride, a kind of – something else. The car lurched back on to
> the main road; he turned the bonnet to Brighton. An enormous
> emotion beat on him; it was like something trying to get in,
> the pressure of gigantic wings against the glass. Dona nobis
> pacem. He withstood it . . . If the glass broke, if the beast –
> whatever it was – got in, God knows what it would do. He
> had a sense of huge havoc – the confession, the penance and
> the sacrament – and awful distraction, and he drove blind into
> the rain.   (239–40)

All Pinkie's emotions except hatred have seemed so atrophied that
I am strangely and powerfully moved when he admits that sex
had been the one thing in his experience he did not "hate". Greene
here provides the first moment of convincingly represented deep
emotion in his work. Characteristically, that moment depends on
the dash in the phrase 'a kind of – something else'. Pinkie does

not know what he feels; an 'enormous emotion' bears down upon him, trying to batter its way into his heart. To Ida sex is 'fun'. She has a name for it, and one distrusts it. But Pinkie has no name for it, and in that omission one paradoxically senses an emotion that lies beyond Greene's own power to conventionalize it. The dash confirms Greene's suspicion of the 'artificiality of his words'. For it is not Pinkie's emotional poverty that prevents the precise naming of what he feels, but the poverty of language itself, of the world and not the soul.

Yet Pinkie continues to fear the 'huge havoc' of his own emotions, for it distracts him from what he believes he must do. And then Ida's pursuit catches up to him, and leads to his suicide, while he's still 'bound in a habit of hate' (231), the reward for which will be Hell's 'slash of razor blades infinitely prolonged' (109). Ida wins; as in *Stamboul Train*, the world still triumphs over the soul. But Pinkie does provide the alternative to that world that Anthony Farrant cannot, and however relieved one feels by his death, one nevertheless mourns him.

Brighton Rock is not Greene's most neatly constructed, or most readable novel. The novel's conclusion does have a narrative drive unmatched in Greene's work, but with its action almost equally divided between Ida and Pinkie, between an entertaining detective story and the tragedy, it seems diffuse until Pinkie's plans to murder Rose bring its various strands together into that suspenseful ending. And while one assumes that Pinkie is damned, Greene's account of him both tastes of what Orwell condemned as 'the cult of the sanctified sinner',[32] and lies dangerously close to Norman Mailer's romantic celebration of the criminal's existential situation. It is not all that far from Pinkie Brown to Jack Abbott. *Brighton Rock* is nevertheless Greene's great step forward – the first novel in which he finds the terms to make this world answer to his conception of its possibilities. In doing so he provides as well his most sustained examination of the condition of England, a country sapped by its accession to convention, by Ida Arnold's pieties, and embodied in Pinkie's rival, the rich old gang leader, Mr Colleoni, who:

> looked as a man might look who owned the whole world, the whole visible world that is, the cash registers and policemen and prostitutes, Parliament and the laws which say 'this is Right and this Wrong'. (65)

Brighton Rock, like *England Made Me*, is very much a novel of the time just before Munich, an account of a country whose self-satisfied ownership of 'the whole visible world' has led it to abdicate its moral responsibility. And Pinkie Brown, whose murders suggest his capacity for action and emotion, provides Greene's most effective criticism of it.

Brighton Rock made Greene known as '– destestable term! – a Catholic writer' (*Ways of Escape*, 77). Yet its religion seems less an assertion of faith than a coldly calculated attempt to lend his work substance, a substance that in *Brighton Rock* is not so much emotionally felt as intellectually grasped. But one nevertheless accepts Greene's desire, a decade after his conversion, to 'examine more closely the effect of faith on action' (*Ways of Escape*, 79), and accepts it in particular because that same desire sent him to Mexico. There his bloodless commitment to Catholicism was supplanted by the emotional conviction out of which he wrote his first masterpiece, *The Power and the Glory*. That novel's power does not, however, grow from any radical shift in Greene's material, but from the way he uses faith to fulfil the 'pattern' of his early work. The nameless Mexican priest whom Greene takes as his hero seems but a more complex version of Francis Andrews in *The Man Within*, a man both hunted and haunted. He is hunted by the government of the coastal state in which he lives, which has so aggressively persecuted the Church that he is the only cleric left in it; and haunted by the sins his fear has led him to commit, first with alcohol, and then with a woman.

As he does with Pinkie and Anthony Farrant, Greene organizes the priest's experience around a crucial memory. But the priest's memory is not a childhood one, but one of the man he no longer is, the man whose picture is pinned to the police station's wall:

> It was a newspaper photograph of a first communion party taken years ago; a youngish man in a Roman collar sat among the women. You could imagine him petted with small delicacies, . . . plump, with protuberant eyes, . . . a well-shaved, well-powdered jowl much too developed for his age. The good things of life had come to him too early – the respect of his contemporaries, a safe livelihood. The trite religious word upon the tongue, the joke to ease the way, the ready acceptance of other people's homage . . . a happy man.[33]

So the picture appears to the priest's enemy, the atheistic police lieutenant who wants to exterminate the Church and make the whole world anew. Yet when he recalls his first years as a priest, Greene's protagonist sees the same man the lieutenant does. The young priest had lived in safety, with a smug awareness of right and wrong, of the conventions of piety. And he had wanted to be promoted – but only after 'leaving the right kind of debts behind' (138), for as a young man he believed a priest was judged by his debts, the new vestments purchased and renovations undertaken.

After his final capture the priest listens patiently to the lieutenant's condemnation of the Church:

> "Sell all and give to the poor – that was the lesson, wasn't it? And Senora So-and-so, the druggist's wife, would say the family wasn't really deserving of charity, and Senor This, That and the Other would say that if they starved, what else did they deserve, they were Socialists anyway, and the priest – you – would notice who had done his Easter duty and paid his Easter offering . . ."
> The priest said, "You are so right." He added quickly, "Wrong too, of course."   (231–2)

The lieutenant's charges are just, if one's conception of the Church remains bound by that first communion picture. And yet wrong as well, for the Church is more than Easter offerings and first communion dresses. Such conventions have allowed the priest to lead a conventionally moral life. But as the persecution continues, the conventions of his vocation begin to disappear: the vestments, the haggling over the price of a wedding or a baptism, his altar stone, his own chastity, above all his smug sense of his own virtue. All that remains is faith and the gift of transubstantiation. Yet as he does wrong, as he comes to believe his sins will damn him, the priest also unconsciously reveals, more fully than ever before, 'the flickers of the Christ' within him.

Hoggart argues that the novel's characters:

> . . . are being constantly pushed around, put into positions which are more effective for the pattern than probability; for example the half-caste finally betraying the priest to the soldiers, simply saying 'Father' from the clearing as the priest reaches the door – it is too obviously the Judas kiss.[34]

Yet Hoggart misses the reason for the book's power – or, rather, objects to the very source of it. Greene writes in *Ways of Escape* that *The Power and the Glory* is the 'only novel I have written to a thesis' – written to demonstrate the theological distinction between 'the man and his office', embodied in this story of 'the drunken priest who continued to pass life on' (88–9). In posing that thesis Greene does, admittedly, sacrifice some of the complexity of characterization Hoggart values. Yet such complexity, and its attendant 'probability', are irrelevant to Greene's purpose. *The Power and the Glory* is not a realistic novel, however closely it describes the surface of Mexican life. It is instead an attempt to enact a myth about individual freedom and commitment, a book whose characters and action Greene has made simple and unambiguous in order to achieve the sufficiently 'representative and public terms' that such a myth requires.

Toward the end of the novel for example, the priest escapes over the mountains into a province where the Church is tolerated. His life on the 'dangerous edge of things' has made him a good man, however 'wrong' his behaviour. Once over the mountains, however, he begins to become the man in that first communion photograph once more, and his 'inner critic' grows uneasy. Then, just as he prepares to leave for an even safer state, the 'half-caste' that Hoggart refers to appears to summon him back over the mountains to hear the confession of an American criminal dying from a police bullet. The priest suspects a trap – and yet goes anyway, realizing as he does so that 'he felt quite cheerful; he had never really believed in his peace . . . that he would ever get back to parish work and the daily Mass and the careful appearances of piety' (216, 223). The possibility of new danger supports him, and the 'flickers of the Christ' within him increase with each step he takes toward it. And as the priest approaches the hut where he knows he will be betrayed, conscious that at any moment he can save himself by denying his vocation, Greene achieves a fusion of physical and moral suspense like that found in the best of Dostoevsky.

Early in the novel the priest delivers a hasty sermon in which he says:

". . . heaven is here: this is part of heaven just as pain is a part of pleasure . . . The police watching you, the soldiers gathering taxes, the beating you always get from the jefe because you are too poor to pay, smallpox and fever, hunger . . . that is all part of heaven – the preparation. Perhaps without them, who can tell, you wouldn't enjoy heaven so much. Heaven would not be complete. And heaven. What is heaven?" Literary phrases from what seemed now to be another life altogether – the strict quiet life of the seminary – became confused on his tongue: the names of precious stones: Jerusalem the Golden. But these people had never seen gold.

He went rather stumbling on. "Heaven is where there is no jefe, no unjust laws, no taxes, no soldiers and no hunger. Your children do not die in heaven . . . Oh, it is easy to say all the things that there will *not* be in heaven; what is there is God. That is more difficult. Our words are made to describe what we know with our senses. We say 'light' but we are thinking only of the sun . . ." (80)

The priest's sermon suggests the way his society moves, suggests the underlying laws that govern his people's lives. Only religion, Greene suggests, can allow them to bear and to love this hateful world, because only religion makes it an extension of another and more important one, of the heaven that they can know only by negation, a place that is all the earth is not. Greene here sheds 'literary phrases' for concrete words, and yet in so doing acknowledges language's inability fully to name the world, to describe the God whom the priest knows without the use of his senses. For both the priest's and Greene's own sense of life rests on a knowledge of that which they cannot express, and their awareness of that inability serves more powerfully than could any description to bring a sense of heaven before us. The priest's sermon contains Greene's art in miniature. It provides a theological justification for his concentration on the visible world to which his characters are bound, rather than on a description of the soul, of that longed-for sense of 'everlastingness', that by definition remains inaccessible to those words "made to describe what we know with our senses". Greene uses the religious sense to make the world not a reminder of man's 'comic existence', as it had been in *Stamboul Train*, but the arena in which man's spiritual life, his 'tragic fate', is enacted. He writes of Dickens that the places in which his characters 'damned themselves were lent importance by their presence',[35] endowed with a right to exist. So too with Greene, who in the novels that follow *The Power and the Glory* treats the physical world with a seriousness and a care for detail unmatched by any other novelist of his generation, creating the possibility of tragedy through his fidelity to the surface of things.

That sermon also offers a key to Greene's characterization of the priest. The reader feels the priest is very like a saint, not because of his virtues but because of the intensity with which he feels his own vices, as heaven exists in the consciousness of what it is not. Greene's work depends, as far back as *The Man Within*, upon his protagonists' self-deception. The priest believes that his faith will damn him in both this world and the next, and yet remains committed to it. But the characters whom Greene makes distrust their own virtue are, as Terry Eagleton has argued, those whom the reader most credits with it.[36] The priest so distrusts his own emotion, his own commitment, that one paradoxically becomes as suspicious of his slickly presented self-condemnation as of Mabel Warren's romantic formulations in *Stamboul Train*. Just as Mabel's conventional sentiments both mask her vacancy from herself and reveal it to us, so the priest's absolute certainty of his own sinfulness keeps him from realizing the extent of his own humility, sanctity, and capacity for love.

The Power and the Glory, unlike *Brighton Rock*, is not a polemic on behalf of Roman Catholicism. By setting it in a country where Catholicism is both the norm and the object of persecution by a relentlessly secular state Greene makes the novel instead a plea for the necessity of the religious life in general and an assertion of the value of the individual human spirit in an age caught between Hitler and Stalin. Yet, just as Greene had to go to Mexico to feel something more than an intellectual commitment to his religion, so too he had to go there to achieve that sense of the value of individual experience. Greene needs a world where 'one lives between God and the Devil' (*The Lawless Roads*, 184) rather than the 'sinless graceless chromium world' of Ida Arnold, in which nothing seems to matter much. England seems too comfortable to offer an objective correlative for his sense of life's 'dangerous edge', and he has therefore set the vast majority of his later work outside it. *The Power and the Glory* has little to say about the way English society moves. But it says a great deal about the way the modern world does. In it, Greene's own sensibility becomes homologous with the melodrama of modern history, and so achieves the totalization that Eagleton defines as a process of extending 'the materials of a directly personal response . . . into confidently public and representative terms'.

In making that extension Greene found the subject that has absorbed him for the rest of his career, a description of life in the world's 'foully governed'[37] places now collectively known as 'Greeneland'. The physical danger that characterizes such places provides a convincing setting for Greene's sense of life's spiritual dangers, and particularly for his sense of the knife edge between man's 'comic existence' and 'tragic fate'. Before leaving *The Power and the Glory* I want, then, to look briefly at its comedy. When the priest finally reaches that dying criminal, he finds that the man won't confess. "Beat it, father", he says, not because he rejects the priest's faith, but because their shared criminality creates an odd solidarity between them. "You take my gun, father . . . you look after yourself. You take my knife . . ." (226–7). What makes me laugh here is the incongruity of the dying man being a good enough Catholic to remember to say "father" even as he commands the priest to kill the police who lie in ambush for him; a grim, death's-head laughter that threatens to rob Greene's characters of the full dignity of the 'tragic fate' their situation creates.

That thin line between comedy and tragedy will remain for Greene the most dangerous edge of all. But in his next major novel, *The Heart of the Matter*, he uses that comedy only in the genre scenes of colonial life in Sierra Leone, which create a sense of the conditions under which his protagonist Henry Scobie lives. *The Heart of the Matter* is Greene's most ambitious attempt to write a tragedy, to seize the emotional grandeur he has always felt his themes required. The novel deals with what in his superb 1943 thriller about wartime London, *The Ministry of Fear*, Greene called 'the horrible and horrifying emotion of pity' (66). There he describes the adventures of a man who kills his terminally ill wife, out of pity for her sufferings. Or was it pity? Wasn't it, Greene's protagonist asks, his own inability to bear her pain? *The Heart of the Matter* deals with the Catholic convert Scobie's inability to bear the thought of giving other people pain, which makes him kill himself to spare them the continued pain of his presence. Yet Scobie's sense of pity is but a mask for his 'almost monstrous pride' (*Ways of Escape*, 125), for the one whom he can't stand hurting is not his wife Louise, or his mistress Helen, but God. And even though Greene maintains the orthodox belief that suicide, by causing one's own damnation, gives God more pain than anything else, he nevertheless makes Scobie a 'sanctified sinner', whose near-saintly humility has convinced him of his own unworthiness to stand in God's presence.

In the scene on which the novel turns, Scobie prays by the hospital bed of a dying child:

He could hear the heavy uneven breathing of the child. It was as if she were carrying a weight with great effort up a long hill; it was an inhuman situation not to be able to carry it for her. He thought: this is what parents feel year in and year out, and I am shrinking from a few minutes of it. They see their children dying slowly every hour they live. He prayed again, "Father, look after her. Give her peace." The breathing broke, choked, began again with terrible effort. Looking between his fingers, he could see the six-year-old face convulsed like a navvy's with labour. "Father", he prayed, "give her peace. Take away my peace forever, but give her peace." The sweat broke out on his hands. "Father . . ."

He heard a small scraping voice repeat, "Father," and looking up he saw the blue and bloodshot eyes watching him. He thought with horror: this is what I thought I'd missed. He would have called Mrs Bowles, only he hadn't the voice to call with. He could see the breast of the child struggling for breath to repeat the heavy word; he came over to the bed and said, "Yes, dear, don't speak, I'm here." The night-light cast the shadow of his clenched fist on the sheet and it caught the child's eye. An effort to laugh convulsed her and he moved his hand away. "Sleep, dear," he said, "You are sleepy. Sleep." A memory that he had carefully buried returned and taking out his handkerchief he made the shadow of a rabbit's head fall on the pillow beside her. "There's your rabbit," he said, "to go to sleep with. It will stay until you sleep. Sleep." The sweat poured down his face and tasted in his mouth as salt as tears. "Sleep." He moved the rabbit's ears up and down, up and down. Then he heard Mrs Bowles' voice, speaking low just behind him. "Stop that," she said harshly. "The child's dead."   (125)

The few sentences here that deal specifically with Scobie's thoughts all allude to his absence from his own child's deathbed several years before the events the novel describes. Those allusions make this incident stand, not as a brief taste of 'what I thought I'd missed', but as part of his life's central experience. As he begins to pray, our attention turns to the child, whose face, 'convulsed like a navvy's' we see through Scobie's camera eyes, objectified. The word "father" makes the child think her own dead father has come to her, and repetition of that word unleashes the 'memory he had carefully buried'. He makes a shadow rabbit 'fall on the pillow'; the child's innocent delight in it as she dies gives the scene an extraordinary power. Then Mrs Bowles returns and her harsh voice tells not only Scobie but us of the child's death, breaking the sad still beauty of the scene. Her interruption makes Scobie's rabbit seem ridiculous, so that it's impossible, in a way characteristic of Greene's generation, to linger over the sentiment of the scene. Yet by denying us that Dickensian deathbed indulgence, Greene makes the scene all the more authentically moving.

It is, Scobie feels, 'an inhuman situation not to be able to carry' the weight of the child's pain for her, and his thought implicitly addresses the disjunction in man's experience that *Stamboul Train*'s epigraph had suggested. Man's fate is tragic, and yet his existence remains comic. The soul's desires have no power over the objective world. Greene and Scobie both want to create an accommodation between the soul and the world, an accommodation that they can find only through an appeal to God. "Give her peace", Scobie prays. "Take away my peace for ever, but give her peace." And so the child dies happily, and Scobie's life begins to fall apart. As such the consequences of this moment may seem schematic, and the scene is indeed a great one partly because within it the God to whom Scobie prays remains at best a possibility, rather than the certainty that by the end of the novel Greene's insistence on his 'pattern' has made Him. More important, however, is the fact that Scobie prays out of a belief, similar to that on which realism itself depends, that there be some metonymic link between the word and the world; out of the belief, and the hope, that his prayer may be translated into action, that he can conquer the 'antagonistic duality of soul and world' by invoking a God whose hand moves through both. And as Scobie prays, that belief steals over the rest of the novel as well, restoring to it something like the old equilibrium of the nineteenth-century novel through a prose that gives equal weight both to the world and to one's experience of it. It is a scene whose power is unmatched in Greene's work, one that recalls the great set pieces of the Victorians, such as Thackeray's description of old Osborne brooding over the family Bible in *Vanity Fair*.

Scobie's prayer contains in miniature the issues and conflicts on which Greene's work had until that time depended. It contains them, and reconciles them, and in doing so both clarifies and justifies his use of religion to recreate realism's fluid mediation between the soul and the world. The rest of the novel proceeds from this scene – not from Scobie's prayer so much as from the capacity for pity that the prayer reveals. Through Scobie's sacrifice of his peace for hers, Greene suggests both the grandeur and the tragedy of pity. For even here, Scobie's sense of pity grows less from a disinterested care for the unfortunate than from his own inability to bear the sight of her pain, to accept the world's 'inhuman situation'. Scobie loves the world, loves West Africa down to its vultures and ugly laterite roads, and yet cannot commit himself to it. He cannot accept the rules of his world as did the priest in *The Power and the Glory*, cannot accept Czinner's dilemma as an essential part of human life. For Scobie cannot finally accept God, and so accept this world's injustice in the belief that the balance will be redressed in another. He rebels against his knowledge that others will suffer for his sins, that he must hurt either Louise or Helen by choosing between them. And yet he finally hurts them all the more by killing himself in order to avoid that choice.

Greene forces the novel's conclusion by allowing Scobie's religious scruples, which for most of the novel have played a minor role in his characterization, to dominate its last chapters. Scobie refuses to receive absolution for his adultery, because he intends to go on committing it. But he must also receive communion, even though he's in a state of mortal sin, so that his wife won't think there's anything wrong. Yet just as his sense of pity won't let him give pain to the women, so he cannot bear the thought of giving God pain by receiving the sacrament without absolution. Greene's performance for much of the novel seems very nearly as brilliant as in that crucial deathbed scene – his account of Scobie's loveless marriage, for example, or the genre scenes in which some colonial officials try to conquer boredom by seeing who can kill the most cockroaches. Everything works, except that most important thing of all, Greene's attempt to make the reader believe in Scobie's psychology. Early in the novel Scobie reflects on a promise to his wife that:

He would still have made . . . even if he could have foreseen all that would come of it. He had always been prepared to accept the responsibility for his actions, and he had always been half aware too, from the time he made his terrible private vow that she should be happy, how far *this* action might carry him. Despair is the price one pays for setting oneself an impossible aim. It is, one is told, the unforgivable sin, but it is a sin the corrupt or evil man never practises. He always has hope. He never reaches the freezing point of knowing absolute failure. Only the man of goodwill carries always in his heart this capacity for damnation.   (60)

Scobie's move toward suicide grows out of that 'terrible private vow'. In dealing with Scobie's attitude toward his own experience, however, Greene ignores the lesson of that scene over the child's deathbed – that he can best depict deep emotion through a concentration upon physical detail. His prose here depends on aphorisms rather than images, relies on terms like 'despair', 'sin', and 'hope' to suggest the contents of Scobie's mind, rather than attempt to find an objective correlative for it. Yet in doing so he sacrifices the visual clarity, the ability, in Conrad's words, 'to make you *see!*'[38] that is his own best gift, to underline a point about Scobie's motivations. In doing so, Greene opens himself to the charges that Hoggart makes against him. For Scobie is only 'half aware' of his vow's possible consequences. The full awareness of the paragraph's second half belongs to Greene himself. His own compelling essayistic voice takes over, amplifying Scobie's sense of his situation, and yet Greene draws no clear line between the two. One feels him masquerading as Scobie, feels the hot heavy breath with which he imposes his own sensibility upon the character. And in consequence one can't fully believe in Scobie's interior life, in the overly scrupulous conscience in which Greene demands that one does believe.

Orwell writes that beneath 'the cult of the sanctified sinner . . . there probably lies a weakening of belief, for when people really believed in Hell, they were not so fond of striking graceful attitudes on its brink'. His criticism seems to me essentially unanswerable. The 'graceful attitudes' Greene makes Scobie strike produce what Orwell calls a set of 'psychological absurdities'[39] whose mark is the degree to which one feels Greene's own voice behind what is alleged to be the character's rhetoric. Greene tries to evade those absurdities by concentrating on the ungraceful aspects of Scobie's desire to kill himself, his middle-aged reflection that 'it was no use pretending as a young man might that the price was worthwhile' (258), that damnation is worth the pain he might spare others.

Scobie, of course, does believe in his own damnation. 'If one was a Catholic,' he thinks, 'one had all the answers: no prayer was effective in a state of mortal sin . . .' (257). Yet his decision to kill himself rings false because the cadences of his voice are those of Greene's own, the confident voice of a survivor who does, in fact, know 'all the answers', and perhaps Orwell's comments can best be applied to the creator who masquerades as Scobie. For Greene has written that 'I have small belief in the doctrine of eternal punishment (it was Scobie's belief, not mine)' (*Ways of Escape*, 126). One admits his distinction between author and character – insists upon it, in fact, because the novel's final failure grows from a refusal to observe it. For Greene includes no awareness of his own lack of belief in the novel, and so offers no perspective on Scobie's actions. Are we supposed to think Scobie is damned, or aren't we? Do we take the novel's theology seriously, or is the novel merely a case study of Scobie's psychology? Greene's admission of his own 'small belief' makes the novel's conclusion seem factitious, the clever manipulation of a literary 'pattern', rather than the authentic tragedy it purports to be. It suggests, finally, that for Greene religion is but a crutch to lend his work an emotional power he cannot otherwise attain.

IV

Greene's later career involves an attempt to address the factitiousness of the religious sense on which he built the 'trilogy'. Novels such as *The Quiet American* or *The Comedians* contain a sense of doubt that *The Heart of the Matter* lacks, for in them Greene knows that the real tragedy belongs to those who outlive their own answers, who survive their hopes and aspirations and illusions. They seem the work of a man drawn toward a God in Whom he cannot quite summon faith, filled with a longing for 'that city called Peace of Mind', in whose existence he cannot finally believe. That sense of doubt first becomes prominent in *The End of the Affair* (1951). The book turns on the discovery made by its narrator, the writer Maurice Bendrix, of a diary belonging to his former mistress, Sarah Miles. In it she writes that she has abandoned him not for another man, but for God. The end of their affair grows from a day when Bendrix was buried by rubble in the V-I blitz of London, and Sarah, believing him dead, began to pray to a God in Whom she didn't believe:

> I said very slowly, I'll give him up forever, only let him be alive
> with a chance, I pressed and pressed and I could feel the skin
> break, and I said, people can love without seeing each other,
> can't they, can't they, they love You all their lives without seeing
> You, and then he came in at the door, and he was alive, and I
> thought now the agony of being without him starts, and I wished
> he was safely back dead again under the door.   (117)

But was Bendrix dead, or merely stunned? Sarah continues to want
'ordinary corrupt human love' (152), and fights against her growing
belief in God because it requires the sacrifice of what she most
craves. Yet that belief paradoxically springs from her love for
Bendrix. 'Sometimes I've hated Maurice', she writes, 'but would
I have hated him if I hadn't loved him too? O God, if I could really
hate You what would that mean?' For one can't, Sarah writes, hate
a 'vapour' (136).

Sarah's diary is all the more moving because she remains
uncertain that the God to Whom she prays exists, uncertain of the
necessity of her sacrifice. But Greene isn't satisfied with describing
faith's partial victory over doubt. After Sarah dies of pneumonia
Greene supplies a string of carefully stage-managed miracles, that
both bring Bendrix himself to faith and provide an independent
confirmation of the novel's 'official beliefs' – confirmation not just
of God's existence, but of a specifically Catholic God at that. It is
as if Greene feels his own beliefs to be too unstable, too much in
danger of 'dissolving like sandcastles' to risk uncertainty. He has
since admitted the way in which this 'cheating' harmed the novel,
writing that 'every so-called miracle . . . ought to have had a
completely natural explanation' (*Ways of Escape*, 143). For those
miracles remove the doubt on which Sarah's agonized wonder
about the possibility of God's existence depends and hence make
faith impossible, for the one depends upon the other, as love upon
hate.

Greene will not satisfactorily resolve that issue until his late
novel, *Monsignor Quixote* (1981). In its dogged attempt to enact
belief, *The End of the Affair* inadvertently poses the question of his
later career: that of the difficulty of belief itself. It is the same issue
in fact, as that posed by the assistant commissioner in *It's A
Battlefield*, who cannot feel any 'faith, any conviction, that [he

is] on the right side'. But Greene's 'cheating' mars his success in examining that question here, and *The End of the Affair* seems most successful not in its admittedly moving religious sequences, but in its confident exploration of Bendrix' – of Greene's own – voice.

Believing Sarah to have another lover, Bendrix arranges to have her followed, and thinks:

> What an odd collection the trusted professions are. One trusts one's lawyer, one's doctor, priest, I suppose, if one is a Catholic, and now I added to the list one's private detective. Henry's idea of being scrutinized by the other clients was quite wrong. The office had two waiting rooms, and I was admitted alone into one. It was curiously unlike what you would expect in Vigo Street; it had something of the musty air in the outer office of a solicitor, combined with a voguish choice of reading matter in the waiting room, which was more like a dentist's – there were *Harper's Bazaar* and *Life* and a number of French fashion periodicals – and the man who showed me in was a little too attentive and well dressed. He pulled me a chair to the fire and closed the door with great care. I felt like a patient and I suppose I was a patient, sick enough to try the famous shock treatment for jealousy.   (20)

By writing in the first person Greene found a way out of the technical dilemma the seductive power of his own voice had posed in *The Heart of the Matter*. One trusts this worldly unillusioned voice to get the details of the office right, as one trusts Greene's account of boy's adventure fiction; trusts it to know what one 'would expect in Vigo Street', but doesn't find here – a voice whose wise cynical urbanity can encompass both man's comic existence and his tragic fate. Bendrix makes one accept his conclusions about 'What an odd collection the trusted professions are' even before he offers any evidence about them, or even says just what that oddness consists of. It caresses the surfaces of the private detective's waiting room just as in *A Gun for Sale* Greene's third-person omniscience had caressed the shabby shops and streets of London itself. Yet if this confident description has the strengths of Greene's early style, it carries its limitations as well. This voice assumes it knows the world, assumes as Hoggart says that one 'has seen this kind of thing before',[40] and so rules out the possibility of surprise. It belongs to a man determined to take the world in a particular way whether or not the world deserves it, to impose a 'pattern' on experience, as Greene did in making the assumption from which his whole religious involvement grows, that Hell exists because he went to a public school. Bendrix even slides over the fact that the private detective's office isn't what he thought it would be. The office doesn't surprise him, but is only 'curiously unlike' what he had expected – and suspect because of it.

Greene's voice has all of Lawrence's confident mastery of experience, but none of his ability to describe sensations we'd not before been able to name. It can only typify what is already familiar. Yet as his early novels suggest, Greene distrusts his work's slick surface. His position on the leaning tower both makes him overemphasize his vision of the world and admit that it is, after all, only his vision. At the end of the novel, Bendrix, like Czinner, acknowledges that 'my own words were overcharged. I could detect their insincerity' (238); even as Greene detected his own cheating with the novel's structure. It is, perhaps, a tacit acknowledgement of the enormous gap between the actual situation of his childhood and the burden his sensibility places on it. And in recognizing the essential insincerity of his own prose, Greene finds a technique that allows him to evade the deficiencies of his own sensibility. His narrators proclaim their own emptiness, and yet the actions Greene plots for them make one distrust their protestations of their own moral exhaustion. And yet a crucial question remains. Bendrix recognizes his own insincerity. Does he also recognize, as Greene surely intends his readers to, that such self-knowledge makes him oddly admirable?

That question becomes particularly important in *The Quiet American*, Greene's 1955 novel about the French colonial war in Indochina. Halfway through that novel, its narrator, the English journalist Thomas Fowler, and the title character, the CIA *agent provocateur* Alden Pyle, get bombed out of a guard tower. They spend the night hiding in the surrounding paddy, and are rescued in the morning, but the badly wounded Fowler says that he does not remember:

". . . what Pyle later described to others: that I waved my hand in the wrong direction and told them there was a man in the tower and they had to see to him. Anyway I couldn't have made the sentimental assumption that Pyle made. I know myself, and I know the depth of my selfishness. I cannot be at ease (and to be at ease is my chief wish) if someone else is in pain, visibly or audibly or tactually. Sometimes this is mistaken by the innocent for unselfishness, when all I am doing is sacrificing a small good – in this case postponement in attending to my hurt – for the sake of a far greater good, a peace of mind when I need think only of myself." (114)

To Fowler no disinterested quest for abstract justice, no 'great love' or 'great hate' can supersede the desire to 'be at ease', from which he claims all action grows. Fowler describes his own motivations with the same confidence which Mabel Warren in *Stamboul Train* claims to be 'one of those . . . who love and remember always', and his description is fully as suspect as hers, as unreliable as the priest's self-condemnation in *The Power and the Glory*.

When he's wounded Fowler prays to 'the God I didn't believe in' (114) – doesn't believe in because he is 'a reporter. God exists only for leader writers.' (60) As a reporter Fowler takes no stands, chooses no sides, claims to form no opinions. His only commitment is to fact, to understanding the world as it is. Yet as both a French fighter pilot and a Vietnamese Communist tell him, "Sooner or later . . . one has to take sides. If one is to remain human." (174) Sooner or later one must become 'engagé' rather than 'dégagé' (*passim*), must participate in the tragedy of man's fate rather than watch the comedy of his existence. For Fowler the moment of choice comes when Pyle, hoping to create a 'Third Force' (25) in the struggle between the French and the Vietminh provides the explosives for a bomb that goes off at mid-morning in a Saigon square:

The legless torso at the end of the garden still twitched, like a chicken which has lost its head. From the man's shirt, he had probably been a trishaw driver.

Pyle said, "It's awful." He looked at the wet on his shoes and said in a sick voice, "What's that?"

"Blood," I said. "Haven't you ever seen it before?"

He said, "I must get them cleaned before I see the Minister." I don't think he knew what he was saying. He was seeing a real war for the first time.

I forced him, with my hand on his shoulder, to look around. I said, "This is the hour when the place is always full of women and children – it's the shopping hour. Why choose that of all hours . . ."

He said, "[General] Thé wouldn't have done this. I'm sure he wouldn't. – Somebody deceived him. The Communists . . ." (162–3)

Pyle's discomfort at the carnage he's caused makes him retreat into an ideological formulation. He has chosen his side, and the fact of choice itself keeps him from seeing the world before him, gives him the cold callous strength to watch other people's pain without disturbing his own ease. And Fowler cannot stand it. Yet his final betrayal of Pyle to the Communists, his accession to the world's demand that he take sides, can offer him no comfort. Unable to laugh at the comedy of his existence, incapable of feeling the tragedy of his fate, Fowler can neither summon a belief in the cause on whose behalf he acts, nor forget how he had valued his now lost detachment. Having once acted, having once taken sides and become a 'leader writer', Fowler can never again be at 'ease', and in an ironic variation on Henry James, it is the tired and cynical middle-aged Englishman and not the idealistic young American who loses his innocence.

Yet Fowler knows too fully the way in which his words are 'overcharged' to think as well of himself as the reader does. Even his rage over the bombing feeds off his earlier anger at Pyle for luring away his Vietnamese mistress, Phuong. Fowler knows how little he can claim to be a disinterested judge of Pyle's actions, and so learns how impossible the detachment he values has always been; which paradoxically makes him regret its loss all the more. He so fully recognizes the confusion of his own motives that when Pyle's death returns Phuong to him, he feels not happy but empty, admitting in the novel's last words: 'how I wished there existed someone to whom I could say that I was sorry.' (189)

Pyle's death not only creates that desire, in this novel haunted by the absence of God, but precludes it. Yet the reader, who compares Pyle's callousness to Fowler's delirious words in front of the shattered guard tower, treats the narrator more generously than he does himself. The novel's success depends, then, on Fowler's final lack of any real self-knowledge. For if he suspected that his betrayal of Pyle is at all admirable, a demonstration of his own humanity and not a defeat of the principles by which he's tried to live, then Fowler's self-condemnation would be merely the posturing of a secretly self-righteous man. Is it? To what degree has Greene made a distinction between the author and the character to whom he has given his own voice? For an answer one must look to the novel's cunning structure, which shows the lessons Greene learned from his long study of Ford's *The Good Soldier*. Greene opens the novel with Fowler receiving the news of Pyle's murder, and then deploys a series of flashbacks, concealing the narrator's involvement from us until the moment when, as the novel approaches its own present, Fowler decides to act. That structure allows Greene to take advantage of the vacancy of his own voice. On a first reading, the weary emptiness of Fowler's voice seems in excess of its cause. Yet one's perceptions change on rereading *The Quiet American*, as they do with *The Good Soldier*, and in retrospect Fowler's sense of defeat seems justifiable in one who's just caused an assassination.

The Quiet American occupied a crucial place in Greene's own development. In the 1950s, he began to search for 'ways of escape', as he called his 1980 volume of reminiscences, escape from his own unshakeable *ennui*, by travelling to places like Vietnam, whose political situations ensured that one 'lived between God and the Devil', on the 'dangerous edge of things', independent of any religious commitment. That independence allowed Greene to discover the value of uncertainty, and to redress the mistakes he had made with the conclusion to *The End of the Affair*. Like Fowler, he is too much a part of his own generation fully to believe in the terms of the 'great love' and 'great hate' to which religion committed him. His reputation was founded on his religious novels, but only *The Power and the Glory* bears an aesthetically satisfactory witness to faith.

Greene writes out of what is at most a half-belief, and writes best when he can build that half-belief into the structure of the novel, as he could not in *The Heart of the Matter*. Yet he retains a trace of the longing for transcendence and commitment that one catches in Czinner's desire to escape the 'artificiality of his words'. In recent years that longing has taken the form of an interest in leftist governments in the Third World, in Latin America in particular. His 1984 memoir, *Getting to Know the General: The Story of an Involvement*, is but the latest example of that interest, a celebration of a real-life doomed romantic hero, Panama's General Omar Torrijos. Greene's involvement with such movements seems, however, to grow less from a reasoned commitment to Marxism than from his hatred of the 'sinless graceless chromium world' that he finds embodied in the United States, even more fully than in 1930s England. That loathing first takes form in his characterization of Alden Pyle, and in making his case against Pyle Greene does slide over Vietminh atrocities comparable to that bomb in the Saigon square. Nevertheless *The Quiet American* has an importance beyond its place in Greene's own career. For it was one of the first novels to present America as a source of the world's evils, a characterization that has by now become a commonplace even in the works of America's own novelists. But Greene suggests that such evil springs not from malice but from innocence. "I wish", Fowler tells Pyle, "sometimes you had a few bad motives. You might understand a little more about human beings. And that applies to your country too." (133) For Greene, the best and the brightest had no bad motives; they simply had no idea "what the whole affair's about" (31), of the full complexity of international affairs. His attack upon the murderous simplicity of American foreign policy was attacked in turn, and yet thirty years later how prescient the novel seems, and how fair. Ten years before America's full involvement in Vietnam, *The Quiet American* both predicted that involvement and some of the causes of its failure, and in doing so defined the naiveté and the confusion behind the American presence in Vietnam with a clarity which no other novel has yet attained.

With Greene's novels after *The Quiet American* it becomes even more possible than before to speak of Greeneland, and in particular of a typical Greene protagonist. He writes in *The Comedians*, *The Honorary Consul* (1973), and *The Human Factor* about characters who profess no faith, but must nevertheless take action on behalf of a cause they cannot quite believe in. Yet 'He who forms a tie is lost', as Greene quotes from Conrad in the epigraph to *The Human Factor*. However much he sees the necessity of becoming 'engagé', Greene still suggests that doubt and detachment are preferable. In the 1948 pamphlet 'Why Do I Write?' he claims that 'disloyalty'[41] saved him from the burden of being an orthodox Catholic novelist. And in his short story 'Under the Garden', Greene's grotesque mouthpiece, the old man Javitt, says:

> "Be disloyal. It's your duty to the human race. The human race needs to survive and it's the loyal man who dies first from anxiety or a bullet or overwork. If you have to earn a living, boy, and the price they make you pay is loyalty, be a double-

agent – and never let either of the two sides know your real name . . . The same applies to women and God."[42]

The only way to survive in a world where treachery seems inevitable is to embrace it. Spurling argues that Javitt's disloyalty underlies Fowler's journalistic commitment to facts.[43] Facts are disloyal to everything, and so to nothing; can betray nothing because they owe allegiance to nothing except the objective world itself. To Fowler they take the place of belief, and it's only in the attempt to act on behalf of a cause that he learns of the emptiness those facts have created in him. And perhaps in Greene as well. For in the end Greene's only commitment is to that same objective world; hence his move away from religious themes after *The End of the Affair*, whose miracles undermined his disloyalty, and his subsequent use of the world's 'foully governed' places to supply the 'dangerous edge' that religion had once afforded.

That move away from religion may have been accelerated by the enthusiasm Greene's readers felt for his description of Scobie's and Bendrix's spiritual troubles, and the opportunities they took to tell him of their own. In a letter to Evelyn Waugh Greene deplored the confusion in 'some Catholic criticism',[44] and in some Catholic readers, between the functions of a novelist and those of a moral teacher or theologian, a confusion he felt distorted his work and reputation. It is a distinction he explored in his 1962 novel, *A Burnt-out Case*. In *Ways of Escape* Greene calls it 'the blackest book' of his career, a novel about a man in whom emotion appears to have died, the Church architect Querry who in losing his faith believes he has lost his artistic vocation as well. But it is also, Greene notes, the novel in which he 'discovered comedy' (267), the book that brought him to 'that tragicomic region of La Mancha where I expect to stay' (266). All the same the novel so drained Greene that he thought after finishing it he would not have the stamina to write another one. But discovering that 'tragicomic world' proved liberating, and gave him the new strength that enabled him to write *The Comedians*, his largest and most richly conceived novel.

The Comedian's narrator, the expatriate Anglo-Monagesque Brown (he has no first name) has also arrived at the end of belief. As a child Brown let the 'official beliefs' of his Catholic schooling dissolve before the gambling tables and older women of Monte Carlo, where he was born. As an adult, he knows that 'Cynicism is cheap

. . . it's built into all poor-quality goods' (21), because he knows himself so well, knows that he has 'a hollow where a hollow should not have been' (222–3). The novel describes the events that lead Brown to accept that hollow at last. They began, Greene makes him recall, with a journey by ship from New York back to the depressingly 'empty hotel' Brown owns in Papa Doc Duvalier's Haiti, and to 'a love affair which was almost as empty' (9). In New York Brown had hoped to sell the hotel, and counted on his absence to end the love affair. Neither plan works, and so he decides to return to Haiti and all its problems, to the terrors of Duvalier's rule and his weary affair with a diplomat's wife; to accept what Terry Eagleton calls 'a quotidian world which is hated but which cannot be changed'.[45]

On ship he meets two men whose lives will intersect his own in Haiti. One is an American named Smith, who had once run for President on a vegetarian ticket and now wants to spread his gospel in Haiti. The other is an Englishman named Jones, a would-be swashbuckler in whose military title of 'Major' no-one on board can ever quite believe. To Brown their three common surnames seem 'interchangeable like comic masks in a farce' (23), just as life itself is:

a comedy, not the tragedy for which I had been prepared . . . we were all driven by an authoritative practical joker toward the extreme point of comedy. How often, in the crowd on Shaftes-bury Avenue or Broadway, after the theatres closed, have I heard the phrase – 'I laughed till the tears came.'   (31–2)

Brown's sense of life as a comedy corresponds to the slick surfaces of Greene's early novels, books committed only to craft, incapable of rising to the tragedy they feel they should express. Here Greene suggests that tragedy through his description of life in Duvalier's Haiti, where nightmare forms an essential part of the 'quotidian world'. On his return, for example, Brown finds that his friend Doctor Philipot, the country's Secretary for Social Welfare, has fallen from political favour and cut his own throat in the bottom of the hotel's drained swimming pool, rather than wait for Duvalier's secret police, the Tontons Macoute, to do it for him. Greene's description of the way in which Haitian life struggles painfully on through year after terrifying year of murder, graft, poverty, and disease, stands as his most comprehensive portrait of the way a society moves. But for all its description of the horrors of Papa Doc's reign, the novel remains a comedy, albeit one driven to that 'extreme point' at which one cries over one's inability to feel. Brown can only look dispassionately at the passion of other people. He cannot rise to man's tragic fate, but can only appreciate his comic existence, in a way that his comment on Philipot's death makes clear. 'We had only to turn on the water to wash the blood away', Brown recalls. 'He had been as considerate as possible' (53).

Toward the end of the novel Brown provides an explanation for his own way of life:

> Perhaps there is an advantage in being born in a city like Monte Carlo, without roots, for one accepts more easily what comes. The rootless have experienced, like all the others, the temptation of sharing the security of a religious creed or a political faith, and for some reason we have turned the temptation down. We are the faithless. We admire the dedicated, the Doctor Magiots and the Mr. Smiths for their courage and their integrity, for their fidelity to a cause, but through timidity, or through lack of sufficient zest, we find ourselves the only ones truly committed – committed to the whole world of evil and of good, to the wise and the foolish, to the indifferent and to the mistaken. We have chosen nothing except to go on living, 'rolled round on Earth's diurnal course, With rocks and stones and trees.'
>
> The argument interested me; I daresay it eased the never quiet conscience which had been injected into me without my consent, when I was too young to know, by the Fathers of the Visitation.   (279)

Brown cannot bring himself to act, cannot bring himself to join the struggle against Duvalier, however much he loathes his rule. He knows of the existence of deep emotion, of the possibility and indeed the 'security' of the 'great love' or 'great hate' offered by 'a religious creed . . . or political faith'. But he cannot feel it himself. In him the sense of the world is so strong as to exclude the soul. That exclusion troubles him, but he does find some consolation in what Javitt in 'Under the Garden' calls his 'duty' to accept 'the whole human race' as it is.

Such a plea makes the best case possible for what Greene calls the 'splinter of ice'[46] not only in Brown's but in the novelist's own

breast and the disloyalty that grows from it. Yet Greene nevertheless implies his dissatisfaction with that splinter, and perhaps with
his own vocation. Through Brown, Greene suggests the limitations
of his own commitment to craft; suggests what happens when the
emotional conviction that marked *The Power and the Glory* vanishes,
leaving only the priest's love of the physical world without the
faith that could give that love meaning. In that inability to commit
himself, Brown shares with his creator what Philip Stratford
describes as the situation of the novelist 'condemned to inaction
except through sympathy and love',[47] by his need to find room in
his work for all the evil and the good, the wise and the foolish,
whom 'fidelity to a cause' might exclude. Greene has here absorbed
Conrad's definition of art as 'a single-minded attempt to render
the highest kind of justice to the visible universe.[48] Yet for Greene
the inclusiveness of that 'justice' precludes the possibility of
any great but restrictive passion. It makes the 'visible universe'
essentially comic; ignores the 'tragic fate' that must, in pursuit of
that justice, be relegated to another world. Brown's meditation
both explains Greene's move away from religious themes and
justifies his early concentration on the conventional surfaces of the
visible world. It suggests a reason for the extraordinary sureness
of Greene's descriptive passages in comparison with his handling
of emotion; his mastery of a world, rather than of the people to fill
it.

Yet Brown's concluding allusion to his own 'never quiet conscience' acknowledges the limitations of that point of view, and
transforms *The Comedians* into a condemnation of its own style. For
Greene won't allow Brown's self-satisfied account of his own
peculiar form of commitment to stand. He punctures it through
the eulogy given at Jones's funeral in the Dominican Republic –
Jones who has improbably became a guerilla leader in the fight
against Papa Doc, and found himself adequate to his own fantasies.
The priest says:

"The Church condemns violence, but it condemns indifference
more harshly. Violence can be the expression of love, indifference
never. One is an imperfection of charity, the other the perfection
of egoism. In the days of fear, doubt, and confusion, the
simplicity and loyalty of one apostle advocated a political solution. He was wrong, but I would rather be wrong with St.
Thomas than right with the cold and the craven." (283)

That night Brown remembers that 'When I was a boy the Fathers of the Visitation had told me that one test of belief was this: that a man was ready to die for it . . . but for what belief did Jones die?' (286–7) The priest's words show Brown the degree to which his own 'indifference' precludes the dignity that lies beneath the vegetarian Smith's absurd surface, or that Jones gains in his fatal commitment to playing the 'part' his fantasies suggest. For 'Death', Brown admits, 'was a proof of sincerity', even for one like Jones, who dies because "It's in my part old man, it's in my part" (287); fulfils his role in the comedy he has elected to play.

Brown knows that he himself cannot summon that sincerity, even though his unwilling involvement with Jones' escapades costs him his hotel and forces him to leave Haiti. A chance meeting with another old shipmate throws him into a new job – as an undertaker. At the end of the novel Brown begins to treat death with a professional mask that keeps him from taking even his own future seriously. He deals with the sincere, with whose who have suffered life's 'tragic fate', but his own existence must remain comic, that of a spectator to misery. Yet though he ushers other men and women into death, every comedian must someday face it himself, and Brown must therefore continue his search for 'an alternative to the faith' (286) he has lost, even while the novel shows 'polemically the impossibility of acheving [that] necessary object'.

In *The Comedians* Greene presents his *summa* – his fullest exploration of the theme that has absorbed him since he chose that Santayana epigraph for *Stamboul Train*. But novels are not intellectual positions, and *The Comedians* would not seem so rich if it were not, from its first sentence, one of Greene's most masterfully told stories:

> When I think of all the grey memorials erected in London to equestrian generals, the heroes of old colonial wars, and to frock-coated politicians who are even more deeply forgotten, I can find no reason to mock the modest stone that commemorates Jones on the far side of the international road which he failed to cross in a country far from home, though I am not to this day absolutely sure of where, geographically speaking, Jones' home lay. (9)

Incident builds smoothly upon incident; the narrative line moves fluidly from a party on ship, at which condoms are blown up like balloons, to a voodoo ceremony, to a shootout in the Haitian countryside, all without losing the sense of suspense that, in lesser hands, that initial sentence might have destroyed. Paradoxically that sentence contains one of the novel's few allusions to England. Yet while Greene has had once more to set his work abroad, the novel nevertheless bespeaks a deep involvement with his own society. Brown remains an object of history, rather than its agent – loses his hotel not because he wants to, but because he remains one of 'those to whom things are done', rather than a man of 'executive will and intelligence'. In his account of Brown's spiritual powerlessness, his sense of being cheated at the way life has turned out to be a 'comedy, not the tragedy for which I had been prepared', Greene embodies the frustrations of an England shrunk from an empire to an island in a way that makes *The Comedians* a totalizing response, not just to Haitian culture, but to Greene's own.

The Comedians stands as a counterpart to *The Power and the Glory*, and with it as one of Greene's two great novels. For Greene writes best when he can express his loving and fascinated acceptance of the world as it is, with all its horrors. Would he have Haiti be any different? No, not as a novelist, no more than the priest in *The Power and the Glory* would change the world. For as the priest needs the world's misery to prepare him for heaven, so Greene's art requires it as a condition of the 'visible universe' upon which he depends. It is an appalling realization, and one that he has fully managed to make only in these two novels: in *The Power and the Glory* through his representation of a religious faith that can redeem such suffering; in *The Comedians* through his realization of the moral impotence of the 'splinter of ice' the novelist – any spectator – has instead of a heart.

V

Greene has done his best work after *The Comedians* not in his two long and tired political novels, *The Honorary Consul* and *The Human Factor*, but in a pair of exhilarating comic ones, *Travels with my Aunt* (1969) and *Monsignor Quixote* (1982). They are best approached through his 1958 spoof of the Secret Service, *Our Man in Havana*. Greene's early novels had contained a series of elaborate jokes built around his own personal myth, jokes exploring not just his position as a headmaster's son but his own life as a novelist. *Our Man in Havana* takes the process one step further, so that the fiction begins to create the truth. The British Secret Service accidentally recruits Jim Wormold, an English vacuum cleaner salesman, to be its agent in Havana. Wormold has no idea what a spy should do, but rather than lose his attractive salary, he sends in a series of false but impressive reports. And because both his superiors and their enemies believe those reports, the fiction he's created about his life as a spy starts to come true. By the end of the novel Wormold is no longer a fake spy but a real one fighting a real gun battle, imprisoned by the interpretations other people have placed on his own creations, as Greene was himself by that 'Catholic criticism'.

Travels with My Aunt is marked by a similar playfulness about the nature of fiction. It plays with Greene's own myth of himself as a much-travelled writer, and is filled with elaborate jokes upon his own career. In it Greene empties a notebook's worth of anecdotes and aphorisms onto the pages of a picaresque novel about a redheaded retired courtesan, narrated by her 'nephew' (actually son, but he doesn't know that yet), a retired bank manager named Henry Pulling. Henry and his 'Aunt' Augusta travel first to Brighton and later take the Orient Express to Istanbul; her old lover is a Milanese gentleman named Visconti, whose Interpol file describes him as a 'viper' (182); Henry meets a quiet American spy; and Aunt Augusta recalls not just Brown's rakish red-haired mother from *The Comedians*, but Ida Arnold herself.

But while Greene condemned Ida, he has no thought but to enjoy Aunt Augusta. Having plumbed his own weaknesses he can return to the stylized surfaces of his early novels with a new freshness and delight, free at last to write the comedy that had been implicit in them. "I have an impression", Aunt Augusta tells Henry:

'. . . you are really a little shocked by trivial illegalities. When you reach my age you will be more tolerant . . . a little honest thieving hurts no one, especially when it is a question of gold. Gold needs free circulation. The Spanish Empire would have decayed far more quickly if Sir Francis Drake had not kept a portion of the Spanish gold in circulation. (68–9)

– all this as she smuggles a suitcase full of cash out of England, beating both the currency regulations and the taxman. After a long series of novels set in the gloomiest parts of Greeneland, what a surprise and relief Aunt Augusta's genial urbanity must have afforded Greene, and one admires a writer who has both the ability to create so substantial a world, and the confidence to parody it so delightfully.

Greene allows himself some similar allusions to his own work in *Monsignor Quixote*, whose hero is a humble Spanish parish priest suddenly elevated to the rank of monsignor. The novel describes the picaresque journey he makes around Spain with the Communist mayor of his village, whom he calls Sancho, in quest of a monsignor's purple socks and pechera. It is the only one of Greene's books that could be described as gentle. And it contains as well what one takes to be Greene's final resolution of the tension between man's tragic fate and his comic existence, between faith and doubt, commitment and disloyalty. One day the monsignor dreams that:

. . . Christ had been saved from the Cross by the legion of angels to which on an earlier occasion the Devil had told Him that He could appeal. So there was no final agony, no heavy stone which had to be rolled away, no discovery of an empty tomb. Father Quixote stood there watching on Golgotha as Christ stepped down from the Cross triumphant and acclaimed. The Roman soldiers, even the Centurion, knelt in His honour, and the people of Jerusalem poured up the hill to worship Him. The disciples clustered happily around. His mother smiled through her tears of joy. There was no ambiguity, no room for doubt and no room for faith at all. The whole world knew with certainty that Christ was the Son of God.

It was only a dream, of course it was only a dream, but nonetheless Father Quixote had felt on waking the chill of despair felt by a man who realizes suddenly that he has taken up a profession which is of use to no one, who must continue to live in a kind of Saharan desert without doubt or faith, where everyone is certain that the same belief is true. He had found himself whispering, "God save me from such a belief." Then he heard the mayor turn restlessly on the bed beside him, and he added without thought, "Save him too from belief," and only then he fell asleep again.[49]

"It's an awful thing not to have doubts (74), he tells the mayor the next day. Without doubt the Church gives rise to a Torquemada, and Marxism throws up a Stalin – the demons with whom the mayor and the priest reproach one another. Without doubt one knows 'all the answers', and so lives in a nihilism of the truth. Without doubt, faith itself is impossible. For faith requires that one believe in spite of uncertainty, the uncertainty the monsignor's dream would abolish. Faith requires that one continue to believe even while admitting one might be mistaken; Kierkegaard's position, and Dostoevsky's, and more particularly that of Unamuno, whose grave the mayor insists upon visiting. So Greene reconciles the terms that have governed his career, but *Monsignor Quixote* doesn't insist upon the resolution. Greene puts it delicately instead, as if the very need for doubt makes him know better than to insist, as he has so often insisted, in making the statement toward which his work has tended.

And yet there is more. While insisting on the necessity of doubt, *Monsignor Quixote* finally chooses faith, and so makes a statement about the power of belief, and of its expression through art, to create a world. "I shall always remember how under this fig tree I was able to entertain for a short while a descendant of the great Don" (195), an old Spanish patriarch tells the monsignor. His bishop insists that Cervantes' hero is only a fictional character, but the monsignor nevertheless believes that he is in fact descended from him. Greene resolves the tension between the two positions at the end of the novel. The monsignor, now sick and old, is convalescing in a monastery. In his sleep he gets out of bed and walks into the monastery's church, where without waking up he begins to say mass. "When he finds no paten and no chalice, surely he will wake" (215), says Father Leopoldo, one of the monastery's priests, who has followed him into the church. But the monsignor does not wake. He moves 'steadily on without hesitation to the consecration of the non-existent wine in the non-existent chalice' (215), until at the end of the mass he takes 'from the invisible paten the invisible host and [with] his fingers laid the nothing on his tongue' (217). He then beckons the watching mayor to communion – and collapses, and dies.

Afterwards, the mayor, Father Leopoldo, and an American professor argue about the scene. The American does not believe that consecration took place, that mass was said. Yet as Father Leopoldo argues, Monsignor Quixote quite obviously believed in the presence of the bread and wine. "Which of us was right?" he asks. ". . . Do you think it's more difficult to turn empty air into wine than wine into blood? Can our limited senses decide a thing like that?" (219–20). The mass has been imaginary, yet has nevertheless happened. Is it a comedy, or a tragedy? But perhaps those terms don't matter. By making the monsignor believe in his own communion, Greene fuses the two, as in one of Shakespeare's late romances, into a moment whose wholeness answers to Santayana's sense of life, in the other half of that quotation with which I began, as "lyrical in its ideal essence". *Monsignor Quixote* testifies to the salvific power of art: its power to create a world of its own. The monsignor's belief that he is in fact saying mass creates truth out of fiction, just as he is descended from a character in a novel. Art creates life; the spiritual world takes visible form. Greene has written that his books seem to have shaped the course of his own later life; in 'J'Accuse', his 1982 pamphlet about the way organized crime in Nice has affected his friends, he seems, for example, to have entered the world of *Brighton Rock*. Greene has since written other books, including the enjoyable 1988 novel *The Captain and the Enemy*, but *Monsignor Quixote* still stands as a fitting conclusion to any consideration of a writer whose great achievement has been the creation of his own distinctive world.

5
Evelyn Waugh
(1903–1966)

I

Just before the end of *Decline and Fall* (1928) Evelyn Waugh makes Paul Pennyfeather attend a lecture on church history, at which he learns about:

> . . . the heresies of the second century. There was a bishop of Bithynia, Paul learned, who had denied the Divinity of Christ, the immortality of the soul, the existence of good, the legality of marriage, and validity of the sacrament of Extreme Unction. How right they had been to condemn him! (288)

But should one take this passage, and Pennyfeather's concluding comment in particular, at face value, as a Kiplingesque plea for what Alvin Kernan calls the need for 'ceaselessly manned walls protecting sense, order, and meaningful life from riot and savagery'?[1] For Pennyfeather's sentiments seem out of place in a novel written with the *brio* of *Decline and Fall*. They seem, in fact, to belong to the older Waugh, who in *Brideshead Revisited* replaced the anarchic comedy of his early work with an assertive Catholicism, a vision of the Roman Church as civilization's only defence against the terrors of the modern world. This passage does provide a foreshadowing of Waugh's later beliefs, but one need not in reading *Decline and Fall* take its implications seriously, need not view it as a condemnation of the world in which the novel is set. Waugh's work may, as Terry Eagleton writes, be 'built around a conflict between a sense of morality and a sense of style',[2] but the young Waugh sees no need to resolve that conflict.

In fact, *Decline and Fall* posits two kinds of morality: one for the 'static' (288) like Pennyfeather, who 'would never have made a hero' (164), and another for the 'dynamic' (288) like Margot, Lady Metroland, whose energy can make those 'heresies' acceptable, just as she makes the priggish Pennyfeather accept the idea of sex before marriage. The very structure of the sentence in which Paul condemns the bishop reflects his static nature – flat, drawn-out by a reliance on monosyllables, over-emphatically punctuated. The sentence detailing the bishop's activities, in contrast, carries a dynamism in which each of the tenets he denies is less important for the church than its predecessor, but more important for the rhythm of the prose, so that it builds to an incongruous anti-climax against whose comedy Pennyfeather's comment seems a poor second. Laughter serves as a liberation from orthodoxy. The early Waugh is too attracted by the dynamism of heresy to side with the static. For as Edmund Wilson writes, 'the savagery he is afraid of is somehow the same thing as the audacity that so delights him',[3] and in his early novels the audacity prevails. They may pose the terms of a stern morality that provides a frame through which to see the novel's action, but Waugh does not insist on that frame, and Paul's condemnation of heresy is much more a judgement of him than of that ancient bishop.

Graham Greene has written that Edmund Campion's words upon the scaffold, 'We are made a spectacle unto God, unto his angels, and unto men' can serve as a motto for Waugh's work as a whole.[4] But if Waugh's novels from *Decline and Fall* to *Put Out More Flags* (1942) contain some version of his later social and religious beliefs, they do so ironically, for in them Waugh exempts nothing from that spectacle. Everything, religion above all, becomes target of a comedy that recognizes the bounds of propriety only to draw attention to the delight with which it breaks them. One needs, then, a way of relating the comic spectacle of his early books to the religious faith of his later ones. After the Second World War Waugh fused his Catholicism with conservatism to produce a condemnation of what he considered an atheistic and unbearable present, a condemnation summed up in *The Ordeal of Gilbert Pinford* (1958) as an abhorrence of 'plastics, Picasso, sunbathing, and jazz – everything in fact that had happened in his own lifetime' (11). The sharpness – the rudeness – with which he expressed such opinions made Waugh into what Greene describes as a public figure so capable of 'exploitation by journalists' that even now the 'legend' threatens to 'supersede the work'.[5] But no one could play upon that legend as successfully as Waugh did himself in *Pinfold*, his merciless attack on his own pose as what J.B. Priestley called 'a Catholic landed gentleman . . . quietly regretting the Reform Bill of 1832'.[6] Waugh's comedy gave him, throughout his life, an extraordinary capacity for the exposure not just of the absurdities around him, but of the inadequacies of his own vision as well. And he used that comedy to expose not just Pennyfeather's or Pinfold's pretensions, but the limitations of comedy itself. To understand him one needs to see how and why the scathing comic nihilism of his early novels led him finally to becomes a Catholic novelist, rather than remain a novelist who happened to be Catholic.

II

"With his laughter", argues Brother Jorge in Umberto Eco's *The Name of the Rose*, "the fool says in his heart 'Deus non est'."[7] Waugh would recognize the sentiment. He wanted to believe that people have souls, but predicated his comedy on the supposition that they don't. Toward the end of *Decline and Fall*, Margot has Pennyfeather spirited away from prison to her villa on Corfu. There he meets the architect Professor Silenus, who volunteers to tell him "about life", describing it in terms of an amusement park ride. "Life", Silenus says, is:

> . . . like the big wheel at Luna Park . . . a great disc of polished wood that revolves quickly. At first you sit down and watch the others. They are all trying to sit in the wheel, and they keep getting flung off, and that makes them laugh, and you laugh too. It's great fun . . . Of course at the very centre there's a point completely at rest, if one could only find it . . . Lots of people just enjoy scrambling on and being whisked off and scrambling on again . . . But the whole point about the wheel is that you needn't get on it at all . . . People get hold of ideas about life, and that makes them think they've got to join in the game, even if they don't enjoy it. It doesn't suit everyone. Now you're a person who was clearly meant to . . . sit still and if you get bored watch the others. Somehow you got onto the wheel, and you got thrown off again at once. . . . It's all right for Margot, who can cling on . . . but you're static. Instead of this absurd division into sexes they ought to class people as static and dynamic. There's a real distinction there, though I can't tell you how

it comes. I think we're probably two quite different species spiritually.   (282–4)

Waugh here outlines the conditions under which his comedy takes place, in terms similar to those used by such theoreticians of the comic as Henri Bergson or Wyndham Lewis, the latter of whose 'observations about the "Outside and Inside" method of fiction', Waugh wrote, 'no novelist . . . can afford to neglect'.[8] Lewis writes in *The Wild Body* that the comic artist's task lies in exposing the mechanical quality of the rhythmic scheme on which social life depends, just as Waugh's metaphor does here. One then sees, in Bergson's words, 'something mechanical encrusted on the living',[9] and laughs – just as do those trying to sit on the wheel, who see, as they are spun off it, the way in which the amusement has made them mechanical. What matters to Waugh are not his characters' emotional lives but what he called 'the knockabout farce of . . . [their] outward behaviour',[10] whose patterns are those of a big wheel, a machine in which people are at best the raw materials the machine is meant to process. People become things – or, as Lewis says, things behave like people – in an essentially absurd motion that explains most of the local comic effects in Waugh's novels, such as little Lord Tangent's slow dismemberment in *Decline and Fall*, the details of which are reported at intervals throughout the novel in his mother's fox-hunting bray – first the foot comes off, then the leg, and so on.

Silenus's metaphor is an ordering one, but its order is rhythmic, purely descriptive, of a piece with what Lewis calls 'non-moral satire'. It emphasizes the characters' 'outward behaviour', their puppet-like lack of volition in an objective world whose mechanical motion makes their subjective experience irrelevant. After reading this passage one understands the means through which Pennyfeather falls off time and again, and understands as well the reasons why one doesn't much care when he does. For in getting on the wheel Pennyfeather has stopped being what Waugh calls a 'real person' (164), and has become mechanical instead – 'cannon fodder', as Lewis writes in *Men Without Art*, one of 'those to whom things are done'. The paradox, of course, is that to Waugh real persons remain estranged from the life that the wheel embodies. 'The only interest' one has in Pennyfeather, Waugh writes, 'arises from the unusual series of events of which his shadow was a witness' (164). Real people are 'static', in some sense dead. Only their shadows, their surfaces, are 'dynamic' enough to be alive.

But *Decline and Fall* no more insists on its ordering metaphor than it does on Paul's condemnation of heresy. Waugh presents it casually, and steps away from it immediately. Silenus says that generalizations about life such as the one he's just made are 'boring and futile' (284) and goes back to bed. The frame dissolves; Waugh has toyed with some larger meaning, but done no more than that. For while its open admission of the terms on which its art depends does stamp *Decline and Fall* as a modernist novel, it is nevertheless a curiously modest modernist production. Short, accessible, and apparently slight, it has about it none of the air of the difficult new that one associates with modernism; seems marked not by what Eagleton calls the failure to totalize characteristic of Waugh's generation, but by the failure – or the refusal – to make the attempt. The novel appears to have been written not out of a sense of artistic mission, but as an escape from the ennui and frustration of looking for a job. At the time Waugh didn't think of writing as a career but simply as one of a number of things he might do. He had already tried and abandoned teaching, and still thought of cabinet-making and illustration as other possibilities.

The novel doesn't look to modernism for inspiration, not even to a satirist like Lewis, however useful his critical writings are in understanding it, but to the deliberately narrow, and deliberately frivolous, dandy–aesthete tradition of perfect but decidedly minor writers, of whom Oscar Wilde is the progenitor, with Max Beerbohm, Saki, and Ronald Firbank as his most important successors. Waugh's work transcends that tradition, but his debt to it is marked. He shares its material – Oxford seen as a 'kingdom of Cokayne',[11] country house comedies, brittle records of the conversation of clever young men – and shares its style as well, taking from that tradition the smooth, gleaming, amoral surface of his prose, so different from the creaking portentousness of Lewis's or Aldous Huxley's satires. Waugh joined Firbank to the Vortex. The combination of the dandy–aesthete's emphasis on glitter and style with Lewis's comic machine gave him the basis for a precarious creative equilibrium, not dependent upon the novel's conventional sense of morality, in ways suggested by Silenus's distinction between the static and the dynamic. Christopher Sykes, has written that 'Waugh admired and wished to belong to the world of Tony Last, but . . . he felt more at home in Lady Metroland's',[12] and he used that contradiction to keep the frames of his early novels from becoming as rigid and confining as most criticism has tried to make them. His work posits a world in which there are two clear and mutually exclusive alternatives, in which a character is either static or dynamic, Catholic or non-Catholic, innocent like Tony Last in *A Handful of Dust* or irresponsible like his wife. But in his early novels, which position should one prefer? The knowledge that in *Decline and Fall* Margot is dynamic and Paul static doesn't give much help to a reader in search of an evaluative criticism of life. They are 'two quite different species' and the ordinary morality that binds Pennyfeather and that early Bithynian bishop has nothing to do with Margot, even though – or perhaps because – she is a white slaver. Neither is preferable; both are essential and in fact take on their meaning from the other's presence. Waugh's terms aren't moral, but descriptive, and so he doesn't have to commit himself to either alternative, to exclude anything from the spectacle at which he makes us laugh. Instead, he leaves the reader to choose between Margot and Pennyfeather, knowing that the choice will prove impossible, and that the impossibility will be liberating.

In reading *Decline and Fall*, one isn't, in consequence, bothered by the need to pay attention to the standards by which Waugh's comedy might seem, as Bernard Bergonzi writes, 'characteristically cruel'.[13] On the novel's first page, for example, Waugh writes:

> At the last dinner, three years ago, a fox had been brought in in a cage and stoned to death with champagne bottles. What an evening that had been! This was the first meeting since then, and from all over Europe old members had rallied for the occasion. (1)

But in Waugh's early novels, as in Saki's stories, one doesn't pause to shudder at such details. The fox's death is merely noted in passing, a detail of a memorable evening, but no more. The exclamation mark follows not the beast's demise, but the narrator's fond remembrance of the evening as a whole, and the prose moves so quickly past the incident that it keeps one from stopping to consider the actions it describes. Waugh's comedy can make any cruelty delightful rather than troubling, so long as it comes off with an imperturbable insouciance, absolutely unruffled by that chorus of champagne bottles.

Decline and Fall is the final and funniest book in the dandy–

aesthete tradition, and is in many ways a perfect novel – perfect above all in the ease with which it remains inside its boundaries. Only once does Waugh try to force its comedy outside these boundaries. That exception comes in Silenus's speech. He describes the mechanism of the wheel and then adds that "Of course at the very centre there's a point completely at rest, if one could only find it" – a point from which the world's workings are revealed, and from which they make sense. Waugh doesn't here take that idea seriously, and yet one can't forget that the novel's crucial passage acknowledges the need for such a place, even if the perspective on human affairs it provides is not that of the religion on which he later depended, but of a comedy in which people are things. For Waugh cannot completely delight in the flux and change that the wheel at Luna Park embodies. He longs instead for one spot of immobile stability from which to see the whole mechanical world revolve, a place exempt from the limitations of the life he describes – a place that is not, in itself, comic.

Decline and Fall does not insist on either that point or its absence. *Vile Bodies* (1930) does. It has what its predecessors in the dandy–aesthete tradition do not: both an ability to be disturbed by the implications of its own style, and a critical relation to history, to that society in which 'the official beliefs were dissolving like sandcastles'. Toward the end of the novel, Waugh sends some of his characters up in an aeroplane, from which:

> Nina looked down and saw inclined at an odd angle a horizon of straggling red suburb; arterial roads dotted with little cars; factories, some of them working, others empty and decaying; a disused canal; some distant hills sown with bungalows; wireless masts and overhead power cables; men and women were indiscernable except as tiny spots; they were marrying and shopping and making money and having children. The scene lurched and tilted again as the aeroplane struck a current of air.
> "I think I'm going to be sick," said Nina. (284)

She sees the scene at an 'odd angle', as a satirist does, but she nevertheless sees a scene that both she and the reader recognise, the familiar landscape of industrial England, so different from the 'precious stone' and 'blessed plot' which earlier in the scene Waugh had had her quote from John of Gaunt's apostrophe to England in *Richard II*. Waugh's description is very much of its time; both

William H. Pritchard and Samuel Hynes have commented on its similarity to the landscape of 'Auden country'.[14] But Waugh follows Nina's statement with one from her companion: "That's what the paper bags are for" (284), and the passage turns comic, keeping one from feeling any sort of Lawrencian disgust at the rape of rural England. What one does feel is the lack of a point of view. The 'odd angle' of Nina's vision, the 'lurching and tilting' to which the aeroplane subjects her, suggest that while she sees 'the real world' she sees it from Woolf's 'leaning tower'. The aeroplane – modernity – won't allow her to look at the world either steadily or wholly. She is instead filled with what Woolf described as 'the consciousness of things changing and things falling' characteristic of the period in which Waugh writes, so that it's not the actual conditions of life below that make her sick, but the absence of stability, of a settled system of belief from which to view those conditions.

Yet is it history that causes that absence, or Waugh's own style, or both? Waugh's comedy is homologous with the world in which he lives. Earlier in the novel Waugh has Father Rothschild, Lord Metroland, and Mr Outrage, the Prime Minister, gather over champagne to talk about 'the younger generation'. Outrage claims that "There's something wanton about these young people today", and the priest replies:

"Don't you think . . . that perhaps it is all in some way historical? I don't think people ever want to lose their faith either in religion or anything else. I know very few young people, but it seems to me as if they are all possessed with an almost fatal hunger for permanence. I think all these divorces show that. People aren't content just to muddle along nowadays . . . We long for peace, and fill our newspapers with conferences about disarmament and arbitration, but there is a radical instability in our whole world order . . ."   (183–5)

Rothschild adopts an historical argument that precludes holding the young responsible for their actions. But Waugh won't let that argument rest, won't excuse his own generation. He brings Rothschild down with Metroland's blunt objection that "I don't see how all that explains why my stepson should drink like a fish and go about everywhere with a negress . . ." (185). And by the standards of the novel, Metroland is absolutely right, for

Rothschild's appeal to history cannot explain why these particular people behave in this particular way; it explains the general case but doesn't excuse this specific one. Yet Waugh doesn't suggest that his "young people" could act any differently. His characters cannot take control of their own experience, as Nina cannot stop the aeroplane from lurching, and one sees through their situation to Waugh's sense of the vast and manic spectacle of England as a whole, to a country and a generation that cannot be blamed for its failings but that cannot be excused them either. Yet Metroland's comment is also a joke. It makes Rothschild not wise, but merely pompous – spins him off the revolving wheel. Like Silenus's disclaimer about "boring and futile" generalizations, Metroland's words defeat serious enquiry with laughter. With a "radical instability" of their own they militate against Waugh's "hunger for permanence", and so make the novel liable to the same limitations as its characters.

These two scenes provide a microcosm of *Vile Bodies* as a whole. The novel's energy grows from the tension between Waugh's febrile delight in the parties he describes – parties that embody his comic style by turning people into things – and his growing despair over their mad depressing gaiety; over his sense of the inadequacy of Silenus's comic vision, of the terms his imagination most readily suggests. *Vile Bodies* escalates from party to party, a shout welling into a scream, with war a 'Happy Ending' (314) because it solves the problem of what to do with the peace. It is an extraordinarily funny book, and yet also a disturbing one, in a way suggested by the novel's parenthetical revulsion from its own world. "Oh, Nina, *what a lot of parties*", says the novel's protagonist, Adam Fenwick-Symes. And then Waugh writes:

> (. . . Masked parties, Savage parties, Victorian parties, Greek parties, Circus parties, parties where one had to dress as somebody else, almost naked parties in St. John's Wood, parties in flats, and studios and houses and ships and hotels and night clubs, in windmills and swimming baths, tea parties at school where one ate muffins and meringues and tinned crab, parties at Oxford where one drank brown sherry and smoked Turkish cigarettes, dull dances in London and comic dances in Scotland and disgusting dances in Paris – all that succession and repetition of massed humanity . . . those vile bodies . . .) (171)

Waugh's use of the parenthesis is crucial. In removing the passage from the normal flow of the novel it supplies information that one would customarily expect the characters to provide themselves – and draws attention to the fact that they cannot. But why not? What isn't present in the novel, what do the characters lack that could give them the capacity to reflect on the novel's action in the way this passage suggests?

The novel's title, Jeffrey Heath points out, comes from Philippians 3:20–21: 'For our conversation is in heaven, from whence also we look for the Saviour, the Lord Jesus Christ: Who shall change our vile body, that it may be fashioned like unto his glorious body, according to the working whereby he is able even to subdue all things unto himself.'[15] But that transformation is impossible here. The novel describes a world in which bodies are vile because that is all they are, bodies, things that should be people but whose participation in that 'succession and repetition of massed humanity' ensures that they are not; ensures not just that they can only be known by their outsides, but that those outsides are all they have. Waugh's interest lies not in the 'adventure of interiority' with which Lukacs says the novel as a genre is traditionally concerned, but with the spectacle of its absence in a world in which the body supersedes the soul, with life seen from the point of view of Lewis's 'Great With-Out'. Waugh's parenthesis announces his refusal to make the novel's conventional metonymic extension, to allow us to assume the presence of what's not actually on the page – of the interior life he does not describe. The novel's characters are, as its epigraph from *Through the Looking Glass* suggests, incapable of crying "real tears", for its subject is the soul they do not have, the interior life that Waugh's comic style does not allow them to sustain.

It is, however, absurd to worry very much about the 'thingness' of such characters as Agatha Runcible or Miles Malpractice, the "Bright Young People" (14) in whose pranks one delights, the wild bodies whose antics provide the occasion for this frantic comedy. They are simply part of what Waugh called the novel's 'furniture', very much things behaving as if they were people.[16] Stephen Spender even finds them attractive, unlike Hemingway's Lost Generation, because of their 'refusal to be tragic'.[17] Such characters establish the tone of the novel. But its edge comes from its more or less 'straight' treatment of Adam and Nina:

"Adam, darling, what's the matter?"

"I don't know . . . Nina, do you ever feel that things simply can't go on much longer?"

"What d'you mean by things – us or everything?"

"Everything."

"No – I wish I did."

'I daresay you're right . . ."   (273)

Adam and Nina, like Waugh himself, live in the post-Great War world of the leaning tower, in a world in which, as the aeroplane scene suggests, a settled, stable point of view is unattainable. It is in consequence "right", as Adam says, to wish for the capacity to believe that "things simply can't go on much longer" – and equally right to admit that one doesn't have that capacity. Adam and Nina are just conscious enough to be aware of their own shallowness, of the way their interior lives have withered away. Despite Waugh's obvious delight in his process, despite the novel's refusal to assign blame or make a conventional judgement, *Vile Bodies* insists, however lightly, on two things: that the worst fate of all is to be conscious that one is not a person but a prop; and that no style, no glittering surface of wit, can save one from that emptiness, for which one bears the punishment if not the blame.

Waugh's comic style makes his characters subject to the limitations of their period – helps, in fact, to create one's sense of those limitations, of an age in which one cannot control one's own experience. That style, then, becomes itself a metonymy for its period, and through that style *Vile Bodies* does achieve something very like the totalization of which Eagleton speaks, extending 'the materials of a directly personal response to the quality of a whole society . . . into confidently public and representative terms'.

Waugh's comedy, his capacity to puncture any official belief with laughter, keeps his characters, and perhaps himself, from achieving the stable point of view for which they hunger. In *Decline and Fall*, for example, he gloats over the consternation of Margot's neighbours at her decision to tear down her uncomfortable Tudor house – they had enjoyed its quaintness so. In *Black Mischief* (1932), his third novel, he makes one laugh at Basil Seal's unwitting enjoyment, at a cannibal feast, of a stew made from his mistress. Waugh can make any action seem funny and bright and gay and absolutely without moral consequences. One says of such a writer that he holds nothing sacred, that his comedy is so pervasive and corrosive that it can find and exploit the weak parts of any orthodoxy so completely as to deny it any validity at all. But to laugh at everything is to believe in nothing – and suppose one finds such laughter disturbing? Suppose, that is, one wants to hold something sacred, wants that stable point that in making sense of all else, cannot, must not, be punctured by laughter.

Waugh's first marriage, to the Hon. Evelyn Gardner, fell apart while he was writing *Vile Bodies*. The causes of the marriage's failure are complex, but what made him file for divorce was her confession of infidelity.[18] Her betrayal, Sykes writes, made Waugh 'feel lost again in a world where he believed . . . he had found safety. He fell into a state of absolute despair', a despair that colours all his later work.[19] During the divorce proceedings he told his brother Alec that 'the trouble with the world today is that there's not enough religion in it. There's nothing to keep people from doing whatever they want.'[20] *Vile Bodies* does not, however, suggest religion as an answer to the problems of its world, even though its characters are unconscious of any moral restraints on their actions, and even though Waugh became a Catholic shortly after its publication. Instead, it has at its core a lament that belief is impossible, that there is nothing to keep its characters from being mere soul-less things.

That lament grows from Waugh's relentless examination of the premises upon which his comedy is based; an examination that, in Lukacs' words, shows 'polemically the impossibility of achieving' the belief that the book so desperately wants to create. Waugh's novels can at first seem disappointing if one comes to them expecting, as after Henry James most critics do, that a novelist should approach his world through the interior lives of his characters. Even his main characters, the ones such as Adam or Paul who are meant to be more than 'furniture', seem 'flat',[21] one-dimensional, so that his work seems at first to lack the weight, the 'seriousness of purpose' one expects of major fiction. Waugh's external approach is indebted to the modernists' shattering of the novel's traditional requirement that the novelist mediate between the soul and the world. But he has no sympathy with Woolf's demand that novels present life as a 'luminous halo' of consciousness. He has no interest in consciousness as such, except insofar as his characters' lack of it, and their consequent flatness, can be made to tell. He eschews the intimacy between character and reader sought by a writer like Woolf, and finds his imagination drawn instead to his characters' external lives as bodies, bumping other bodies into uncomfortable positions. Waugh's aesthetic is different from Woolf's, but not less serious. Its guiding principle is this: that through a non-committal description of a character's external life in a world without conventional morality, one can make powerful if oblique statements about human incapacity. *Vile Bodies* uses comedy to subvert the premises on which that comedy is based. Laughter may serve as a liberation for orthodoxy, but for Waugh it is finally a reminder of his world's inability to sustain and express a genuine and deeply-felt emotion.

In its refusal to express such emotion, Waugh's style is the perfect instrument for capturing the last great days of the stoic English gentleman, of the stiff upper lip. In his fourth novel, *A Handful of Dust* (1934), Waugh has Tony Last spend weeks alone at home in the country while his abhorrent wife Brenda cavorts adulterously in London. Waugh writes that Tony:

> . . . dozed a little; then he went up to change. At dinner he said, "Ambrose, when I'm alone I think in future I'll have dinner at a table in the library." Afterward he sat with a book in front of the fire, but he was unable to read. At ten o'clock he scattered the logs in the fireplace before going upstairs. He fastened the library windows and turned out the lights. That night he went into Brenda's empty room to sleep.   (102)

One infers the pain and loneliness of Tony's interior life, but nothing in the passage states it directly. Waugh does not allow his readers the comfort, however bare, that comes from intimacy with a character's mind. Instead he attempts, like his friend Graham Greene, to suggest emotion through a precise notation of physical detail. Tony remains a thing – but not one at which we laugh, for Waugh here divorces laughter from comedy to make his style serve the purposes of a more delicate characterization, to suggest the stunted emotional life that nothing in Tony's background has prepared him to articulate. Bergonzi writes that *A Handful of Dust* is filled 'with an intense pathos that would be tragic if the characters involved had a sufficient degree of humanity to support tragedy',[22] if Waugh's conception of their vile bodies did not entail their inability to express deep feeling. Yet tragedy provides a reassuring catharsis. It says that people have souls as well as bodies, that human action may be noble and fine. Waugh's comic sense requires that he ignore that possibility. But while the thingness of people can be funny, Waugh knows in this passage that it is not always so, and the collective catastrophe of his world is that individual tragedy is impossible.

III

Waugh's move toward Catholicism, as a novelist if not as a man, is best described in terms of that Yeatsian quarrel with the self to which I alluded in this book's introduction, the quarrel from which poetry is born. He is the most sceptical English novelist of this century, a writer kept in his early books from blank despair only by the liberating power of a comedy whose premises propelled him toward that same despair. *Vile Bodies'* hysteria revealed the inadequacies of Silenus's conception of life, and yet Waugh does not in that novel have anything with which to replace it, no antidote to it, no conception of the world that can make people more than mere bodies struggling for a place upon the wheel. In *Black Mischief* he finds a temporary respite both in the invention of Basil Seal, a character endowed with his own gifts, and in the opposition of England to the black African nation of Azania, "two quite different species", like Paul and Margot in *Decline and Fall*. Basil serves as the novelist's stand-in (his 'alter-id', in Joseph Epstein's inspired phrase),[23] one who can treat the novel's other characters as things and get away with it, even at that concluding cannibal feast. Yet at the end of the novel, after Basil's return to England, Sonia Trumpington says, "D'you know, deep down in my heart, I've got a tiny fear that Basil is going to turn serious on us too" (305–6). It is as if he, as if Waugh himself, recoils from the novel's comedy, as the reader recoils from his own laughter at the cannibal feast; as, in fact, Waugh's own prose does in registering a final fascinated horror with the cannibals' 'glistening backs heaving and shivering in the shadows' (302) that is quite different in tone from the cool irony with which he had earlier regarded Azania.

But while Waugh's comic imagination does allow him to conceive of *Black Mischief*'s concluding horrors, it cannot encompass them. He does not, can not, show the reader Basil's reaction to the knowledge of what he's done; has nothing to say about the cannibalism except that he has nothing to say about it. Waugh has here reached the limits of the comedy on which he built his early novels. He must begin that 'quarrel with himself', must assess the implications of what he has already done, and begin the search for a moral basis from which to respond to the inhumanity of his own style. For, unlike Lewis, Waugh could not revel in man's spiritual poverty. He feared and tried to escape from the emptiness of Tony Last, an emptiness and a sense of disconnection for the expression of which his style was perfectly suited. The story of his career is one of a search for that "point completely at rest" to which Silenus referred, of that "hunger for permanence" to which Father Rothschild alluded. For in an age of "radical instability" only such a point could allow him to make sense of the world and so afford him the sense of human possibility he otherwise lacked.

Waugh found that necessary and sustaining relationship in the Roman Catholic Church. In his 1935 biography *Edmund Campion*, he writes that Campion 'makes the claim, which lies at the root of all Catholic apologetic, that the Faith is absolutely satisfactory to the mind, enlisting all knowledge and all reason in its cause; that it is completely compelling to any who give it "an indifferent and quiet audience" '.[24] Having decided that modern society entailed a choice between 'Christianity and Chaos',[25] Waugh chose Christianity, and so entered the Roman Church 'on firm intellectual conviction but with little emotion',[26] because it seemed to offer the 'most complete and vital form'[27] of Christian faith. Catholicism for him made the world comprehensible, set straight the leaning tower. It redeemed man from his spiritual poverty and gave him the soul Waugh's characters had so conspicuously lacked. But Waugh was also infected by what Conor Cruise O'Brien calls a 'deep English romanticism'.[28] One might, in fact, say that his comedy fed off a set of romantic aspirations that he could not allow himself to take seriously; that, as in the description of Etna I quoted in my introduction, his irony was so sure because he understood the romanticism it undercut so well. But when Waugh did allow himself to entertain those romantic hopes and dreams, his language summoned what O'Brien describes as a whole 'Gothic world . . . come to grief, menaced by some element of modernity'.[29] Waugh was drawn to all periods of the past. He delighted in the clutter and *bric a brac* of any time not his own and, after the Second World War in particular, romanticized any age in which he could imagine that classes had been fixed and people lived in intimate relation with the land. His political and cultural beliefs became a simplistic

version of the Tory Radical tradition of social criticism outlined by
Raymond Williams in *Culture and Society*;[30] simplistic, because he
presented those beliefs with the exaggeration from which he could
never escape. In 1959, for example, Waugh wrote that he would
not vote in general elections because he did not presume to advise
his 'sovereign on her choice of servants'.[31] The idea is deliberately
comic – but as with Basil Seal in 'Basil Seal Rides Again' (1963), in
whom 'The performance had become the persona', it is not entirely
so.[32]

Waugh believed that modern civilization's loss of the discipline
of what T. E. Hulme calls 'order and tradition'[33] had led inevitably
to the spiritual poverty of which his own work is, paradoxically, a
product. In consequence, his Catholicism became a refuge to which
he could flee from the spectacle of the present. For Waugh did not
love the doctrines of the Church so much as he did its historical
continuity, which seemed to assuage his "hunger for permanence".
To Waugh that very continuity seemed to guarantee the truth of
Church doctrine. Its ability to withstand the ridicule of nineteen
hundred years provided a test of its truth. Having stood so long,
it could presumably stand against both his own laughter and the
forces that were dissolving the other official beliefs of his society.
When, after the Second Vatican Council, the Church seemed to
break with its own history, Waugh feared that he might apostasize,
for the Church itself seemed then to shake its own foundations,
the foundations of the one thing that had resisted his own
laughter's nihilism, and kept him from despair.

As a result, the explicit literary manifestations of his faith were
not, on the whole, those of the Catholic Church so much as
those of what O'Brien calls a 'private religion' on which Waugh
'superimposed Catholicism, much as newly converted pagans are
said to superimpose a Christian nomenclature on their ancient
cults of trees and thunder'.[34] Waugh's 'private religion' depends
on a chivalric conception of the Catholic world, in which civilization
is embodied in Tony Last's 'Gothic world . . . [of] armour glittering
through the forest glades . . . embroidered feet on the greensward
. . . cream and dappled unicorns' (209), country houses and the
cult of the aristocracy. He identifies the Church and the civilization
around it almost exclusively with an aristocracy whose country
houses, Frank Kermode argues, stand as types of the City of God;[35]
an aristocracy whom, Bergonzi suggests, Waugh saw as 'the
custodians of the traditional values in a world increasingly threat-

ened by the barbarians'.[36]

Such a conception of civilization both dominates and damages *Brideshead Revisited*; Waugh treats it ironically in *Sword of Honour*, but it nevertheless mars that trilogy as well. When he wrote *A Handful of Dust*, however, Waugh had not yet coupled Catholicism with chivalry. There he attacks the idea that any civilization could offer a refuge from, or have the power to withstand, the threat of modernity. *A Handful of Dust* describes what happens to characters like those in *Vile Bodies* when a war doesn't come to solve their problems, and so they marry and have children instead. Most of Waugh's characters in *A Handful of Dust*, as in his earlier novels, treat each other as if they were things. But he complicates its world by introducing one 'problematic' character, Tony Last, who believes, however impotently, that they should be something more. Tony believes in his country house, Hetton Abbey, in the ordered, stable, pre-capitalistic society it embodies, and in the necessity of behaving decently "to people less fortunate" than himself (25) that ownership of such a house implies. Yet while the novel acknowledges the attraction of Tony's own private religion, Waugh's comedy also tests and finds it wanting.

Tony and Brenda Last's friends believe that they are 'pre-eminently successful in solving the problem of getting along well together' (28). But they haven't. For Tony, as Brenda says, is "madly feudal" (49):

> "We've always lived here and I hope John will be able to keep it on after me. One has a duty towards one's employees, and towards the place too. It's a definite part of English life which would be a serious loss if . . ." Then Tony stopped short in his speech and looked at the bed. Brenda had turned on her face and only the top of her head appeared above the sheets.
>
> "Oh God," she said into her pillows, "What have I done?"
>
> "I say, am I being pompous again?"
>
> She turned sideways so that her nose and one eye emerged. "Oh, no, darling, not *pompous*. You wouldn't know how." (19)

Not pompous, but antiquated. Tony is charming and 'amusing' (128) and when Brenda teases him about 'posing as an upright God-fearing gentleman of the old school' (36) he sees the joke – which doesn't at all diminish the pleasure he takes in his weekly routine of unbelieving but ceremonious attendance at Sunday services, followed by the ritual selection of a buttonhole in the greenhouse, and a 'solemn' glass of sherry in the library (35). He recognizes Brenda's boredom with their life in the country, but doesn't imagine it's possible for them to live in any other way.

Yet Hetton represents an attempt to live in a manner that Tony's historical moment will not allow. As Brenda's awful brother, Reggie St Cloud, argues, "There's a lot in what these Labour fellows say, you know. Big houses are a thing of the past in England I'm afraid." Reggie has sold his own family's estate, but one's laughter at the offhandedness with which he describes it as a "nasty wrench at the time of course, old association and everything like that" (206), merely discredits the speaker and not the point he makes. Forster's characters in *A Room with a View* (1908) consider thirty acres enough for a place in the country. By the 1930s, Orwell argues, the rentier-professional classes of which Waugh was a member were ceasing to have any relationship at all with the soil;[37] old Mr Plant in Waugh's splendid, war-interrupted fragment, *Work Suspended* (1942), even calls himself a member of the 'landless, moneyless, educated gentry'.[38] Waugh's achievement in *A Handful of Dust* is to describe, as it begins to happen, the process through which the world on which Hetton's values were based comes at last to die. Yet caught in the space between the last disease and the death-rattle Waugh does not yet have to write the elegies for architecture that both he and his friend John Betjeman produced after the Second World War.

Waugh affirms the value of the ideal Tony tries to live by, of his traditional conception of what it means to be a gentleman and a landlord. But he nevertheless insists on the madness of trying to maintain that ideal in the modern world, with an irony that checks the novel's romanticism, and keeps it from becoming sanctimonious about Tony's "madly feudal" attempt to live as his ancestors had. Instead, Waugh takes as his theme the impotence of the past to sustain one in the present. Modernity catches Tony up short. Neither Hetton's values nor its broad acres can keep him from being what Lewis calls 'cannon-fodder', one of 'those to whom things are done'. They cannot prevent Brenda from fleeing the *ennui* Hetton makes her feel for the shelter of an affair with John Beaver, the boorish son of an interior decorator. And yet Waugh prevents one from blaming her, this Nina Blount with a husband and child, however much one loathes and condemns her. For nothing in Brenda's world has suggested that adultery might be anything more than inconvenient if discovered. She finds her infidelity accepted as a matter of course – as an inevitability – by everyone except the man it most affects. Brenda's emotions are entirely social, those of the world and not the soul. She understands boredom, embarrassment, and even shame, but remains absolutely unaware that there is such a thing as suffering. Nothing has prepared her for Tony's obstinate pain, which she and her friends can only see, in social terms, as a "too monstrous" (210) affront to good taste.

Yet Tony's problems aren't caused by Brenda's actions alone. Hetton fails on its own terms as well, and not just in its inability to prevent Brenda's adultery. Nothing about Hetton, nothing in that world of 'cream and dappled unicorns', can prepare Tony for the 'Hard Cheese' (84) of his wife's infidelity, or more importantly, for their son John Andrew's death out fox-hunting. Hetton cannot provide the solace in extremity Tony needs, gives him only a childhood card game of 'Animal Snap' with which to pass the hours between the boy's death and Brenda's arrival from London. Tony can only react to his son's death with an inhuman self-control, a solicitiousness for how "awful" (147) the situation must be for everyone else: for the girl whose shying horse caused the accident; for his friend Jock Grant-Menzies, who goes to London to break the news to Brenda; for Brenda herself. For his attempt to live up to his sense of the duty and self-sacrifice Hetton's values require keeps him, as the novel's comic style keeps Waugh himself, from going beyond the stock and stoically wooden responses to death that are all his gentleman's education has provided.

Waugh's handling of that death's aftermath is as powerful and delicate as anything he ever wrote. Jock finds Brenda closeted with a fashionable fortune teller, talking about her lover:

> "What is it, Jock? Tell me quickly, I'm scared. It's nothing awful, is it."
> "I'm afraid it is. There's been a very serious accident."
> "John?"
> "Yes."
> "Dead?"
> He nodded.
> She sat down on a hard little Empire chair against the wall, perfectly still with her hands folded in her lap, like a small, well-brought up child introduced into a room full of grown-ups. She

said, "Tell me what happened. Why do you know about it first?"

"I've been down at Hetton since the week-end."

"Hetton?"

"Don't you remember? John was going hunting today."

She frowned, not at once taking in what he was saying. "John . . . John Andrew . . . I . . . Oh thank God . . ." Then she burst into tears.   (161–2)

Waugh never wrote a better scene; one feels here the combination of psychological subtlety and firm judgement that Lewis's 'Great With-Out' can convey. Waugh customarily uses that technique to describe a character whose subjective life has withered. Here, however, he shifts its emphasis to describe a situation in which Brenda's consciousness is absolutely irrelevant to one's judgement of her. One knows precisely why Brenda says what she does here, and no amount of internal explanation, of dramatized consciousness, could add to that knowledge. What it could affect, however, is the categorical judgement Waugh wants his readers to make of her, whatever her psychological confusion may be. Some things, his objective description of her insists, must remain unforgivable, and so he uses her "Oh thank God" to place Brenda completely beyond the pale of one's sympathy.

Brenda's words reveal Waugh's conception of the poverty of the modern world. Yet Tony can only keep Hetton by acceding to that world, can keep it only by sacrificing his idealized conception of it. He decides to let Brenda divorce him to marry Beaver, and is even willing, after arranging the customary faked evidence of a dirty weekend in Brighton, to be the defendant himself. Then Beaver insists that Brenda ask for a settlement whose payment would force Tony to sell Hetton. Tony refuses. He stops what in *Men at Arms* (1952) Waugh makes Virginia Crouchback calls this "chivalrous nonsense . . . of playing the guilty party" (16) and decides to "divorce Brenda without settlements of any kind" (210). Tony can preserve either the house, or the refuge, but not both, for that accession to modernity, however necessary, also betrays the ideal on which he believes Hetton is founded. It thrusts him from Hetton's inadequate protection against the inhumanity of Brenda's modern world into that inhumanity itself. (His successors there, his cousins the Richard Lasts, choose the house over the refuge, and turn the stable area into a profitable silver fox farm.) There is for Tony no possibility of an accommodation between the soul and the world. Nothing can make that modernity more bearable, not even the execution of his long-postponed and carefully meditated plan to add more bathrooms.

He decides to travel instead, to lose himself in movement. And so, in the South American chapters that conclude the novel, Tony begins a Lukacsian search for a fabled city, a citadel, an Eldorado to replace the sullied Hetton:

> He had a clear picture of it in his mind. It was Gothic in character, all vanes and pinnacles, gargoyles, battlements, groins and tracery, pavilions and terraces, a transfigured Hetton, pennons and banners floating on the sweet breeze, everything luminous and translucent; a coral citadel crowning a green hill-top sown with heraldic and fabulous animals and symmetrical, dispropor- tionate blossom.   (222)

Tony's vision of the City holds out the promise that life can be noble and fine, that people need not be things. It affords an emotional richness that serves as an antidote to the waste land of England, a waste land that Waugh suggests, in part, through the very modern Mrs Beaver's profession. John's mother stands for an age in which social life is shaped not by taste and tradition but by an interior decorator's decisions about what ought to be fashion- able, like the drawing room at Hetton she plans to re-do for Brenda in white chromium plating.

And yet the richness that Tony seeks remains illusory. *A Handful of Dust* fulfils the classic pattern of the novel as a genre in its account, like that of *Père Goriot* or *Great Expectations*, of the failure of its protagonist's search for authentic values among what Trilling calls 'the inferior objects of the social world'. Down with fever in South America, Tony calls out, in a hallucinatory delirium surely modelled on the 'Circe' section of *Ulysses*, that "There is no City. Mrs. Beaver has covered it with chromium plating and converted it into flats." (288) There is no City, not because of modernity alone, but because that 'Gothic' dream remains inadequate to Tony's experience. It had 'come to grief' (209) in England but it had given him no terms for that grief, and his pursuit of into the South American jungle leads him into the living damnation Waugh describes in the novel's conclusion, reading Dickens aloud to his illiterate half-caste captor for the rest of his life.

In describing Tony's 'coral citadel' Waugh's language grows

unironically rich, and the fullness of his prose clashes with the clipped perfection of his earlier work, which had so effectively taught one to suspect such nobility. In reading that description, however, one senses that Waugh wants Tony's vision to be adequate. The novel attempts to enact belief in an ordered and stable society through the power of art alone – tests the limits not just of Tony's private religion but of Waugh's own. *A Handful of Dust* disturbs because in writing it Waugh was searching for the same fabled City as his protagonist, and knew he had not found it. His classical insistence on the inadequacies of Tony's attempt to understand the present through a romantic conception of the past ensures that while the novel contains the religious impulse towards transcendence, it cannot offer the possibility of transcendence itself. One can say that Waugh's early novels describe a world without God, in that the comforts of religion, the assurance that men are more than things, are not available in them. The sermons the Reverend Tendril delivers at Hetton's church are imperialist tracts; after his son's death Tony says that "the last thing one wants to talk about at a time like this is religion" (158). And yet religion is precisely what fiction's essential metonymy makes one expect to find in the novel after John Andrew's death – an expectation that Waugh defeats. Religion in this novel is like the interior life in *Vile Bodies*. It has a thwarted presence, of which one is made aware only by its absence; provides a point of contrast, however inaccessible, to the spiritual waste land of which the novel's landscape actually consists. *A Handful of Dust* takes place in a world like the one I. A. Richards described in *Science and Poetry*, one marked by 'a sense of desolation, of uncertainty, of futility, of the groundlessness of aspirations, of the vanity of endeavour, and a thirst for a life-giving water which seems suddenly to have failed'.[39] But Richards argues that one can, that one must, get used to such a world, and praises Eliot's *The Waste Land*, from which Waugh takes the novel's title, for making order out of a world without belief, in such a way that the reader does not feel that lack to be an absence. Yet Waugh could not save himself through style alone, as Eliot could. His style lay itself at the heart of his 'desolation', and so in reading *A Handful of Dust* one feels that absence above all. In his quest for the City Tony attempts to find the comforts of religion in secular form. But it is Waugh's attempt as well, and those comforts remain as unavailable to the readers of this merciless novel as they are to its characters.

In its sense of a spiritual emergency without a solution, of a fear that one cannot grasp and conquer because it is located in an evanescent handful of dust, the novel is homologous to England's political emergency of the 1930s. In its description of the changing basis of English life it fulfils what Lukacs describes as the genre's essential aim, the totalizing 'representation of the way society moves', that Eagleton claims the writers of Waugh's generation could not achieve. *A Handful of Dust* stands as Waugh's greatest achievement. Yet in writing it he must have felt once again the cost of a comic vision, must have felt comedy's nihilistic power not just to liberate one from orthodoxy but to destroy belief as well. *A Handful of Dust*, like *Vile Bodies*, holds nothing sacred, and so drains all sustenance from the secular terms in which Waugh couches his vision of a romantic past and a dehumanized present. It would be ten years before Waugh found a way to keep from laughing, however grimly, at Tony's vision of that 'coral citadel', coupling it in *Brideshead Revisited* (1944) to a Catholicism that exempted it from his sense of the ridiculous. Yet why assume that the present is dehumanized and the past was not? Why doubt just the terms of a romantic vision and not that vision itself?

IV

Waugh's first marriage was annulled in 1936 and he married Laura Herbert the next year. In 1938 he published *Scoop*, his most good-natured novel, which contains the mechanism of his early novels, but without their sense of animated despair. Waugh had mastered a formula and could play upon it with a too-perfect ease, a situation addressed by the mystery novelist John Plant in his war-interrupted fragment, *Work Suspended* (1942). "It seems to me that I am in danger of becoming mechanical", he tells his publisher, "turning out year after year the kind of book I know I can write well; I feel I have got as good as I ever can be at this particular sort of writing. I need new worlds to conquer" (132). The novel's characters may be mechanisms; the novelist should not be. But while both *Work Suspended*'s first-person narration, and its use of what Cyril Connolly in *Enemies of Promise* called 'a reasoned extravagance'[40] of prose, did make a substantial gesture towards those new worlds, Waugh's concentration on it was shattered by the start of the war in 1939. His next book, *Put Out More Flags*, returned to his old world and even his old characters for a self-consciously wistful farewell. The novel is in places as farcical as *Decline and Fall*, but Waugh's overall frustration· with its world seems obvious. One senses that he would rather be working on something else, would rather be exploring the possibilities suggested by Tony Last's situation, which in *Put Out More Flags* he embodies in the aesthete army officer, Cedric Lyne.

Late in the novel Cedric recalls the way he met his wife Angela, who has since become Basil Seal's mistress:

> Cedric was accomplished; he was a beautiful horseman but hated the rigours of fox-hunting; he was a very fine shot and . . . that formed a single tenuous bond with his brother officers . . . Angela's father had a celebrated shoot in Norfolk; he had also, Cedric was told, a collection of French impressionists. Thither that autumn ten years ago Cedric had gone and had found the pictures too obvious and the birds too tame and the party tedious beyond belief, except for Angela, past her debutante days, aloof now and living in a cool and mysterious solitude of her own creation . . . quite suddenly, she had accepted Cedric as being like herself a stranger in these parts, as being, unlike herself, full of understanding of another more splendid, attainable world outside . . .
>
> And this was the way they had gone. Cedric stood by the spring, enshrined, now, in a little temple. The architrave was covered with stalactites, the dome was set with real shells and the clear water bubbled out from the feet of a Triton. Cedric and Angela had bought this temple on their honeymoon at a deserted villa in the hills behind Naples.
>
> Below in the hillside lay the cave which Cedric had bought the summer that Angela had refused to come with him to Salzburg; the summer when she met Basil. The lonely and humiliating years after that summer each had its own monument.
>
> (215–17)

Waugh is as skilful as Graham Greene at making his characters' sadness colour a description of the physical world; makes those temples an objectification of Cedric's emotional state, just as his style had embodied Tony Last's loneliness in the superficially similar passage I quoted earlier. Yet there is an enormous difference between the sad cadences of this passage and Waugh's casual,

offhand tone in *A Handful of Dust*. Tony's emptiness and confusion
had in part been dictated by Waugh's sense of the limitations of
his own style – by his technique, that means 'of evading the
personally impossible'. Waugh could not allow one the comfort of
knowing Tony's thoughts because he didn't quite trust himself
with them. He could not in 1934 allow any character the dignity of
fine emotion because he both did not believe and yet wanted badly
to believe in such dignity, and was consequently afraid of losing
his controlling irony. Writing *A Handful of Dust* nevertheless made
this description of Cedric's loneliness possible. Hetton's failure
taught Waugh the limitations of the sterile aestheticism represented
by Cedric's collection of pagan tombs and temples, so that while
he sympathizes with Cedric's situation as a cuckolded husband,
he feels no temptation to exalt him. The result is a distanced but
unironic and poignant assent to the validity of Cedric's feelings,
yet one so aware of the character's limitations as to be untinged
by sentimentality.

Yet this passage's richness makes one wonder how Waugh might
write if he lost that distance. It points, that is, to *Brideshead Revisited*,
and in particular to such passages as the narrator Charles Ryder's
description of his first sexual encounter with Lady Julia Flyte
Mottram:

> So at sunset I took formal possession of her as her lover. It
> was no time for the sweets of luxury; they would come, in their
> season, with the swallow and the lime-flowers. Now on the
> rough water, as I was made free of her narrow loins and, it
> seemed now, in assuaging that fierce appetite, cast a burden
> which I had borne all my life, toiled under, not knowing its
> nature – now, while the waves still broke and thundered on the
> prow, the act of possession was a symbol, a rite of ancient origin
> and solemn meaning.   (261)

Waugh said in his introduction to the novel's revised edition (1960)
that he wrote the novel during:

> . . . a bleak period of present privation and threatening disaster
> . . . and in consequence the book is infused with a kind of
> gluttony, for food and wine, for the splendours of the recent
> past, and for rhetorical and ornamental language.[41]

But in his reworking of the seduction passage I've quoted above, Waugh could only change Julia from an exalted sexual object into an exalted piece of real estate, 'a property I would enjoy and develop at leisure'.[42] For what he described in 1960 as the novel's 'grosser passages', are nevertheless 'essential to it', however 'distasteful' he finds them;[43] essential because, as Waugh's comments suggest, the novel is not, in Bergonzi's words the 'sober chronicle of grace and adultery and aristocratic folly' that its traditionally realistic surface suggests, but 'an almost uncontrolled fantasy'.[44]

In 1939 Waugh had joined the Royal Marines as a lieutenant and quickly fell in love with the army, finding in regimental life a sense of fellowship he had never before known and never would again. He was promoted captain in 1940, exchanged into a commando unit, and saw combat during the British evacuation of Crete in 1941. Yet despite the physical courage his superior officers acknowledged he displayed, the capricious sensibility on which Waugh's comedy depended made him such an atrocious regimental officer that they feared his own men would kill him. When his unit sailed for North Africa in 1943 he was left behind, shunted from one training course to another because nobody could find anything else for him to do. The experience shattered him, making him feel as unwanted as had his first wife's adultery.

Waugh fell out of love with the army and into a gloom for which *Brideshead Revisited*'s romantic 'gluttony' provided an antidote. He wrote the novel in 1944, during a long leave granted because it was the easiest way to get rid of him. It is his longest novel, a book in which he courts ambition as relentlessly as he had avoided it in *Decline and Fall*, and courts it finally without success. *Brideshead Revisited* contains many marvellous scenes and characters. One remembers in particular the hundred-page sequence with which it opens, describing Ryder's life at an Oxford in whose

. . . spacious and quiet streets men walked and spoke as they had done in Newman's day; her autumnal mists, her grey springtime, and the rare glory of her summer days – such as that day – when the chestnut was in flower and the bells rang out high and clear over her gables and cupolas, exhaled the soft vapours of a thousand years of learning. It was this cloistral hush which gave our laughter its resonance . . .   (21)

One accepts this deliberately romantic vision, accepts the purple

prose of youth because youth has, after all, to end. So long as
Brideshead Revisited sticks to the charm of youth, to the novelty of
"a motorcar and a basket of strawberries and a bottle of Chateau
Peyraguey" (23), it works; even Ryder's undergraduate homosexuality maintains a convincing and celebratory innocence. The novel's
failure lies, rather, in Waugh's attempt to extend that vision to
adult life, as he does in describing Ryder 'made free', in his mid-
thirties, of Julia's 'narrow loins'. But if *Brideshead Revisited* is not
Waugh's best novel, it is nevertheless the most crucial book in his
development. It is the novel toward which his early work leads
and on which his later books depend, and so a detailed account of
his intentions in it remains a necessity.

Brideshead Revisited breaks with Waugh's earlier work in its
attempt, as he wrote in his 1946 essay, 'Fan-Fare', 'to represent
man more fully, which, to me, means only one thing, man in his
relation to God'. Waugh argues that:

> . . . you can only leave God out by making your characters pure
> abstractions. Countless admirable writers, perhaps some of the
> best in the world, succeed in this. Henry James was the last of
> them. The failure of modern novelists since and including James
> Joyce is one of presumption and exorbitance. They are not
> content with the artificial figures which hitherto passed so
> gracefully as men and women. They try to represent the whole
> human mind and soul and yet omit its determining character –
> that of being God's creature with a defined purpose.[45]

A comedy that treats people as things cannot pretend to 'represent
the whole human mind and soul', and so Waugh had in his early
novels been 'content' with those 'artificial figures', with characters
who only 'passed . . . as men and women'. But Waugh did not
remain 'content' with them and his descriptions of Julia's husband
Rex Mottram suggests why. Rex, Julia says, isn't "a complete
human being at all . . . [but] a tiny bit of a man pretending he [is]
whole" (200). Rex isn't, she tells Ryder, "a real person at all . . .
He couldn't imagine why it hurt me to find, two months after we
came back to London from our honeymoon, that he was still
keeping up with [his old mistress] Brenda Champion." (257) Like
Brenda Last, Rex lacks the capacity for reflection, for the interior
life that one must possess to understand another's pain, because
he himself "isn't a real person" but a thing masquerading as one;

as Paul Pennyfeather had become in joining, however briefly, the
world of Margot Metroland. Yet Waugh predicates Rex's failure to
be a 'real person' upon what the Catholic Julia discovers when Rex
receives instruction in the catechism before their wedding: that he
is entirely without the sense that man has a soul, a relation to
God. As Greene has to make his characters believe in something
outside themselves before they can believe in themselves, so
Waugh needs to give his characters an awareness of the religious
life before they can seem 'real' – something more than 'furniture',
not only to each other but to Waugh himself.

The use of religion allowed Waugh to create a sense of human
possibility, embodied in the richness of his prose, that is otherwise
absent from his world. It makes his characters aware of the soul's
existence and so redeems their vile bodies, and in doing so gives
his fiction a sense of the purpose and value of individual experience
that the social conditions of his period, as well as his own style,
had destroyed. Perhaps, given the extremity of the war's 'present
privation and threatening disaster', Waugh had to believe in that
sense, just as Woolf had to believe in the possibility of her own
mind's free play. What, however, does it mean for a character in a
novel to have a soul? Waugh tries to give *Brideshead Revisited*'s
characters souls in the religious sense of the word, taking their
spiritual lives both within and without the Catholic Church as the
novel's subject. But how can a novelist persuade his readers that
those spiritual lives exist? I've already mentioned Waugh's review
of Powell's *The Kindly Ones*, in which he wrote that 'we know
much more about [Powell's] characters' appearance than their
souls'.[46] Religion in Powell's work, I've argued, is tellingly conspi-
cuous by its absence. Yet Waugh's opposition of 'appearance' to
'soul' also suggests an opposition between the objective world and
subjective experience – suggests that Waugh, like Lukacs, equates
the soul and the interior life. Waugh's treatment of Rex does
suggest that to him an awareness of the soul in a religious sense is
a prerequisite for the existence of an interior life. Yet in writing it
is surely the other way around. A novelist can only persuade a
reader that his characters have souls by making that reader believe
in those characters' interior lives, and so in *Brideshead Revisited*
Waugh presents his characters' souls not through an account of
their religious beliefs but through the conventions of first-person
narration.

First-person narration has in Waugh's generation a greater

importance than for writers of earlier generations. Because such narration is by definition the product of an individual and not an omniscient voice; because it contains an awareness that, as Ryder notes, the narrator 'can only say' (235) how events looked to him, it provides an implicit acknowledgement of the way in which Woolf's leaning tower has made one unable to see life steadily and see it whole. This is especially true with Powell's *A Dance to the Music of Time*. More importantly, it allows the novelist to present the interior life without requiring him to depend upon either the Victorians' sense of an accommodation between the soul and the world, or the modernists' attempt to transcend it. By the time he wrote *Brideshead Revisited* Waugh had already, with *Work Suspended*, made an experiment in the first-person. If his characters in that fragment are bodies, it's only because the conventions of the first person require the narrator to view them from outside, which he does with a detached but tolerant amusement at their outward behaviour. Yet such a narrator's necessary revelation of his own interior life tacitly asserts, as Powell does in the *Dance*, that the novel's other characters have such a life as well, that men are not things. By accepting that convention, then, Waugh steps in literary if not theological terms around the dilemma of *Vile Bodies*. He gives his characters 'souls'. In creating the possibility of the interior life he creates the possibility of the spiritual life as well, of describing 'man in his relation to God', through a simple account of his characters' religious opinions.

Brideshead Revisited's stated theme is 'the operation of divine grace upon a group of diverse but closely connected people'.[47] But in examining that theme the novel makes a joint appeal to both a religious and an aristocratic tradition, fusing Catholicism with Tony Last's vision of a 'coral citadel', and making them sit together in judgement on the present. The crucial question to ask of the book, then, is that of the connection between the two. The novel opens in the middle stages of the Second World War. Ryder's army unit has moved into a new camp built in the grounds of Brideshead Castle, the ancestral home of the Catholic Marquess of Marchmain, with whose family, the Flytes, Ryder's pre-war life has been bound. As morning breaks on his first day in the new bivouac, Ryder, a fashionable painter of country houses, recalls his long involvement with the family, in a flashback that fills all but the novel's last few pages. There are, in effect, two Charles Ryders, the narrator and the character. Ryder the character has, as Martin Green points out,[48] to make a choice between two temptations: between the Flyte's easy, comfortable, English charm, and the dangerous promise of art proffered by his Oxford contemporary, the dandy-aesthete Anthony Blanche. But Ryder hasn't the strength of will that Blanche's way demands, and he succumbs to the Flytes' charm, even though he knows it can only harm his art. He falls in love with the family, not with their faith but with their beauty and wealth and rank; and in fact has affairs with both Sebastian, the Marquess's second son, and Sebastian's sister Julia. Yet both he and Blanche miss what Waugh suggests is the most important thing about the Flytes – that they are Roman Catholics. Ryder the narrator does not make that mistake. His attitude toward the family is coloured not just by his romantic memory of their splendour, but by Waugh's implication that after his relations with both Sebastian and Julia have been frustrated by their religion, Ryder has himself converted to it. And that conversion makes him see Brideshead Castle, the seat of the Flyte's earthly splendour, as but a type of the City of God, a Hetton irradiated with divine grace.[49]

Or so the novel would have it. Yet Ryder identifies Catholicism almost entirely with families like Lady Marchmain's, whose:

. . . family history was typical of the Catholic squires of England; from Elizabeth's reign until Victoria's they lived sequestered lives among their tenantry and kinsmen, sending their sons to school abroad; often marrying there – inter-marrying, if not, with a score of families like themselves, debarred from all preferment; and learning, in those lost generations, lessons which could still be read in the lives of the last three men of the house . . . men who were, in all the full flood of academic and athletic success, of popularity and the promise of great rewards ahead, seen somehow as set apart from their fellows, garlanded victims, devoted to the sacrifice. These men must die to make a world for Hooper; they were the aborigines, vermin by right of law, to be shot off at leisure so that things might be safe for the travelling salesman, with his polygonal pince-nez, his fat wet handshake, his grinning dentures. (139)

In *Work Suspended* Waugh had begun to find a way, deeply informed by a sense of the past, to criticize the present without becoming contemptuous of it. There he describes the death in an car accident of the narrator's father, the last Victorian narrative painter, who had so refused to acknowledge such a modern monstrosity as the motor car that he took no pains to avoid being run over by one. The salesman who drove the car argues that "no one can blame it on me" (139), and he's right. No blame attaches to anyone, neither to the painter who cannot be bothered to get out of the way of the present, nor to the salesman who mows down the past. Like the static and dynamic in *Decline and Fall*, both are essential; both are intractable; the crash is inevitable. The narrator's calm meditation on that inevitability offered a solution to Waugh's dilemma in *A Handful of Dust* – gave him the chance to create that longed-for 'point completely at rest' through the power of style alone.

But Waugh's experiences in the army made him hate his personal present in a way that he extended to modern society as a whole. The Hooper for whom Lady Marchmain's brothers presumably died, a subaltern in Ryder's company, is the product of state schools where 'The history they taught him had had few battles in it, but instead, a profusion of details about humane legislation and recent industrial change.' (9) – a type of the Common Man whom Ryder sets against those three dead heroes, victims of the Great War. What, however, is the necessary connection between these 'aborigines', Catholicism, their deaths in the Great War, and the rise of the travelling salesman? Waugh implies that these men died because they were Catholics, that a family history of sequestered lives and marriages abroad made them more expendable than a Protestant. Yet Waugh's vision of these men as 'garlanded victims' has nothing to do with religion as such. It is simply a heightened version of the standard post-Great War Rupert Brooke, Fine-Flower-of-the-Nation, Lost Generation mythology that I discussed in my chapter on Powell.[50] The memorial volume in which Lady Marchmain celebrates her brothers' memory resembles nothing so much as the *Pages from a Family Journal* in which Lady Desborough commemorated the deaths of her two Protestant sons.[51] And one would in any case hesitate to describe their deaths as a sacrifice the modern world required to make things 'safe for the travelling salesman', any more than it required the innumerable deaths of the salesmen and clerks and labourers and servants whom they led out of the trenches.

Waugh's lament here isn't so much for the extinction of an old recusant family as for the social order he has identified with them; a lament for the end of the old English agricultural and aristocratic order, for Hetton. Because Waugh wishes to defend that society, wishes to preserve the refuge the thought of it affords, he exempts the novel's Catholic characters from any sustained criticism. In consequence, he never fully examines the subject on which the novel seems to depend: the connection between Sebastian's alcoholism and his parents' sundered marriage. It is a subject perfectly suited to the cold eye with which Ryder dissects Rex Mottram, or even his own wife Celia, but his account of it is vague. Eagleton argues that this vagueness comes from the fact that 'To suggest that the Marchmain family has literally reduced its younger son to a burnt-out alcoholic wreck would interfere somewhat with that nostalgic apologia for English ancestral seats which it is *Brideshead*'s declared purpose to launch';[52] and while one recognizes the polemical overstatement in his words one nevertheless admits their justice.

Or does the novel depend on that subject? Eagleton claims that Sebastian is surely the novel's hero, and certainly its opening chapters, in which Ryder is most concerned with him, are by far the book's most successful. Yet in the novel's second half Ryder's attention turns abruptly to Julia, where it remains until the end of the novel, when she decides that even though she's not been a good Catholic, she can't divorce Rex to marry him, because divorce would mean shutting herself 'out from His mercy . . . [by setting] up a rival good to God's' (340). And Ryder, passive as ever, lets her pass out of his life with the suggestion that she has been "only a forerunner" (303) for something else, as he claims his love for Sebastian was a forerunner for his love for her. But for whom or what? Ryder's conversion suggests that she could only have been a forerunner for God Himself, that his long involvement with the Flytes has been but a way to bring him into the Roman Catholic Church. His baptism pays for their pain. Perhaps in some divine economy it does. But it doesn't here, first because Ryder isn't self-absorbed enough to regard the people he loves as but means to an end, and so can't persuade us to look at them that way either; and second, because his actual conversion takes place offstage and so seems extraneous to the events he describes, however much it proceeds from them.

Ryder doesn't, that is, quite manage to fill the novel that is, inevitably, about him. That structural confusion ensures that what we most remember about *Brideshead Revisited* are not its legitimate attractions – Ryder's evocation of the majestic and languid sensuality of late adolescence, or its many pages of sharp comedy, or even its final appeal to the 'small red flame' (351) of faith – but by its odd fusion of Debrett and divinity. While the novel corrects Ryder's lack of religion, it does not correct either his snobbery or his sentimentality. Instead Waugh uses them to establish a link between the Church and the cult of knights and unicorns. Ryder's new Catholicism doesn't make him revise his romantic estimation of the Flytes, but merely reinforces it, sanctifying his empurpled sense of the fine promise of Julia's 'narrow loins'. And Ryder's mistake is Waugh's as well. The novel's first-person narration allows him to suspend the suspicion of orthodoxy that had earlier checked and controlled his broad streak of sentimentality, in favour of a direct presentation of a personal myth of the past. Waugh's imagination works best, however, when he turns it against an ideal; is better at undercutting a position than at affirming one. *Brideshead Revisited*'s most memorable passage is, in fact, the denunciation of Hooper's world I quoted above – but its sentiments are hardly ones that the reader can endorse. Only on the last page does Waugh make Ryder acknowledge that the present still has both meaning and value, that the sanctuary flame at Brideshead burns 'anew among the old stones', so that the 'garlanded victims' are not 'the last word' (351). But that admission comes too late to save the novel; it is just enough to keep one from making a case for Ryder as an unreliable narrator as well as an unreliable character.

In *The End of the Battle*, the conclusion of the war trilogy whose one-volume 1965 redaction he called *Sword of Honour*, Waugh makes Guy Crouchback summon a vision of the Church's indifference to the modern world:

> Guy took his leave and was at Matchet when Italy surrendered
> . . .
>
> "That looks like the end of the Piedmontese usurpation," he said to his father. "What a mistake the Lateran Treaty was. It seemed masterly at the time – how long? Fifteen years ago? What are fifteen years in the history of Rome? How much better it would have been if the Popes had sat it out and then emerged saying, 'What was all that? *Risorgimento*? Garibaldi? Cavour? The house of Savoy? Mussolini? Just some hooligans from out of town causing a disturbance . . .' That's what the Pope ought to be saying today." (5–6)

The Church provides a refuge for a character whose dissatisfaction parallels Waugh's own at the time he wrote *Brideshead Revisited*: unwanted, refused employment by his superior officers, rejected by the army on whose fellowship and sense of tradition he had depended. All Guy has left is his personal honour and a romantic vision of history. But his old father says, " . . . you're really making the most terrible nonsense, you know. That isn't at all what the Church is like. It isn't what she's *for*." (6)

Mr Crouchback's comment provides the best criticism of *Brideshead Revisited* imaginable. It is precisely what Waugh did not know while writing the novel: that the Church is not intended to 'strike attitudes and stand on its dignity' (8), but to save souls. In coupling religion to his romantic vision of the City Waugh succumbs completely to the charm of a Gothic dream he had found inadequate in *A Handful of Dust*. He does not pause to ask whether his romanticism is an essential part of his faith, does not question the value of his search for a time of innocence before the desolation of the present. Waugh's identification of Catholicism with a dying aristocratic tradition means that for him Catholicism can only deal with the modern world by rejecting it. O'Brien writes that 'There was once an Irish priest who refused to pray for the conversion of England, and Mr Waugh, I fear, might refuse to pray for the conversion of Hooper.'[53] Waugh's private religion requires that Hooper be a thing with 'grinning dentures', for if he admitted that the Church could speak to Hooper he would have to ask if the present is any more contemptible than any other period. But one refuses to accept the thingness of Hooper in a novel whose subject is 'the operation of divine grace', and *Brideshead Revisited*'s great flaw is that for all its concern with faith and grace, it finally fails to take its Catholicism seriously.

Edmund Wilson predicted that the novel's 'gluttony' would make it a bestseller, and so it did.[54] Its success brought Waugh to Hollywood to discuss the possibility of filming it. No movie came of the trip, but the novella *The Loved One* (1948) did, the only one of his books sufficiently directed against a specific target – Southern California's version of what Greene calls the 'sinless graceless chromium world' – to fit the generic requirements of satire. Waugh's prose carries an *ex cathedra* tone whose pronouncements one enjoys, but there is nevertheless a touch of the straw dog about his target, and *The Loved One* is extraneous to an assessment of his later career. For as *Brideshead Revisited*'s failures suggest, the central issue in that assessment is not the role that Catholicism plays in his novels, but the process through which Waugh clears away what O'Brien calls his 'bulky memorials . . . to other gods'[55] in order to let it play any role at all. Each of Waugh's major novels attempts to correct the inadequacies of its predecessors. As *A Handful of Dust* made *Brideshead Revisited* necessary, so that novel's flawed vision of the Church required its own correction in *Sword of Honour*, in ways that Mr Crouchback's reproof of his son suggests.

But it is not until its last volume that the trilogy finally becomes an attack on the ethos of *Brideshead Revisited*, and indeed its first two volumes, *Men at Arms* and *Officers and Gentlemen* seem like nothing so much as an affirmation and extension of that ethos. After the publication of *Officers and Gentlemen*, in fact, Waugh announced that he had completed his intentions in the space of two volumes, and would not proceed with his plans to write a third. Only after the bout of hallucinations he described in *The Ordeal of Gilbert Pinfold* did he change his mind and write *The End of the Battle* (1961), a novel that not only completed his original design but qualified and undercut the first two volumes' attitude toward Guy Crouchback and his experience.

Sword of Honour is rich in incident and atmosphere: rich in its recreation of the ritual exuberance of the officer's mess, the chaos of battle, and army red tape; in its description of commando training with well-born daredevils in the Highlands, and bombings in London, and embassy life in Egypt; in Waugh's gallery of minor characters, from Guy Crouchback's Uncle Peregrine, 'a bore of international repute' (*Men at Arms*, 12), to his commanding officer, Brigadier Ritchie-Hook, who calls warfare the art of "biffing" (*Men at Arms*, 157); rich above all in Waugh's handling of the comedy of military life. The army is made for laughter. Combat fulfils the promise – or the threat – latent in Waugh's comedy: that people are just things, no more than bodies fit to spin around a wheel, to be blown around and blown up and used up. In consequence, combat frees Waugh from having to explore the implications of his comedy himself, and so his description of the 'knockabout farce' of military training maintains an oddly liberating innocence that makes some sequences as blithe and as carefree as anything in *Decline and Fall*.

But not even Guy's brother-officer, the marvellous Apthorpe of *Men at Arms*, always obsessed with his private thunderbox, calls for as much commentary as Waugh's attempt to see his Catholicism steadily. One turns, therefore, from Waugh's comedy to a consideration of *Sword of Honour*'s central theme, the vanity of the belief that perfect harmony can be found in any way except through God. Guy comes from an old Catholic family, like Lady Marchmain's, one that has held the same manor in unbroken male succession since the time of Henry I. In his mid-thirties when *Men at Arms* begins, Guy lives in Italy after the end of his marriage to the subsequently much-wedded Virginia Troy, 'a bright, fashionable girl' (13), but not a Catholic. As war looms Guy leaves Italy to join the army, a vision of knights and unicorns before him, dedicating himself to battle before he goes on the sword of an English crusader buried in the local church. Guy believes that after a decade of political confusion the Russo-German alliance has put 'the enemy plain in view, huge and hateful, all disguise cast off. It was the Modern Age in arms', embodied in both fascism's and communism's irreligion (7–8).

Guy hates modernity and so welcomes a war that allows him to fight it. Yet as the novel progresses he finds himself increasingly unable to make that fight. At the end of *Officers and Gentlemen* he learns simultaneously about the desertion of his comrade Ivor Claire, whom he has earlier considered an embodiment of the "fine flower of the Nation" (132), and of Russia's entrance into the war on the British side:

> It was just such a sunny, breezy Mediterranean day two years before when he read of the Russo-German alliance, when a decade of shame seemed to be ending in light and reason, when the Enemy was plain in view . . .
>
> Now that hallucination was dissolving . . . and he was back after less than two years' pilgrimage in a Holy Land of illusion, in the old ambiguous world, where priests were spies and gallant friends proved traitors and his country was led blundering into dishonour.   (325)

Guy had imagined that the world had resolved itself into simplicity. And yet England too now stands revealed as part of the Modern Age Guy hates – and so he burns the evidence that could incriminate Ivor Claire. There seems no point in making a stand for justice in such a world, a world in which, as Guy tells his father at the start of *The End of the Battle*, it doesn't seem to matter much who wins. Only personal honour remains.

But Guy's father rebukes him. "You mustn't sulk" (8), he writes, and yet sulking is precisely what both Guy and Waugh had seemed to be doing at the end of *Officers and Gentlemen*. Waugh's decision to complete the trilogy radically alters the way in which one reads the first two volumes. By themselves they seem to affirm *Brideshead Revisited*'s position, to reject Hooper's world, but in the light of Mr Crouchback's words one must read that rejection ironically, as a sign of Guy's own limitations. Yet the trilogy's first two volumes do not quite support that irony. They may undercut Guy's belief that the war is a 'time of glory and dedication' (*Men at Arms*, 77), but they do so with a wistfulness, a melancholy regret that the world is not as simple as Guy believes it to be. Guy cannot imagine human guile, and cannot imagine that other people's advice isn't always good. When someone suggests that whiskey is a suitable gift for a man in hospital, he doesn't hesitate to bring Apthorpe the bottle that helps cause his death. In *Men at Arms* the Catholic antiquary Mr Goodall tells Guy that in the eyes of the Church he is still married to his ex-wife, Virginia, and can therefore sleep with her without sin. So Guy not only propositions her – that she minds not at all – but tells her his motive without bothering to consider that she might " . . . far rather be taken for a tart . . . You wet, smug, obscene, pompous, sexless lunatic pig" (178), than be the sexual object of a Jesuitical distinction. One senses the accuracy of Virginia's epithets, and yet Guy's naiveté attracts Waugh. He makes mistake after mistake, and yet never receives the full weight of Waugh's censure. Each of his mistakes does, admittedly, grow from someone else's suggestion, but Waugh never scrutinizes the deficiency in Guy's character that makes him so foolishly trusting, so open to other people's stupidity. For to Waugh it is not precisely a deficiency, and in reading the trilogy's first two volumes, one senses in his tone a certain petulant irritation with the world for being a more complicated place than either he or Guy had imagined it could be.

The last volume, does, however, force Guy to realize that one's personal honour is itself nothing more than vanity, that he too is part of the spectacle of the modern age in arms. Towards the end of the volume a Jewish refugee asks him:

"Is there any place that is free from evil? It is too simple to say that only the Nazis wanted war. These Communists wanted it to. It was the only way in which they could come to power.

Many of my people wanted it, to be revenged on the Germans, to hasten the creation of the national state. It seems to me there was a will to war, a death wish, everywhere. Even good men thought their private honour would be satisfied by war. They could assert their manhood by killing and being killed. They would accept hardships in recompense for having been selfish and lazy. Danger justifies privilege. I knew Italians – not very many perhaps – who felt this. Were there none in England?"

"God forgive me," said Guy, "I was one of them." (305)

Waugh isn't here occupied with the creation of the soul *per se*. He had achieved that in *Brideshead Revisited*, and even though Guy's interior life has a negligible presence in *Sword of Honour*, we do nevertheless credit him with having one. His concern lies, rather, in eliminating the myths that he had placed between that soul and its God. Guy's prayer for forgiveness makes *Sword of Honour* an ironic dissection of Waugh's Gothic dream. The trilogy comes round, like *A Handful of Dust*, to acknowledge the inadequacies of a romantic conception of life, to recognize that the modern world can neither be fought against nor excluded from one's life. Guy learns that he is not a 'garlanded victim' set off from Hooper's world, but a part of that world himself. *The End of the Battle* sustains an awareness of the individual's dual complicity in and impotence before the nightmare of modern history that stands as one of Waugh's most powerful and disturbing achievements. And that awareness seems all the more powerful for being expressed not through the dislocating, fragmented form with which most novelists have tried to capture that post-modernist sense of history, but through Waugh's tight and measured realism.

Bergonzi writes that 'with complete honesty [Waugh] accepted the collapse of the myth that had sustained a sizeable segment of his fiction'.[56] However regretfully, one makes what the English title of the trilogy's last volume calls an 'Unconditional Surrender' to the modern age. And if, Waugh implies, one's faith is genuine it remains in the absence of unicorns, strengthened, in fact, by the flight of temporal vanities. In a coda to the trilogy set in 1951, Guy's pompous brother-in-law, Box-Bender, says that "Things have turned out very conveniently for Guy" (*The End of the Battle*, 319). One shudders at the irony. Surely it is neither convenient nor pleasant to lose all one's illusions. Yet Box-Bender is absolutely if unconsciously right. For if the chastening spirit of the war has

destroyed the vanity with which Guy entered the army, if it has
brought him to the simplicity of his father's faith, then haven't
things turned out far more than conveniently? One may, perhaps,
bemoan a world in which the myths and dreams of Waugh's
private religion are impossible to sustain. But Mr Crouchback
doesn't need those myths. He lives in the present for the future,
interested in the past but not regretting it, secure in his belief that
God will enable the soul to withstand whatever armies the world
may send against it. In him Waugh embodies his realization that
no belief can substitute for a religious one, that neither class nor
profession nor some intimate relation with the land make man
into something other than a thing. Only faith can – and faith is
what remains when everything else has failed, when one cannot
seem to tell right from wrong and personal honour turns to ashes.
Historical conditions change. Neither Hetton nor the idea of a
gentleman's honour can mean what they once did. History always
makes the tower lean. For Waugh only religious truth stands still,
steady and firm upon its foundation, the only certainty in the 'old
ambiguous world'.

V

The End of the Battle's honesty depends not so much on the trilogy's
first two novels as on the book Waugh wrote about the bout of
hallucinations (the result of mixing liquor with his sleeping
draught,) from which he suffered while working on *Officers and
Gentlemen. The Ordeal of Gilbert Pinfold* (1958) is Waugh's best post-
war novel, a supremely self-knowing book in which Pinfold's
character and experiences are openly based upon Waugh's own:

> He wished no one ill, but he looked at the world *sub specie
> aeternitatis*, and he found it flat as a map; except when, rather
> often, personal annoyance intruded. Then he would come
> tumbling from his exalted point of observation. Shocked by a
> bad bottle of wine, an impertinent stranger, or a fault in syntax,
> his mind like a cinema camera trucked furiously forward to
> confront the offending object close up with glaring lens; with
> the eyes of a drill sergeant inspecting an awkward squad, bulging
> with wrath that was half facetious, and with half-simulated

incredulity; like a drill sergeant he was absurd to many but to some rather formidable . . .

It was his modesty which needed protection and for this purpose, but without design, he gradually assumed this character of burlesque. He was neither a scholar nor a regular soldier; the part for which he cast himself was a combination of eccentric don and testy colonel and he acted it strenuously, before his children at Lychpole and his cronies in London, until it came to dominate his whole outward personality. When he ceased to be alone, when he swung into his club or stumped up the nursery stairs, he left half of himself behind and the other half swelled to fill its place. He offered the world a front of pomposity mitigated by indiscretion that was as hard, bright and antiquated as a cuirass. (12–13)

Waugh's prose in this novel is as cold and tight and elegant as any he ever wrote – a prose that could well be described by Waugh's account of Pinfold's 'front' in this passage's last sentence. Nothing Pinfold does can surprise Waugh. No corner of his mind remains hidden or unexplained. A bad bottle of wine produces an automatic response, for his standard of human behaviour is that type of the human automaton, the drill sergeant. So long as one sees the Pinfold-thing in these terms there seems no point in making any judgement upon him. What could one say? That Pinfold has befuddled his mind and blotched his hands with drugs and drink? What criticism could one suggest that doesn't dissolve before the hilarity of the novel's assertion that 'all was not well with' Pinfold, as if he were a car in need of a tune-up? (26)

Waugh never created the comedy of 'the mechanical encrusted upon the living' so completely as he did in this novel. Yet that is precisely its point. For *Pinfold*, like *Vile Bodies*, depends on Waugh's persistent questioning of the assumptions on which his comedy depends. Gilbert Pinfold is a successful novelist in middle age, an insomniac who uses a sleeping potion mixed with creme de menthe to escape from himself into 'welcome unconsciousness' (26). The combination makes him ill and he takes an ocean voyage to recover. During his trip, however, he begins to hear the voices of a vicious family whom he calls the Angels, whose gossiping about him provides the book's main action. Yet at the end of the novel, after his hallucinations have fled, one thing remains unclear. Why,

Pinfold wonders, "if I was supplying all the information to the Angels, why did I tell them such a lot of rot? I mean to say, if I wanted to draw up an indictment of myself, I could make a far blacker and more plausible case than they did" (229). For Pinfold's voices don't play off the private fears from which his sleeping potion allows him to escape, but off the persona he's created to protect his 'modesty'. And they say all the things one might conventionally say to discredit such a figure: that Pinfold is a homosexual who poses as an Old Etonian and an ex-Guards officer; that his debts are enormous and his Catholicism a way of sucking up to the aristocracy; that he pretends to be a gentleman but lets his mother starve; in short, that he deserves to be horse-whipped.

Such hallucinations don't display self-knowledge so much as a knowledge of the way the self is perceived by others, and are in fact an exaggerated catalogue of the sorts of things people said about Waugh himself throughout the 1950s. Against that public *persona* Waugh sets Pinfold's conception of his private self, balances the world against the soul. Not all the voices he hears are his enemies. One of the friendly ones says, "You just pretend to be hard and worldly, don't you? And you can't blame people if they take you at your own estimate. . . . But I know better." (165–6) The claims of Pinfold's tormentors are patently absurd, but this one voice is not all 'rot' and it hints at that 'far blacker and more plausible case'. In his *New Statesman* review of the novel, Priestley wrote that Pinfold's hallucinations spring from 'the fundamental self telling the ego not to be a mountebank'.[57] True – but Priestley fails to recognize that the problem lies not with the specific role as a Jacobite country squire Pinfold has adopted, but with the fact of performance itself: with making the self, the soul, into a mechanism, however comic. In 'Basil Seal Rides Again', Waugh writes that Basil's 'conscious imposture . . . had become habitual to him . . . the parody had become the persona' from which he cannot escape, making the 'antiquated' beliefs he had once uttered in jest into his 'settled opinions'.[58] The same has happened with Pinfold. His voices don't make a blacker case against him because they can't. Pinfold's performance so dominates the private self that there's no reason for anyone to suspect that self even exists. And does it? For by drowning the self in sleeping potions when he's not performing, Pinfold does his best to keep it from living.

The Ordeal of Gilbert Pinfold is a novel of existential doubt, built around this harrowing suggestion: that it might be possible to destroy one's own soul. It contains the fear voiced by Graham Greene that I quoted at the start of this chapter: that the legend will supersede the work, that the writer will become no more than a character in a journalist's anecdote; that as with the frustrated metonymy of *Vile Bodies*, the part the public sees of Waugh himself will not imply a whole. Against that fear stands only Waugh's faith that people do have souls beneath their objective surfaces. The novel led Waugh to a re-examination of his persona, and of the private religion to which it was matched. He could not as a writer maintain Pinfold's pose after he had subjected it to the pressures of his comedy, could not settle for the private religion whose absurdities he had so marvellously exposed. The novel made him see that Tony Last's Gothic dream was inessential to his faith, and its result was *The End of the Battle*, which salvages not just the war trilogy but the place of religion in Waugh's work as a whole. He freed himself as a novelist. But it was a Pyrrhic victory, and as Bergonzi writes, 'It was hardly to be expected that he could have gone on writing happily in the absence' of that dream.[59] *The End of the Battle* was Waugh's last novel, and he did not free himself as a man. He ate and drank and smoked too much, and continued to pose, to proclaim the modern world an abomination. He persisted in his belief that the Church should stand against the world rather than in it. The Second Vatican Council, he wrote a month before his death, had 'knocked the guts out of' him,[60] and he felt the abandonment of the Latin mass as a blow in the face. The Church's apparent break with history appeared to him to set the tower leaning once more. He was a deeply unhappy man who, Greene writes in a moving portrait, disguised his own 'inner torment in drollery', hid his misery behind the comedy that caused it.[61] But he did not apostasize, and he died on Easter Sunday 1966, having just heard one final Latin mass.

Conclusion

As the Empire drew in, as England became Little England once more, an island increasingly isolated from the stage of world history, so too did the English novel become increasingly conscious of its own limitations. In the four novelists I've considered here one sees the beginnings of that dwindling toward twilight, of an absorption with its own small size, that characterizes most English fiction after the Second World War. Their forerunner in this is Forster, who in taking as his subject the limitations of gentility has had more influence upon the English novel than any other writer in this century. Yet Forster is an anomaly in his own generation. His was but one of a number of possible ways that the novel could have developed. It took the writers with whom I've dealt to make Forster's individual attitude into a consensus, to turn his material into the material of the English novel as a whole. In their hands the English novel became what, in some words of William H. Pritchard's that I quoted in my introduction, it has been for the last half-century: 'short, cool or opaque in its tone, suspicious of eloquence, committed to terse conversations among characters, neither genial nor "sincere" in its overall manner.' Such an idiom grows from an acute awareness of one's own limitations, that ironic 'consciousness of what [one] cannot do', that we see in the manic plots of Iris Murdoch and the black comedy of Anthony Burgess; in Muriel Spark, Barbara Pym, and Kingsley Amis; William Trevor, Margaret Drabble, and Anita Brookner. And the absence of explicit moral judgement that characterizes Waugh's comedy of externality has been particularly crucial in shaping younger writers like A.N. Wilson and William Boyd.

In creating that aesthetic, nothing seems more important than the fact that these novelists were all members of their culture's establishment, men assured of the comforts of what Woolf calls 'middle-class birth and expensive education'. When England was still a world power, Woolf and Lawrence were able to see their country's situation more clearly than any other English novelists precisely because they were outsiders; knew the extent of that power so well for being excluded from it by sex or class. But in observing England's long slide from power, it helped for the writers I've considered to come from inside the dominant culture. It made the sense of one's impotence all the more acute – acute because it was new, a feeling of one's limitations for which one hadn't been prepared.

I could, of course, construct a different story, find a different way of looking at the fiction produced by novelists of the 'second generation'. I could trace the connection between the Auden generation and the working-class heroes of Amis, Braine, and Sillitoe; could follow the line of descent from Woolf to Lessing. Yet as the sceptical young provincial on the move up the social ladder – either as author or character – is the type for the 1950s, as Lessing's sense of rebellion and innovation provides the type for the 1960s, so these writers stand as the type of the novelist for the 1930s and 40s, when England began to realize that things were never going to be what they had once been, what the whole weight of British culture had taught its children to believe they always would be. Born in an age when the 'official beliefs' of their class 'were dissolving like sandcastles', these novelists express a doubt about the capacities of the individual to affect the world around him that is itself homologous to England's loss of the power to affect world history. One might, perhaps, draw a parallel here between their work and the concentration on will-lessness so characteristic of the American minimalist short story writers of the last decade.

As part of that doubt they maintain as well a central doubt of the relevance, even of the existence, of the interior life, a doubt that their work makes an attempt to combat. In the early Waugh's unwillingness to grant his characters souls, in Graham Greene's final distrust of emotion of any kind, one finds the fictional mirror of an educational system that encourages its pupils to behave as if one's 'interior tumult' (in Powell's words about Henry Green) does not exist; a willed ignorance of emotion, an attempt to maintain a certain posture in the world at the expense of the soul. With these writers the cliché comes true: they are the product of the stiff upper lip English schoolboys are encouraged to wear, or rather of its implications: that if one wears it for long, the mind behind that lip seems so increasingly unimportant as to become non-existent. Waugh, Powell, and Graham Greene all attempt to combat that part of their sensibilities; while in his dialogue novels Henry Green turns to that externality as a way of ignoring his private terrors, of escaping his 'inner . . . landscape'.

England's history, first and last, has been determined by the fact that it's an island. Its separation from the Continent spared it from the worst of the nightmares modern history has created. The Blitz was not the Holocaust. Orwell had, one remembers, to set *1984* in the future. Its grimness may be shaped by his own experience of war-time and post-war austerity, but Orwell could not set that novel's horrors in the English present. Yet aside from his imagination of future technology, the novel did provide a close description of the present – of the present elsewhere. For England after the Second World War, history on a grand scale nearly always happens elsewhere; even its own history has been largely determined by its divestiture of the Empire. What the English novel has, above all, had to offer in this period has been poise. As Powell's Nicholas Jenkins found that the search for a style provided a way to save himself from the confusion of modern life, so most English novelists maintain a belief in the value of style itself, in the importance of an unillusioned self-possession as a way of combatting the world. And the novel that poise has produced has, at its best, offered great pleasure by successfully balancing beauty of form against an appeal to the common reader. What makes that stance possible, however, is the fact that the English novel has been spared the transformations modern history has wrought upon the genre – and suffers from their absence. One cannot often simply relax with a novel by Gunter Grass or Milan Kundera or Salman Rushdie or Gabriel Garcia Marquez, as one can with Trevor or Pym. As a reader one often needs that relaxation, that pleasure. But it must nevertheless be admitted that English writers play little role in the new and powerful stage of the novel's history that the names of those four novelists suggest.

Yet as Rushdie's name implies, if England has lost its Empire, the Empire itself has come to England. The English novel, narrowly conceived, is not now the most important fiction published in England. Almost every other winner of the Booker Prize (and most of those that look like lasting) has been a product of what one can loosely call the Commonwealth or post-colonial novel. The real vitality of the non-American novel in English lies in the fiction created by that history that happens elsewhere, whether its authors are Nigerian like Chinua Achebe or Indian like R. K. Narayan; resident in England like V. S. Naipaul, or in their home countries like Nadine Gordimer or Patrick White. And even the English novel itself has gained immensely from its examination of the legacy of Empire, through works such as Paul Scott's *The Raj Quartet* that examine its divestiture, or like Drabble's *The Middle Ground*, which describes the way immigration from the Commonwealth has changed Britain.

The novelists I've dealt with here have little to do with such developments. They represent, rather, the state of the novel at mid-century when, with the modernists dead or in retirement, and the careers of the younger generation of Amis, Burgess, and Murdoch delayed by the war, they comprised virtually the only generation of significant working novelists in England. They have perhaps little to say about developments in English history after 1950 *per se*, but I hope to have suggested the ways their search for a style both shaped future developments in the English novel and prefigured those in English society itself. The question remains of the scale of their achievement. Pritchett worried in his 1947 essay 'The Future of Fiction' that what he saw as his own generation's narrow perfection of form would finally amount to no more than a Silver Age.[1] In the end he was right – an age in which a great many novelists (these four, but also Elizabeth Bowen, Christopher Isherwood, Ivy Compton-Burnett, Jean Rhys) performed at a very high level, but in which there were, if few valleys, few peaks either. How will history treat these novelists? Henry Green, I think, will always be an acquired taste – a masterful prose stylist, a fascinating 'case' for the critic, but someone who will be read primarily by those with a taste for 'experimental' fiction. To which I would add that those who after writing three or four books are still called 'experimental' are those who have failed – those who have failed to reshape the reading public, and indeed the genre itself, into their own image. No one now calls James or Woolf an 'experimental writer', but their work was in its day at least as radical as Henry Green's. Anthony Powell will stand as the perfect embodiment of the silver age, of the pleasures of major–minor art – Andrew Marvell reborn as a novelist. Graham Greene will live as a superbly entertaining writer, author of two great (*The Power and the Glory* and *The Comedians*) and one near-great (*The Quiet American*) novels, and as the creator of Greeneland, that way station between Conrad and Naipaul.

And Waugh? I began this study with the vague idea that Waugh was the best of the four, and that *A Handful of Dust* was his best book. Everything I have read since beginning the project has only helped convince me of that. Even a silver age can have one novelist of supreme achievement, a writer like the ideal great novelist Pritchett described in his preface to *The Living Novel*:

> . . . the freshest, the most original, the most importunate and living novelist . . . more readable, more entertaining, more suggestive and incomparably more able . . . most sensitive to the situation of [his] time . . . in the finer sense, contemporary.[2]

Waugh's generation belonged to him as much as it did to Auden; and the present of the English novel belongs to him far more than English poetry now does to Auden. He is the most important comic artist England has produced since Dickens – and one important for world literature as well, as Dickens was, for having helped to create black humour, that grisly laughter with which writers everywhere confront the contemporary nightmare. *A Handful of Dust* is as large an achievement as *A Passage to India* or *Women in Love* or *To the Lighthouse*, and Waugh stands, the only English novelist after the modernists whose position now seems securely canonical, as the great writer of his times.

Notes and References

Introduction

1. R. W. B. Lewis uses this term in *The Picaresque Saint: Representative Figures in Contemporary Fiction* (Philadelphia and New York: J. B. Lippincott Co., 1959) to distinguish those novelists born around the turn of the century from their predecessors, the 'first generation' of Joyce, Lawrence, Mann, Proust, *et al.*
2. Samuel Hynes, *The Auden Generation* (New York: The Viking Press, 1977).
3. William H. Pritchard, *Seeing Through Everything: English Writers 1918–1940* (New York: Oxford University Press, 1977), p. 179.
4. Georg Lukacs, *The Theory of the Novel* (Written 1914–15; first published in German 1920) trans. Anna Bostock (Cambridge, MA: MIT Press, 1971), p. 88.
5. E. M. Forster, *Howards End* (New York: G. P. Putnam's Sons, 1910), p. 203.
6. Virginia Woolf, 'The Leaning Tower', in *Collected Essays*, vol. II (London: The Hogarth Press, 1966), p. 171.
7. Ibid., p. 167.
8. Ibid., p. 171.
9. George Orwell, 'Inside the Whale'. In *The Collected Essays, Journalism and Letters of George Orwell, Vol 1*, ed. Sonia Orwell and Ian Angus (New York: Harcourt Brace Jovanovich, 1968), p. 512.
10. Valentine Cunningham, *British Writers of the Thirties* (New York: Oxford University Press, 1988).
11. Evelyn Waugh, 'Two Unquiet Lives'. In *The Essays, Articles and Reviews of Evelyn Waugh*, ed. Donat Gallagher (Boston: Little, Brown & Co., 1984), p. 394.
12. Gilles Deleuze and Felix Guattari, *Kafka: Toward a Minor Literature*, trans. Dana Polan; foreword by Reda Bensmaia (Minneapolis: University of Minnesota Press, 1986).
13. See Lucien Goldmann, 'The Genetic-Structuralist Method in the History of Literature'. In *Toward a Sociology of the Novel*. trans. Alan Sheridan (London: Tavistock Publications, 1975), pp. 156–71.
14. Ibid., p. 159.
15. Lucien Goldmann, *The Hidden God*, trans. Philip Thody (London: Routledge & Kegan Paul, 1964), p. 17.
16. Raymond Williams, *The Long Revolution* (London: Chatto & Windus, 1961), p. 48.
17. Cyril Connolly, *The Unquiet Grave: A Word Cycle by Palinurus* (1945; rpt. New York: The Viking Press, 1957), p. 22.
18. See her essay, 'The Sublime and the Beautiful Revisited' in *The Yale*

203

Review, Winter 1960, pp. 247–71.

19. Iris Murdoch, 'Against Dryness', *Encounter*, January 1961, p. 18.
20. W. B. Yeats, 'Anima Hominis' in *Essays* (New York: Macmillan, 1924), p. 492.
21. Clive James, *From the Land of Shadows* (1982; rpt. London: Picador, 1983), p. 138.

1 The English Novel: Modernism and After

1. Lionel Trilling, 'Forward' to *The Liberal Imagination* (1950); rpt. New York: Charles Scribner's Sons, 1976), p. viii.
2. D. H. Lawrence, 'Why the Novel Matters' in *Phoenix* (1936; rpt. Harmondsworth: Penguin Books, 1978) p. 535.
3. Georg Lukacs, *The Theory of the Novel* (written 1914–15; first published in German, 1920) trans. Anna Bostock (Cambridge, MA: MIT Press, 1971), p. 89.
4. Ibid., p. 78.
5. Ibid., p. 89.
6. Ibid., p. 60.
7. Ibid., p. 80.
8. Ibid., pp. 38–9.
9. Ibid., p. 72.
10. Virginia Woolf, 'Mr. Bennett and Mrs. Brown.' In *The Captain's Death-Bed and Other Essays* (New York: Harcourt Brace Jovanovich, 1950) p. 97.
11. Ibid., p. 114.
12. Woolf, 'Modern Fiction', in *The Common Reader* (New York: Harcourt Brace & World, 1925), p. 154.
13. Graham Greene, 'Francois Mauriac' in *Collected Essays* (1964; rpt. Harmondsworth: Penguin Books, 1970), p. 92.
14. Lionel Trilling, 'Art and Fortune', in *The Liberal Imagination*, p. 268.
15. Roman Jakobson, 'The Metaphoric and Metonymic Poles' in *Critical Theory Since Plato*, ed. Hazard Adams (New York: Harcourt Brace Jovanovich), p. 1113.
16. Ibid., p. 1116.
17. David Lodge, *The Modes of Modern Writing* (Ithaca, New York: Cornell University Press, 1977), p. 76.
18. Malcolm Bradbury, 'The Novel in the 1920s' in *The Twentieth Century*, ed. Bernard Bergonzi (London: Barrie & Jenkins, 1970), p. 181.
19. Woolf, 'Mr. Bennett and Mrs. Brown', p. 96.
20. I. A. Richards, *Science and Poetry* (New York: W. W. Norton & Co., 1926), p. 95.
21. Ibid., p. 76.
22. Lucien Goldmann, *Toward a Sociology of the Novel*. (London: Tavistock Publications, 1975) p. 12.
23. Jane Austen, *Emma* (1817; rpt. London: Oxford University Press, 1971), p. 210.

24. Virginia Woolf, 'The Leaning Tower', in *Collected Essays, Vol. II* (London: The Hogarth Press, 1966), pp. 169–70.
25. Robert Kiely, *Beyond Egotism* (Cambridge, MA: Harvard University Press, 1980), p. 5.
26. From *The Napoleon of Notting Hill.* Quoted in Jefferson Hunter, *Edwardian Fiction* (Cambridge, MA: Harvard University Press, 1982), p. 228.
27. See 'Rudyard Kipling: The Empire Strikes Back', in Martin Green's *The English Novel in the Twentieth Century* (London: Routledge & Kegan Paul, 1984); and 'England After 1918: Our Turn To Cliché' in his *Transatlantic Patterns* (New York: Basic Books, 1977).
28. Jonathan Gathorne Hardy, *The Old School Tie* (New York: The Viking Press, 1977), *passim*.
29. Quoted in Jefferson Hunter, *Edwardian Fiction* (Cambridge, MA: Harvard University Press, 1982), p. 5.
30. Raymond Williams, *Marxism and Literature* (Oxford: Oxford University Press, 1977), p. 176.
31. José Ortega y Gasset, 'Notes on the Novel', in *The Dehumanization of Art*, trans. Helene Weyl (Princeton: Princeton University Press, 1968), p. 58.
32. See *The Essays, Articles and Reviews of Evelyn Waugh*, ed. Donat Gallagher (Boston: Little, Brown & Co., 1984). On Joyce he wrote that 'Modern novelists taught by Mr. James Joyce are at last realizing the importance of re-echoing and remodifying the same themes' (p. 82); on Lawrence that 'The most important work of poetry this year is clearly *The Collected Poems of D. H. Lawrence*' (p. 42).
33. In *The Poetry of Robert Frost*, ed. Edward Connery Latham (New York: Holt, Rinehart & Winston, 1967), p. 120.
34. Anthony Powell, *Messengers of Day*, (New York: Holt, Rinehart & Winston, 1978), p. 1.
35. Virginia Woolf, 'Modern Fiction', p. 154.
36. Graham Greene, 'The Saratoga Trunk', in *Collected Essays*, p. 116.
37. Georg Lukacs, *The Historical Novel*, trans. Hannah and Stanley Mitchell (Lincoln, Nebraska: University of Nebraska Press, 1962), p. 23.
38. Evelyn Waugh, 'The War and the Younger Generation', in *The Essays, Articles and Reviews of Evelyn Waugh*, p. 62.
39. George Orwell, 'Inside the Whale', in *The Collected Essays, Journalism and Letters of George Orwell, Vol. 1*, ed. Sonia Orwell and Ian Angus, (New York: Harcourt Brace Jovanovich, 1968), pp. 505, 514–15.
40. Robert Graves, *Goodbye to All That* (London: Jonathan Cape, 1929).
41. Georg Lukacs, *The Historical Novel*, p. 23.
42. Evelyn Waugh, *Vile Bodies* (Boston: Little Brown & Co., 1930), p. 284.
43. Virginia Woolf, 'The Leaning Tower', p. 170.
44. Ibid., p. 171.
45. Graham Greene, 'The Dark Backward', in *Collected Essays*, pp. 55–6.
46. E. M. Forster, *Howards End* (New York: G. P. Putnam's Sons, 1910), p. 53.
47. Evelyn Waugh, *A Little Learning* (1964; rpt. Harmondsworth: Penguin Books, 1983) p. 170.

48. See Chapter 7, 'Who's Who or The Uncertainties of the Bourgeoisie' in Eric Hobsbawm, *The Age of Empire: 1875–1914* (New York, Pantheon, 1987) for an illuminating discussion of the Edwardian suburbs.
49. Cyril Connolly, *Enemies of Promise* (1938; rpt. Harmondsworth: Penguin Books, 1961, p. 67.
50. Ibid., p. 78.
51. Ibid.
52. Wyndham Lewis, *Men Without Art* (London: Cassell & Co., 1934) p. 41.
53. Ibid., p. 112.
54. Ibid., p. 40.
55. Paul Fussell, *The Great War and Modern Memory* (New York: Oxford University Press, 1975), *passim*.
56. Wyndham Lewis, *Men Without Art*, p. 128.
57. Wyndham Lewis, *The Wild Body* (London: Chatto & Windus, 1927), p. 246.
58. Wyndham Lewis, *Men Without Art*, p. 103.
59. Wyndham Lewis, *The Wild Body*, p. 234.
60. George Orwell, 'Such, Such Were the Joys', in *The Collected Essays, Journalism and Letters, Vol. 4*, p. 366.
61. W. H. Auden, 'The Liberal Fascist', in *The English Auden*, ed. Edward Mendelson (New York: Random House, 1977), p. 325.
62. Martin Green, *The English Novel in the Twentieth Century* (London: Routledge & Kegan Paul, 1984), p. xvi.
63. Ibid., p. 208.
64. Evelyn Waugh, *Labels, A Mediterranean Journal* (London: Duckworth, 1930), p. 169.
65. George Orwell, 'Inside the Whale', p. 515.
66. Corelli Barnett, *The Collapse of British Power* (New York: Morrow, 1972), *passim*.
67. Evelyn Waugh, 'Dedication' (to Randolph Churchill) to *Put Out More Flags* (Boston: Little, Brown & Co., 1942).
68. Michael North, *Henry Green and the Writing of His Generation* (Charlottesville: University Press of Virginia, 1984), p. 42.
69. Georg Lukacs, *The Historical Novel*, pp. 139–44.
70. Ibid., p. 139.
71. Graham Greene, 'The Young Dickens', in *Collected Essays*, p. 83.
72. Terry Eagleton, *Exiles and Emigrés* (New York: Shocken Books, 1970), p. 223.

2 Henry Green

References to Green's works are given in the text. For *Loving, Living,* and *Party Going* I have used the 1978 Penguin omnibus edition; for *Nothing, Doting* and *Blindness*, Penguin's 1980 omnibus. For Green's remaining works I have used the first American editions of *Caught* (1952), *Back* (1950), and *Concluding* (1952); (all New York: The Viking Press); and the 1940 Hogarth Press edition of *Pack My Bag*.

1. V. S. Pritchett, 'Henry Green: In the Echo Chamber', in *The Tale Bearers* (New York: Random House, 1980), p. 115.
2. Philip Toynbee, 'The Novels of Henry Green', *The Partisan Review*, 16 (1949), p. 587.
3. Anthony Powell, *Infants of the Spring* (New York: Holt, Rinehart & Winston, 1977), p. 161.
4. Harvey Breit, 'A Talk with Henry Green – and a P.S.' *The New York Times Book Review*, 19 February 1950, p. 29.
5. Henry Green, 'Apologia', *Folios of New Writing*, Autumn 1941 (London: The Hogarth Press), p. 46.
6. Nigel Dennis, 'The Double Life of Henry Green', *Life*, 33 (August 4, 1952), p. 84.
7. Terry Southern, 'Henry Green', *The Paris Review* 5, no. 19 (1958), p. 73.
8. Henry Green, 'A Novelist to His Readers', *The Listener*, 9 November 1980, p. 506.
9. Frank Kermode, *The Art of Telling* (Cambridge, MA: Harvard University Press, 1983), p. 89.
10. Anthony Powell, *Infants of the Spring*, p. 161.
11. V. S. Pritchett, 'Henry Green: In the Echo Chamber', p. 118.
12. Michael North, *Henry Green and the Writing of His Generation* (Charlottesville: University Press of Virginia, 1984), p. 15.
13. Ibid., p. 10.
14. Ibid., p. 12.
15. Ibid., p. 213.
16. V. S. Pritchett, 'Henry Green: In the Echo Chamber', p. 115.
17. Ibid., p. 117.
18. Valentine Cunningham, *British Writers of the Thirties* (Oxford: Oxford University Press, 1988), pp. 9–10.
19. Walter Allen, 'An Artist of the Thirties', *Folios of New Writing 3*, Spring 1941, p. 149.
20. Evelyn Waugh, 'A Neglected Masterpiece'. *The Essays, Articles, and Reviews of Evelyn Waugh*, ed. Donat Gallagher. (Boston: Little, Brown & Co., 1984), p. 81.
21. Walter Allen, 'An Artist of the Thirties', p. 152.
22. W. H. Auden, 'In Memory of W. B. Yeats', in *The English Auden*, ed. Edward Mendelson (New York: Random House, 1977), p. 242.
23. G. Rostrevor Hamilton, *The Tell-Tale Article* (London: Heinemann, 1949), p. 8.
24. A. Kingsley Weatherhead, *A Reading of Henry Green* (Seattle: University of Washington Press, 1961), p. 88.
25. Henry Green, 'For Jenny with Affection from Henry Green', *The Spectator* 211 (4 October 1963), p. 422.
26. V. S. Pritchett, 'Henry Green: In the Echo Chamber', p. 116.
27. T. S. Eliot, 'The Love Song of J. Alfred Prufrock', *The Complete Poems and Plays, 1909–1950* (New York: Harcourt Brace and World, 1952), p. 6.

28. Giorgio Melchiori, *The Tightrope Walkers: Studies of Mannerism in Modern English Literature* (London: Routledge & Kegan Paul, 1956), p. 189.
29. Terry Southern, 'Henry Green', *The Paris Review* 5, no. 19 (1958), p. 66.
30. Ibid., p. 65.
31. Evelyn Waugh, 'Fan-Fare', *The Essays, Articles and Reviews of Evelyn Waugh*, p. 303.
32. John Russell, 'There It Is', *Kenyon Review*, 16 (1964), p. 451.
33. Ibid., p. 438.
34. Anthony Powell, *Infants of the Spring*, p. 29.
35. Eudora Welty, 'Henry Green: A Novelist of the Imagination', *Texas Quarterly* 4 (1961), p. 249.
36. Quoted from Priestley's 'The Arts Under Socialism', in Robert Hewison, *In Anger: British Culture in the Cold War, 1945–60* (New York: Oxford University Press, 1981), pp. 26–7.
37. Samuel Beckett, *The Unnameable* (1958), in *Three Novels by Samuel Beckett* (New York: Grove Press, 1965), p. 414.
38. John Updike, 'Introduction' to *Loving, Living, Party Going* (Harmondsworth: Penguin Books, 1978), p. 14.
39. Henry Green, 'A Novelist to his Readers', p. 506.
40. Ibid., p. 506.
41. V. S. Pritchett, 'A Literary Letter from the British Capitol', *The New York Times Book Review*, 7 January 1951, p. 14.
42. John Updike, 'Introduction', p. 14.
43. Norman Page, *Speech in the English Novel* (London: Longman, 1973), p. 130.
44. Terry Southern, 'Henry Green' *The Paris Review* 5, no. 19 (1958), p. 67.
45. John Russell, 'There it is', p. 449.
46. Evelyn Waugh, *The Letters of Evelyn Waugh*, ed. Mark Amory (New Haven and New York: Ticknor & Fields, 1980), p. 516.

3   Anthony Powell

References to Powell's novels are incorporated in the text. For his early novels *Afternoon Men* (1931), *From a View to a Death* (1933), and *Agents and Patients* (1936) I have used the Heinemann uniform edition of his works; for *A Dance to the Music of Time* (1951–75), the Fontana paperback edition.

1. E. M. Forster, *Aspects of the Novel* (New York, Harcourt, Brace and Co., 1927), p. 49.
2. G. U. Ellis, *Twilight on Parnassus* (London: Michael Joseph Ltd., 1939), p. 385.
3. Alan Brownjohn, 'Profile 6: Anthony Powell', *New Review* 6, (September 1974), p. 22.
4. James Tucker, *The Novels of Anthony Powell* (New York: Columbia University Press, 1976), pp. 83, 140.
5. Wyndham Lewis, *The Wild Body* (London: Chatto & Windus, 1927), p. 233.
6. Wyndham Lewis, *Men Without Art* (London: Cassell & Co., 1934), pp. 103, 112.

7. Anthony Powell, *Messengers of Day* (New York: Holt, Rinehart & Winston, 1978), p. 112. Except where noted, all other biographical information comes from this volume or its three companions in *To Keep the Ball Rolling: The Memoirs of Anthony Powell* (1977–1983), of which this is volume 2.
8. *The Wild Body*, p. 246.
9. G. U. Ellis, *Twilight on Parnassus*, p. 377.
10. Bernard Bergonzi, *Anthony Powell* (London: Longman Group Ltd., 1971), p. 4.
11. V. S. Pritchett, 'The Bored Barbarians', in *The Living Novel and Later Appreciations* (New York: Random House, 1964), p. 297.
12. James Hall, *The Tragic Comedians* (Bloomington: Indiana University Press, 1963), p. 133.
13. Kingsley Amis, 'Afternoon World', *The Spectator*, 13 May 1955, p. 619.
14. Cyril Connolly, *Enemies of Promise* (1938; rpt. Harmondsworth: Penguin Books, 1961), p. 54.
15. Arthur Mizener, '*A Dance to the Music of Time*: The Novels of Anthony Powell', *Kenyon Review* XXII (Winter, 1960), p. 79.
16. Robert K. Morris, *The Novels of Anthony Powell* (Pittsburg: University of Pittsburgh Press, 1960), p. 51.
17. Powell, *To Keep the Ball Rolling, vol. 3: Faces in My Time* (New York: Holt, Rinehart & Winston, 1980), pp. 212–13.
18. Pritchett, 'The Future of Fiction', in *Penguin New Writing*, 32 (1947), p. 103.
19. James Tucker, *The Novels of Anthony Powell*, p. 95.
20. Marvin Mudrick, *Books Are Not Life But Then What Is?* (New York: Oxford University Press, 1979), p. 282.
21. *Messengers of Day*, p. 116.
22. Alan Brownjohn, 'Profile 6: Anthony Powell', p. 25.
23. Irving Howe, *Politics and the Novel* (New York: Horizon Press, 1957), p. 63.
24. V. S. Pritchett, 'The Bored Barbarians', p. 297.
25. Arthur Mizener, '*A Dance . . .*' p. 85.
26. Wyndham Lewis, *The Wild Body*, p. 246.
27. Anthony Powell, *John Aubrey and His Friends* (London: Eyre & Spottiswode, 1948), p. 66.
28. Michael Barber, 'The Art of Fiction: Anthony Powell', *The Paris Review*, 73 (1977), p. 61.
29. V. S. Pritchett, 'The Bored Barbarians', p. 297.
30. Elizabeth Longford, 'A Talk with Anthony Powell', *The New York Times Book Review*, 11 April 1976, p. 47.
31. James Tucker, *The Novels of Anthony Powell*, p. 161.
32. *Faces in My Time*, p. 2.
33. Benjamin DeMott, 'Ask at the House', *Atlantic Monthly*, April 1976, p. 110.
34. Michael Barber, 'The Art of Fiction', p. 73.
35. Arthur Mizener, '*A Dance . . .*', *passim*.
36. Ibid., p. 86.
37. Evelyn Waugh, 'Fan-Fare', in *The Essays, Articles and Reviews of Evelyn*

Waugh, ed. Donat Gallagher (Boston: Little, Brown & Co., 1984), p. 304.
38. Martin Green, *The English Novel in the Twentieth Century* (London: Routledge & Kegan Paul, 1984), p. xviii.
39. James Tucker, *The Novels of Anthony Powell*, p. 3.
40. Walter Allen, *Tradition and Dream* (London: Dent, 1964), p. 221.
41. John Keegan, *Six Armies in Normandy* (1982; rpt. Harmondsworth: Penguin Books, 1983), p. 58.
42. John Russell, *Anthony Powell* (Bloomington and London: Indiana University Press, 1970), p. 190.
43. T. S. Eliot, 'Tradition and the Individual Talent', in *Selected Prose of T. S. Eliot*, ed. Frank Kermode (New York: Farrar Straus Giroux, 1975), p. 43.
44. Powell's model for Moreland is most obviously his friend, the composer Constant Lambert. But his characters are all composites, and surely there is a touch of Henry Green in Moreland as well, in statements like "Love means such different things to different people", (*The Kindly Ones*, p. 142), as well as in Jenkins' statement that for Moreland "a thick curtain" (*The Soldier's Art*, p. 121) lies between the present and the years before the war.
45. Evelyn Waugh, 'Bioscope', *The Spectator*, 29 June 1962, p. 863.
46. Evelyn Waugh, *The Ordeal of Gilbert Pinfold* (Boston: Little, Brown & Co.), p. 216.
47. Bernard Bergonzi, 'Appendix. Anthony Powell: The Last Quarter', in *The Situation of the Novel*, rev. ed. (Pittsburgh: University of Pittsburgh Press, 1979), pp. 238–41.
48. Some recent criticism has turned to Powell's speculative interest in the occult as a way of understanding the novel; see, for example, Henry R. Harrington, 'Anthony Powell, Nicolas Poussin, and the Structure of Time', (*Contemporary Literature*, Winter 1983, pp. 431–48), which argues suggestively though not to my mind conclusively, that the structure of the Zodiac underlies that of the novel as a whole.

4 Graham Greene

Page references to Greene's novels are given in the text and refer to the Penguin editions of his works except where noted.

1. Graham Greene, *Stamboul Train* (1932; rpt. London: Heinemann/Bodley Head, 1974), p. 198. Further references given in the text.
2. Richard Hoggart, 'The Force of Caricature', in *Graham Greene: A Collection of Critical Essays*, ed. Samuel Hynes (Englewood Cliffs, NJ: Prentice-Hall, 1973), p. 84.
3. Graham Greene, 'Isis Idol', in *Collected Essays* (1969; rpt. Harmondsworth: Penguin Books, 1970), p. 165–7.
4. Martin Green, *Transatlantic Patterns* (New York: Basic Books, 1977), pp. 141–2.

5. See 'Our Turn to Cliché' in *Transatlantic Patterns*.
6. Arthur Calder-Marshall, 'The Works of Graham Greene', *Horizon* I (May 1940), pp. 367–75.
7. Graham Greene, *Ways of Escape* (New York: Simon & Schuster, 1980), p. 80. Further references given in the text.
8. R. W. B. Lewis, *The Picaresque Saint* (Philadelphia and New York: J. B. Lippincott Co., 1959), p. 220.
9. John Spurling, *Graham Greene* (London and New York: Methuen, 1983), p. 62.
10. Richard Hoggart, 'The Force of Caricature', pp. 88, 91–2.
11. Ibid., p. 83.
12. Graham Greene, 'The Young Dickens', in *Collected Essays*, p. 83.
13. Graham Greene, 'The Lost Childhood', in *Collected Essays*, p. 18.
14. Graham Greene, *A Sort of Life* (1971: rpt. Harmondsworth: Penguin Books, 1972), p. 54–5. Further references given in the text. The first volume of Norman Sherry's biography of Greene (New York: The Viking Press, 1989) appeared too late for me to draw on it here. Sherry treats Greene's school years in greater detail, but neither challenges nor greatly enriches the account of them, or indeed of Greene's life and career as a whole, that the novelist himself has given. See my review, *The Boston Globe*, 11 June 1989.
15. Cyril Connolly, *Enemies of Promise* (1938; rpt. Harmondsworth, Penguin Books, 1961), p. 271.
16. George Orwell, 'Inside the Whale', in *The Collected Essays, Journalism, and Letters of George Orwell, Vol 1*, ed. Sonia Orwell and Ian Angus (New York: Harcourt Brace Jovanovich, 1968), p. 517.
17. Graham Greene, *The Human Factor* (1978; rpt. New York: Avon, 1979), p. 116.
18. Graham Greene, 'Francois Mauriac', in *Collected Essays*, p. 91.
19. Graham Greene, *The Lawless Roads* (1939; rpt. Harmondsworth: Penguin Books, 1974), p. 184. Further references given in the text.
20. Graham Greene, *Journey Without Maps* (1936; rpt. Harmondsworth: Penguin Books, 1971), p. 249. Further references given in the text.
21. Lucien Goldmann, *Toward a Sociology of the Novel*, trans. Alan Sheridan (London: Tavistock Publications, 1975), p. 160.
22. From the epigraph to *It's a Battlefield*, taken from Kinglake's history of the Crimean War.
23. Terry Eagleton, *Exiles and Emigrés* (New York: Schocken Books, 1970), p. 136.
24. Quoted from a radio interview with Walter Allen in Peter Wolfe, *Graham Greene the Entertainer* (Carbondale and Edwardsville: Southern Illinois University Press, 1972), p. 5.
25. Julian Jebb, 'Evelyn Waugh', an interview in *The Paris Review*, 8. (Summer–Fall 1963), p. 79.
26. Richard Hoggart, 'The Force of Caricature', p. 91.
27. R. W. B. Lewis, *The Picaresque Saint*, p. 239.
28. 'The Lost Childhood', pp. 16–17.
29. George Orwell, 'The Sanctified Sinner', in Hynes, *Graham Greene*, p. 107.

30. R. W. B. Lewis, *The Picaresque Saint*, p. 248.
31. Graham Greene, 'Frederick Rolfe: From the Devil's Side', in *Collected Essays*, p. 135.
32. George Orwell, 'The Sanctified Sinner'.
33. Graham Greene, *The Power and the Glory* (1940; rpt. London: Heinemann/Bodley Head, 1971) pp. 19–20. Further references given in the text.
34. Richard Hoggart, 'The Force of Caricature', p. 89.
35. 'Francois Mauriac', p. 92.
36. See Eagleton's illuminating discussion of this issue in his chapter on Greene in *Exiles and Emigrés*.
37. John Spurling, *Graham Greene*, p. 74.
38. Joseph Conrad, 'Preface' to *The Nigger of the Narcissus* (1897), in *The Nigger of the Narcissus*, ed. Robert Kimbrough (New York: Norton, 1979), p. 147.
39. George Orwell, 'The Sanctified Sinner'.
40. Richard Hoggart, 'The Force of Caricature', p. 84.
41. Graham Greene, *Why Do I Write? An exchange of views with V. S. Pritchett and Elizabeth Bowen* (London: Percival Marshall, 1948), p. 31.
42. Graham Greene, 'Under the Garden', in *Collected Stories* (New York: Viking, 1973), pp. 215–16.
43. John Spurling, *Graham Greene*, p. 57.
44. Quoted in *Ways of Escape*, p. 265.
45. Terry Eagleton, *Exiles and Emigrés*, p. 136.
46. John Spurling (*Graham Greene*, p. 17) notes the use of this phrase in both *The Comedians* (p. 246) and *A Sort of Life* (p. 134).
47. Philip Stratford, *Faith and Fiction: Creative Process in Greene and Mauriac* (Notre Dame, Indiana: University of Notre Dame Press, 1965), p. 234.
48. Joseph Conrad, 'Preface' to *The Nigger of the Narcissus*, in Kimbrough, p. 147.
49. Graham Greene, *Monsignor Quixote* (New York: Simon & Schuster, 1982), pp. 69–70. Further references given in the text.

5 Evelyn Waugh

References to Waugh's novels are incorporated in the text and refer to the Little, Brown & Co. American editions of his work except where noted.

1. Alvin Kernan, 'The Wall and the Jungle: The Early Novels of Evelyn Waugh', *Yale Review*, 53 (1963–64), p. 199.
2. Terry Eagleton, *Exiles and Emigrés* (New York: Schocken Books, 1972), p. 43.
3. Edmund Wilson, '"Never Apologize, Never Explain": The Art of Evelyn Waugh', in *Classics and Commercials* (New York: Farrar Straus and Co., 1950), p. 146.
4. Graham Greene, 'The Redemption of Mr. Joyboy', in *The Portable Graham Greene*, ed. Philip Stratford (New York: Viking, 1973), p. 557.

5. Graham Greene, *Ways of Escape* (New York: Simon & Schuster, 1980), p. 270.

6. J. B. Priestley, 'What was Wrong with Pinfold', *The New Statesman*, 31 August 1957, p. 244.

7. Umberto Eco, *The Name of the Rose*, trans. William Weaver (New York: Harcourt Brace Jovanovich, 1983), p. 132.

8. Evelyn Waugh, 'Satire and Fiction', in *The Essays, Articles, and Reviews of Evelyn Waugh*, ed. Donat Gallagher (Boston: Little, Brown & Co., 1984), p. 102.

9. Henri Bergson, 'Laughter', in *Comedy*, ed. Wylie Sypher (Baltimore: The Johns Hopkins University Press, 1980), p. 84.

10. Evelyn Waugh, 'Fan-Fare', in *The Essays, Articles . . .* ed. Donat Gallagher, p. 303.

11. Peter Quennell, 'A Kingdom of Cokayne', in *Evelyn Waugh and his World*, ed. David Pryce-Jones (Boston: Little, Brown & Co., 1973), p. 23.

12. Christopher Sykes, *Evelyn Waugh*, rev. ed. (Harmondsworth: Penguin Books, 1977), p. 251. All biographical material in this chapter comes from Sykes except where noted. Martin Stannard's superb *Evelyn Waugh: The Early Years, 1903–39* (New York: Norton, 1987) appeared after I had completed my work on Waugh. But his picture of Waugh, and in particular his discussion of the novelist's dissatisfaction with his own comedy, seems in keeping with my own.

13. Bernard Bergonzi, 'Evelyn Waugh's Gentlemen', *Critical Quarterly* 5 (Spring 1963), p. 191.

14. Samuel Hynes, *The Auden Generation* (New York: The Viking Press, 1977), p. 59; William H. Pritchard, *Seeing Through Everything* (New York: Oxford University Press, 1977), p. 187.

15. Jeffrey Heath, *The Picturesque Prison: Evelyn Waugh and His Writing* (Kingston and Montreal: McGill–Queens University Press, 1982), pp. 89–90.

16. Julian Jebb, 'Evelyn Waugh', an interview in *The Paris Review*, vol. 8 (Summer–Fall, 1963), p. 79.

17. Stephen Spender, *The Creative Element* (New York: British Book Center, 1954), p. 164.

18. The best discussion of the end of Waugh's first marriage is in Stannard, Ch. 6.

19. Christopher Sykes, *Evelyn Waugh*, pp. 139–40.

20. Alec Waugh, *My Brother Evelyn* (New York: Farrar Straus & Giroux, 1967), p. 191.

21. E. M. Forster, *Aspects of the Novel* (New York: Harcourt Brace and Co., 1927), p. 103.

22. Bernard Bergonzi, *The Situation of the Novel* (Pittsburgh: University of Pittsburgh Press, 1970), p. 106.

23. Joseph Epstein, 'The Outrageous Mr. Wu', *The New Criterion*, April 1985, p. 14.

24. Waugh, *Edmund Campion* (1935: rpt. Oxford: Oxford University Press, 1980), p. 117.

25. Evelyn Waugh, 'Converted to Rome', in *The Essays, Articles . . .* ed.

Donat Gallagher, p. 103.

26. Evelyn Waugh, 'Come Inside', in *Essays, Articles* . . ., ed. Donat Gallagher, p. 368.

27. Evelyn Waugh, 'Converted to Rome', in *Essays, Articles* . . ., ed. Donat Gallagher, p. 104.

28. Conor Cruise O'Brien (writing as Donat O'Donnell), *Maria Cross: Imaginative Patterns in a Group of Modern Catholic Writers* (New York: Oxford University Press, 1952), p. 120.

29. Ibid., p. 121.

30. Raymond Williams, *Culture and Society* (New York: Columbia University Press, 1958).

31. Evelyn Waugh, 'Aspirations of a Mugwump', in *Essays, Articles* . . ., ed. Donat Gallagher, p. 537.

32. Evelyn Waugh, 'Basil Seal Rides Again', in *Work Suspended and Other Stories* (Harmondsworth: Penguin Books, 1967), p. 269.

33. T. E. Hulme, 'Romanticism and Classicism', in *Speculations*, ed. Herbert Read (London: Routledge & Kegan Paul, 1924), p. 117.

34. Conor Cruise O'Brien, *Maria Cross* . . ., p. 130.

35. Frank Kermode, 'Mr. Waugh's Cities', in *Puzzles and Epiphanies* (London: Routledge & Kegan Paul, 1962), pp. 171–2.

36. Bernard Bergonzi, *The Situation of the Novel*, p. 105.

37. George Orwell, 'Inside the Whale', in *The Collected Essays, Journals and Letters of George Orwell, Vol. 1*, ed. Sonia Orwell and Ian Angus (New York: Harcourt Brace Jovanovich, 1968), p. 503.

38. 'Work Suspended', in *Work Suspended and Other Stories*, p. 112. Further references incorporated in the text.

39. I. A. Richards, *Science and Poetry* (New York: W. W. Norton & Co., 1976), p. 76.

40. Cyril Connolly, *Enemies of Promise*. (1938; rpt. Harmondsworth: Penguin Books, 1961), p. 94.

41. Evelyn Waugh, *Brideshead Revisited*, rev. ed. (London: Chapman & Hall, 1960), p. 9.

42. Ibid., p. 288.

43. Ibid., p. 9.

44. Bernard Bergonzi, *The Situation of the Novel*, p. 111.

45. In 'Fan-Fare', p. 302.

46. Evelyn Waugh, 'Bioscope', *The Spectator*, 29 June 1962, p. 863.

47. *Brideshead Revisited*, rev. ed., p. 9.

48. Martin Green, *Transatlantic Patterns* (New York: Basic Books, 1977), ch. 11.

49. See Frank Kermode, 'Mr Waugh's Cities' for the best account of this aspect of the novel.

50. See Robert Wohl, *The Generation of 1914* (Cambridge, MA: Harvard University Press, 1979), ch. 3: 'England: Lost Legions of Lost Youth'.

51. Lady Desborough, *Pages From a Family Journal* (Eton College: privately printed, Spottiswode, Ballantyne & Co., 1916).

52. Terry Eagleton, *Exiles and Emigrés* p. 65.

53. Conor Cruise O'Brien, *Maria Cross* . . ., p. 116.

54. Ibid., p. 119.

55. See his 'Splendors and Miseries of Evelyn Waugh', in *Classics and Commercials*, pp. 298–305.
56. Bernard Bergonzi, *The Situation of the Novel*, p. 117. His discussion of *Sword of Honour* as a whole is illuminating, and my account of it is indebted to him throughout.
57. J. B. Priestley, 'What was Wrong with Pinfold?', p. 244.
58. 'Basil Seal Rides Again', p. 269.
59. Bergonzi, *The Situation of the Novel*, p. 117.
60. Evelyn Waugh, *The Letters of Evelyn Waugh*, ed. Mark Amory (New Haven and New York: Ticknor & Fields, 1980), p. 638.
61. Graham Greene, *Ways of Escape*, p. 270.

Conclusion

1. V. S. Pritchett, 'The Future of Fiction', *Penguin New Writing* 32 (1947).
2. V. S. Pritchett, *The Living Novel* (London: Chatto & Windus, 1946), p. viii.

Index